The
Legislator's Companion

A HANDBOOK
for the

National Assembly

State Houses of Assembly
&
Local Government Legislative Councils

b y

Emmanuel O. Anyaegbunam

BookBuilders • Editions Africa

Published by the
BookBuilders • Editions A frica
2 A w osika A venue
Bodija Estate, Ibadan
M obile: 0805 662 9266
bookbuilderafrica@ yahoo.com
w w w.bookbuilderseditionsafrica.com

in cooperation w ith
_____

Parliam entary Publishers Ltd, Lagos
080 5 541 8376 // 080 5 338 8888

Printed by **O luBen** Printers
O ke-A do, Ibadan
0805 522 0209

Please note: The Standing O rders of the Bayelsa State H ouse of
A ssem bly, w ere used w hen m aking reference to state assem bly
procedures.

Dedicated to

Reverend (Dr) Moses Iloh

Contents

Contents cont. . .

PREFACE
to the fourth edition

The fourth edition of the *Legislator's Companion* is a product of Nigeria's recent political experience and substantially updates the material in third edition in (2007). I have devoted additional chapters to the declaration of states of emergency, historical phases of local government in Nigeria and also to elections and electoral petitions.

I have deliberately rewritten most of the chapters and included new decisions on constitutional law in line with our legislative experience as from 2007. Thus, highlighting the salient constitutional issues and cases that summed up our ten year experience in constitutional democracy since 1999.

Friedrich Ebert Stiftung (Foundation) earns my gratitude for her pioneer support and assistance in the production of the first two editions of this book in 2000 and 2003.

I would like to express my deep appreciation to Vincent Ike Uko Esq, Vennat Omiqie, Edwin Anikwem, Dr. Osita Agbu, Maria-Theresa Sofunde, Supo Olaibi, Fola Arthur-Worrey and Rev. Dr. Moses Iloh for their unique assistance and consequent library services.

I wish to particularly acknowledge the entire staff of BookBuilders (Editions Africa), for lending their usual professional expertise to this updated 2009 edition, with special thanks to Chris Bankole and Olajide Olalekan Oyewole.

My real and deepest thanks are due to God Almighty and Lord Jesus Christ as the source of all that now constitute this text.

Emmanuel Obusom Anyaegbunam
December, 2009

Chapter 1

History of Modern Legislature

It is the legislature that lays down basic principles, which the judiciary has to interpret and use as a frame of reference in adjudicating cases, and which the executive has to apply in the implementation of policies and execution of laws.

V alentine H erm an & Françoise M endel

---

*T*he collective interests and communal relationships of man have been expressed through collective deliberation, decision making and execution throughout the ages. Thus, Greek city-states of which Athens was the most outstanding, was organized and legislated for by the Assembly or 'Ecclesia', which comprised all the citizens above the age of twenty who met forty (40) times in a year.

The constitution of Rome in the 3rd century B.C. provided for four classes of lower assemblies. These assemblies were —

- comitia curiata
- comitia centuriata
- comitia tribute
- concilium plebis

One of the lasting legacies of the Roman parliamentary system is the constitution of the Senate as the upper legislative chamber. The Roman Senate comprised of three hundred (300) eminent citizens. The membership was revised by the censors once in five years. The Senate, as the predominant chamber of the Roman era, reviewed the decisions of the lower assemblies. It also issued directions to the magistrates and deliberated on other important matters of governance.

The central assembly

The genesis of the central assembly, congress, parliament or by whatever name it is called, can be traced to the political development of Medieval Europe. In that era, the inability of   the ruling monarchs to cope with the demands of new initiatives and more democratic governance necessitated the formation of advisory councils or bodies.

The burning issue of that period was taxation. The imposition and collection of tax required additional credibility, hence, the monarchs' recourse to advisory councils provided some relief. However, the relief and cooperation, which the kings enjoyed from the enlightened class, who constituted the advisory councils, was short-lived. The ruling monarchs' control of taxation was vehemently and robustly challenged. The cliché 'no taxation without representation' gained popularity and affirmation. Hence, the liberal republican spirit became the bedrock of the representative assembly or parliament.

The birth of the British parliament

The Norman Conquest of 1066, adversely affected the political history of the British. It resulted in the selection of high-ranking nobles and clergy who constituted an advisory body to William the Conqueror and subsequent kings. That initial informal advisory group later graduated into a formal assembly known as the 'Great Council' or 'Magnum Concillium'. The assembly met thrice a year to help the king in public administration and the enactment of laws.

Governance and tax

In the 1200s, King John broadened the membership of the advisory council by extending an invitation to the knights who were elected from the shires (counties). King John's motive was to secure their approval and support to collect taxes which he had levied, thereby, according political legitimacy to his taxation policy.

The turning point in the advancement to representative governance in Britain was the initiative of King Edward I in 1295. The monarch summoned the lay and spiritual peers, the representatives of the lower clergy, two knights from each shire, and some members, generally two, from each town or borough to the 1295 meeting. The peculiar and impressive composition of that meeting earned it the name 'model parliament', because it resembled later parliaments. This assemblage was evidently the root of modern representative parliaments.

The official separation of the parliament occurred in the mid-1300s. That was when the elected representatives began to sit separately from the nobles and bishops. Thus, the parliament was divided into two: the House of Lords and the House of Commons.

The prestige of the parliament appreciated remarkably during the reign of Henry VII in the course of the English Reformation. The king's permission enabled the Commons to meet at St. Stephen's Chapel in the palace of Westminster.

The Petition of Rights

In 1628, a new conflict erupted between the English king and the parliament. The source of that unfortunate development was the refusal of the administration of King Charles I to adhere to the provisions of the Petition of Rights.

The Petition of Rights (among others) declared:

- that taxes could not be levied without the consent of the parliament
- that Englishmen could not be imprisoned without cause shown and trial given
- that soldiers and sailors could not be billeted on private householders without their consents

King Charles I refused to implement the Petition of Rights, moreover, he denied the parliament sitting from 1629 – 1640. In the course of that stalemate, the king was forced to summon the parliament in 1640. The primary reason for the king's concession in summoning the parliament after eleven years was to enable him to obtain parliament's approval to raise funds to run public affairs. However, the parliament exploited the situation fully by refusing to approve funds for the king unless he consented to the Petition of Rights. The crisis degenerated into a Civil War from 1642-1648. The parliament tried, convicted and executed King Charles I in 1649.

The consequent legislature was led by the Puritan general, Oliver Cromwell. The regime declared England a republic and held unto power forcontinuous thirteen (13) years from 1640 – 1653. It was then deservedly referred to as the 'Long Parliament'. Oliver Cromwell later sacked the parliament and evolved into an absolute dictator from 1653 until his death in 1658.

The tense political atmosphere regained normalcy in 1660 when a new parliament restored the old order of monarchy. The parliament by then had wrestled enormous powers from the Crown. In 1689, the parliament's power blossomed with the introduction of the Bill of Rights.

The Bill of Rights

The Bill of Rights (1689) afforded the parliament the right to meet frequently and enjoy freedom of speech during debates. The revolutionary bill also confirmed the right of the House of Commons to control financial legislation. Article IX stated that:

> . . . freedom of speech and debates in proceedings in
> parliament ought not to be impeached or questioned in
> any court or place of parliament.

There were other developments and reforms that made parliamentary sovereignty a basic feature of the British political system. These measures have, in turn, stabilized the Westminster system as a commendable model for the rest of the world. The House of Commons is made up of six hundred and fifty eight (658 – 465 from England, 48 from Wales, 45 from Scotland, 100 from Ireland) members who are directly elected. A general election must be held every five years which is the maximum life of any parliament, although the ruling party can call for election before the expiration of the five year tenure due to political convenience. The House of Lords is not elected and was composed of 740 members as at 2009.

History of the United States Congress

The early colonists, especially those from Britain, arrived on the shores of the new world around the mid 1600s with liberal ideas — charged with the spirit of freedom from oppressive laws. The revolutionary influence of the Petition of Rights, the Bill of Rights and other related experiences informed their ideas of governance.

Their liberal ideals were manifested in the establishment of representative assemblies in their new American base in 1660s. These representative assemblies were the platform from which the colonists expressed their disaffection with the policies of the British-appointed colonial governors. The crux of the matter was the authority of the governors to collect taxes, issue money and provide defence.

The official relationship between Britain and the American colonies deteriorated in the 1760s because of prohibitive tax legislation. The embittered colonists dubbed these obnoxious tax laws 'Coercive Acts'.

The colonial representative assemblies were readily available and equipped to take up the cause of the colonists. It was the meeting of the colonial representatives in Philadelphia on September 5, 1774, that became the historic watershed. That meeting was 'to consult upon the present unhappy state of the colonies'. It has been popularly referred to as the 'First Continental Congress'.

The Continental Congress no doubt   laid the foundation for the first National Assembly in the United States. The fifty-five delegates to the meeting were drawn from all the colonies except Georgia. The meeting concluded with a declaration of rights and grievances, addressed to Great Britain.

The second Continental Congress met in Philadelphia on May 1775 and declared the colonies independent of Britain. It served as the transitory national government until the adoption of the Articles of Confederation by the states in 1781. It was then (1781) that a national legislature called the Congress of the Confederation was inaugurated.

The Articles of Confederation was a formal agreement that loosely unified the colonies through a national legislature. However, the system had neither an independent executive nor a judicial arm. Thus, its inherent weakness was palpable.

In May 1787, the Constitutional Convention convened in Philadelphia State House. The convention deliberated exhaustively for sixteen (16) weeks and produced a workable constitution for the United States. It approved the principle of separation of powers and thereby, created independent legislative, executive and judicial arms of government.

The American Constitution provided for a two-chamber congress unlike the earlier congress of only one chamber. The spectacular initiative of the establishment of that bicameral congress, became known as the 'Great Compromise'. It was a dynamic mechanism that resolved the protracted dispute between the delegates from the small states who favoured equal representation for every state. And those from the large states who wanted representation based on population.

The first meeting of the Congress in New York City in 1789 recorded twenty-six senators and sixty-five members of the House of Representatives in attendance. The increase in the number of states that have joined the union since 1789 is reflected in the increased number of seats in the Congress. At present, there are 50 states, with two senators from each state. Thus, the Senate has one hundred members. The House of Representatives has four hundred and thirty-five members.

The senators are elected for a six-year term and their counterparts in the House of Representatives for a two-year term. One-third of the senators retire every two years to ensure stability. There is no legal limit on the number of times a member of the congress can serve. The Supreme Court endorsed this stance when it declared unconstitutional, in 1995, the laws passed by some states that limited the number of terms or years their congressmen could serve.

Parliamentary rule in Germany

Germany's totalitarian rule and its instigation of two World Wars impinged on her parliamentary history. In 1919, Germany adopted a democratic constitution that was popularly known as the Weimar Constitution or Republic. That constitution, which was in existence from 1919 until the rise of the Nazis to power in 1933, inaugurated a bicameral legislature. It had the 'Reichstag' as the lower House of Parliament and the 'Reichstrat' as the Upper House of Parliament. The dictatorial Nazi regime upturned the democratic virtues of the Weimar Constitution with far-reaching changes. As Appadorai clearly observed, these changes in the constitution were:

> *. . . so fundamental indeed that its makers would probably not recognize their handiwork in its later modified form.*

The consequent turmoil of World War II had a remarkable impact on German political history. Thus, Germany was divided into two: the German Democratic Republic (GDR) on the eastern part under Soviet control and the Federal Republic of Germany on the western side, with the Allied Forces in control.

On May 23, 1949, the Basic Law for the Federal Republic of Germany came into force, while the German Democratic Republic under the Soviet strangle-hold retained her centralized socialist political culture.

---

[1] See A. Appadorai, *The Substance of Politics* (Oxford University Press, New York, 1975): 463.

In 1989, Germany witnessed another historic political turning point. The political winds of change which resulted in the collapse of the Berlin Wall and ultimately in the signing of the treaty on the final reunification of Germany on September 12, 1990. Hence, the return of full sovereignty to reunified Germany. The historic democratic development was legally consolidated on October 3, 1990, as Germany achieved national unity through the adoption of the Basic Law as the constitution of the whole country.

The basic law of Germany recognizes the Bundestag House of Representatives as the democratic parliament of the country. It is composed of 656 members, who are elected for a determinate four-year period. This legislature commands broad powers, which include assistance in the formation of other constitutional institutions, as well as control of the general administration.

The Bundesrat is the upper house and it is through this chamber that the sixteen Länder participate in the legislative process and administration of the federation in matters covering the European Union. The members of the Bundesrat are not elected, but are appointed and recalled by the Land parliaments. The Bundesrat members cannot initiate legislation, they can only advise. They are bound by the instructions from the Land parliaments who appointed them.

Therefore, the Bundesrat serves as a political bridge between the true democratic norms of the Bundestag and the administrative necessities of the Lander. This constitutional compromise aids the integration spirit of the European Union.

The French National Assembly

The revolutionary experiences of France also shaped her parliamentary history. The radical policies of Philip IV, which culminated in the inauguration of the first Estates General in 1302, was the forerunner of the French parliament. This body of Frenchmen rallied together by Philip IV constituted the foundation of the French parliament.

In the course of the French revolution, King Louis XVI summoned the EstatesGeneral in May 1789. The Estates-General were comprised of three estates or classes:

- the clergy
- the nobility
- the commoners

The revolutionary spirit erupted when the third estate, or the commoners, declared themselves a National Assembly in June 1789. They also assumed full powers to write a new constitution for France.

The popular support of the National Assembly, which also resulted in the dethronement of Louis XVI in July 1789, was phenomenal. In 1791, the National Assembly succeeded with the drafting of a new constitution, which transformed France into a constitutional or limited monarchy under a one-chamber legislature. The assembly was elected for one year by restricted suffrage. It was to enact laws, raise taxes, determine public expenditure, ratify treaties and declare rights.

The revolutionary pace advanced in 1792 with the election of a new National Assembly by universal adult suffrage. It was known as the 'National Convention'. It drew up a republican constitution which was never in operation, due to the on-going political crises. In 1795, a new constitution instituted the government popularly referred to as 'the Directory'. The Directory was elected by a restricted suffrage and operated a legislative power shared by two chambers.

The Revolution of 1848 put an end to the monarchy that began in 1830. The liberal stance of this revolution restored the right to vote to all Frenchmen. The revolt against Napoleon III in 1871 resulted in the establishment of the Third Republic. The resultant National Assembly of the Republic became established as the legislative organ of the government in France.

The Constitutional Act of 1875 consolidated the French parliamentary system. The legislative power was bestowed on the bicameral legislature: the Chamber of Deputies and the Senate. The deputies were elected by direct universal suffrage for four years. The Senate enjoyed a tenure of nine years through indirect suffrage. Appadorai testified to the unique qualities of this republic in these words:

> *Some stability was attained during 1870 - 1940, the period of the Third Republic, which was indeed the regime which lasted the longest during the last one hundred and eighty years; the sovereignty of the people also found its fullest expression during this period.*

After World War II, in 1946, a new constitution emerged which ushered in the

---

[2] Ibid, 295.

Fourth Republic. This constitution established parliamentary sovereignty. General Charles de Gaulle surfaced on the French political scene in the course of this constitution. The extensive power of the legislature was not favourable for de Gaulle's disposition for strong executive powers.

Charles de Gaulle resigned as president in 1946. There were numerous political challenges as well as de Gaulle's opposition that led to the demise of the Fourth Republic constitution.

De Gaulle returned to power as a compromise candidate to douse the political tension in 1958. He came in as prime minister with emergency powers for a period of six months. De Gaulle's administration drafted a new constitution which the French voters approved on September, 28, 1958, as the Fifth Republic constitution. The constitution granted enormous power to the president and, at the same time, reduced the power of the legislature. However, de Gaulle was rejected by French voters in 1969.

The French National Assembly, as presently constituted, is made up of the Chamber of Deputies and the Senate. There are 577 deputies who are elected every five years, unless an election is called before the expiration of their tenure. The Senate has 319 members. Senators are elected by regional and city electoral colleges for a nine-year term. The Chamber of Deputies is actually the national assembly. It has greater powers than the Senate. When both chambers disagree on the text of a bill, the ultimate decision lies with the Chamber of Deputies. Moreover, the Council of Ministers must ensure the support of the majority of the deputies. If the council of ministers lacks that vital majority support, the ministers have to resign and the president will appoint a new prime minister.

The president has the constitutional power to dissolve the Chamber of Deputies and call for a new election. Many conveniently refer to the French Chamber of Deputies as the National Assembly and the parliament as comprising of the Chamber of Deputies and the Senate.

Chapter 2

Constitutional Development and the Evolution of the Legislature in Nigeria

Power being almost always the rival of power, the general government will at all times stand ready to check the usurpation of the state governments, and these will have the same disposition towards the general government. The people by throwing themselves into either scale, will infallibly make it to preponderate.

Alexander Hamilton

*T*he centralized administrative structure of the British colonial regime left an abiding mark on the Nigerian political culture and administrative process. This contact laid the foundation for most of Nigeria's democratic experience. The first semblance of a legislature in Nigeria's political history could be traced to the Nigerian Council of 1913. The council was merely an advisory and deliberative council with jurisdiction only over the Colony of Lagos and the Protectorate of Southern Nigeria.

The Clifford Constitution, 1922

In 1922, the Clifford Constitution established the first legislature for the whole country, known as 'the Legislative Council of Nigeria'. It had forty-six members (twenty seven official and nineteen unofficial). Fifteen of the unofficial members were nominated and four were elected (three members from Lagos and one from Calabar). The Legislative Council legislated primarily for Lagos and the Southern Protectorate, while the governor made laws for the Cameroons and the Northern

Protectorate by proclamation. It was only on financial matters that the Legislative Council legislated for the entire country.

The Richard Constitution, 1946

The increased wave of nationalism gave birth to the Richard Constitution in 1946. The constitution unified the whole country for the first time under a central legislative council. The legislative council was composed of forty-five members (twenty-eight unofficial and seventeen official).

The Central Legislative Council also retained the four (4) elective seats formula (three seats for Lagos and one for Calabar). This constitution created the first regional legislative assemblies in Nigeria. The Northern Region, in addition to her legislative assembly, had a House of Chiefs.

The Macpherson Constitution, 1951

The intensified nationalist struggle and attendant clamour for representation and independence scored a landmark victory in 1951 with the introduction of the Macpherson Constitution. The most remarkable innovation of that constitution was the establishment of a central legislative body known as the House of Representatives.

The House of Representatives had one hundred and forty-nine members. These members were selected by the regional legislative assemblies which acted as electoral colleges. The majority of the members of the regional assemblies were elected. The Western Region then joined the North by inaugurating its House of Chiefs.

The Lyttleton Constitution, 1954

The country's march towards independence was catalysed by the introduction of some salient features in the Lyttleton Constitution of 1954. This improvement made the membership of the House of Representatives increase to one hundred and eighty-four. The members were directly elected, except for the Northern Region that retained the electoral college system.

The 1954 Constitution also divided legislative powers into exclusive, concurrent and residual powers. It also granted the regional assemblies the autonomy to pass bills without the consent of the central legislature or the governor-general.

Meanwhile, each regional assembly was empowered to appoint the leader of the party with majority of seats in the house as the premier or head of the government. The Northern and Western Regions continued with their bicameral legislature (House of Assembly and House of Chiefs). The Eastern Region eventually established its own House of Chiefs in 1959.

In the last lap of the transitory process to independence, the central government established an upper chamber (the Senate) in January, 1960. The Senate was constituted with forty-four pioneer members. Thus, a bicameral National Assembly (the Senate and the House of Representatives) was created at the centre. The House of Representatives membership was further increased to 320 members. In 1960, the constitutional legislative powers of the National Parliament resided in the Queen of England, the Senate and the House of Representatives. The assent of the governor-general was required to transform a bill passed by the National Parliament into a binding law.

In 1963, Nigeria became a republic. Hence, the constitutional legislative powers of the National Assembly resided in the President, the Senate and the House of Representatives. The assent of the president was required to transform a bill passed by the National Parliament into a binding law.

Collapse of the First Republic

The collapse of the First Republic in 1966 by military coup terminated the country's democratic institutions. The first in the long series of the military interventions into politics. Three successive military regimes ruled Nigeria between 1966 and 1979[1] when General Olusegun Obasanjo handed the governance of the nation back to the politicians. Democratic governance was restored on the 1st of October, 1979, when Nigeria adopted a presidential constitution with emphasis on the separation of powers. The constitutional legislative powers of the central government was vested in the National Assembly, which was made up of the Senate and the House of Representatives.

The Senate had ninety-five (95) members with equal representation of five senators per state for the then nineteen states of the federation. The House of Representatives had four hundred and fifty (450) members, who were elected on

---

[1] General T.Aguiyi-Ironsi (Jan15 1966-July 29 1966); General Y. Gowon (July 1966 - July 1975); Generals M. Mohammed/O. Obasanjo (1975-1979).

proportional representation basis. The members of the National Assembly were directly elected for a term of four years. Each state operated a unicameral House of Assembly with the same four-year tenure.

Demise of the Second Republic

The Second Republic was, however, short-lived. On December 31 1983 the military once again intervened. Three successively oppressive and ineffective military governments hung unto power for 16 years, until the death of Sani Abacha in June 1998. In- between the Babangida and Abacha regimes, a 3-month interim government, headed by Chief Ernest Shonekan, was put in place to end the political crisis and prolonged strikes after Babangida annulled the election results in 1993. The interim government was not a democratically-elected government and was easily pushed aside by Abacha, who gave the initial ostensible impression that his regime would return the country to civilian rule. This did not happen. Death finally removed Abacha from office in June 1998; a genuine transition to democracy programme was put in place by his successor, General Abdulsalami Abubakar.

On 29 May 1999, Nigeria returned once again to civilian rule with a presidential constitution. The bicameral structure of Senate and House of Representatives was retained at the centre. The Senate has 109 members and the House of Representatives comprises 360 members. The component states retained their unicameral houses of assembly.

The Third Republic

Nigeria is currently under her longest continuous experience of democratic governance since the inception of the Third Republic on May 29, 1999. There have been three general elections in 1999, 2003 and 2007, respectively. The federal and state governments have successfully changed hands based on the outcome of the afore stated elections.

---

[2] The military regimes between 1983 and 1999 were: General M. Buhari (Dec 1983- Aug 1985); General I. Babangida (Aug 1985 - Aug 1993); Sani Abacha, (Nov 1993- 8 June 1998); Abdulsalami Abukbakar from (June 8 1998 to 29 May 1999).

But the April 2007 general elections was severely marred by massive irregularities. The avalanche of petitions by the contestants at the Election Petition Tribunals throughout the country and the overarching outcry of both the foreign and local observers of that exercise is disheartening. That election has put the credibility and the performance rating of the Independent National Electoral Commission (INEC) in bad light.

The nullification of the governorship elections in Kogi, Kebbi, Enugu, Adamawa, Sokoto, Edo, Bayelsa, Cross River, Ekiti and Ondo states, and the order for fresh elections in these states within three months by the various Election Petitions Tribunal and the Court of Appeal strengthen this point. The declaration by the Supreme Court of Rotimi Amaechi as the rightful governor of Rivers State on October 25, 2007, in replacement of Celestine Omehia, the INEC declared governor of that state (from May, 29, 2007, until October 25, 2007) also exposed the general disgraceful outcome of the 2007 elections.

In Edo and Ondo states, the Court of Appeal affirmed the verdict of the Election Petition Tribunals. Thus, Comrade Adams Oshiomole and Dr. Segun Mimiko were declared as the validly elected governors of both states.

The bye-election of 25 April 2009, in the ten affected local government areas, returned Dr. Segun Oni as the governor of Ekiti State. That election in Ekiti State, re-echoed the worrisome violent features of our past electoral history and the uneasy controversies that trailed that exercise. The Idi-Osi Local Government Area election was inconclusive and was concluded few days later.

The Court of Appeal also upturned the decision of the Election Petition Tribunal, and in that wise, upheld the election of Theodore Orji as the valid governor of Abia State.

More so, the Supreme Court's nullification of the Anambra State governorship election of April 14, 2007 and its return of Peter Obi as the incumbent governor of that state, even as at the date of that election, further consolidates these points.

The conduct of the local government election in some states towards the last quarter of year 2007, also deepened these electoral woes. The alarming outcome of that exercise under the auspices of the State Independent Electoral Commission (SIEC) unveiled our unwholesome political culture.

ThisDay newspapers described it thus:

> *Expectedly, the local government polls lived up to the fears of the*
> *opposition as violence and all forms of electoral malpractices*
> *marred most of them. Predictably the ruling PDP swept all the*
> *seats in most of the states just as was the case a fortnight ago*
> *when the ruling ANPP in Kano swept most of the seats in the*
> *state, a situation that led to riots in the state. In Kwara, Ebonyi*
> *and Cross River states that had theirs earlier, the ruling PDP in*
> *these states were expectedly not magnanimous to the opposition.*[3]

The local government election in Plateau State in December 2008, resulted in the Jos crisis that claimed numerous lives and destroyed properties. The general outcry against these deplorable electoral exercises, led to the federal government inauguration of the Electoral Reform Committee led by Justice Lawal Uwais (rtd) in 2007.

But the government's stance on the recommendation of that committee, notably on the president's power to appoint the chairman of the Independent Electoral Commission (INEC), did not receive public support. The committee's suggestion of an independent screening and appointment panel (National Judicial Council), as the appointing authority before Senate confirmation, garnered public support. However, the government white paper maintained the status quo, and the president retained the power of appointment, which dampened public enthusiasm in the electoral reform initiative.

The refreshing note is that these electoral problems have been subjected to the rule of law and constitutionalism. A promising departure from the past experience of recourse to violence and military intervention. Obedience to the rule of law is the bedrock of political stability. It is the gradual teething process towards the attainment of dynamic political equilibrium without loss of balance, through surrendering our political differences and bitterness to the constitutionally ordained institutions rather than thuggery. The current and prospective gains of

---

[3] *ThisDay* newspaper. Local government polls, matters arising. 22 December 2007: 53.

abiding by the decisions of our competent courts and tribunals, holds the future of Nigeria and her democracy as part of the civilized world.

Chapter 3

Historical Phases of Local Government in Nigeria from Native Authority to the Presidential System

In the 21ˢᵗ century, capable, reliable and transparent institutions are the key to success — strong parliaments and honest police force, independent judges and journalists, a vibrant private sector and civil society. Those are the things that give life to democracy, because that is what matters in peoples' lives.

President Barack O bam a
in A ccra, G hana, 11 July 2009

*L*ocal government legislation in Nigeria started with the advent of native authority rule during the colonial era of indirect rule. The Native Authority Act (1916)[1] empowered the colonial governor vide section 4 to:

> Appoint any chief or other native of any native tribunal to be a native authority for the purpose of this Act.

The nationalist struggle for independence and its attendant fervent winds of change, found favourable consideration in the Macpherson Constitution of 1951. That constitution, granted autonomy to the then existing three regions and yielded

---

[1] The Native Authority Act of 1916 was amended in 1933 and repealed by the Native Authority Act of 1943.

control of local government to the respective regional government. This development was affirmed by Mike Adeleye in these words:

> *...with the inauguration of the 1951 Macpherson Constitution, responsibility for local government was transferred to the nascent regions under the control of Nigerian nationalists, who lost no time in introducing changes in the system.* [2]

It was in this context, that the different regions operated different local government administrations and structures until the 1976 local government reforms.

Eastern Region

The colonial system of indirect rule was very unpopular in the Eastern Region. Thus, the Eastern Region Local Government Act of 1950 was enacted. That legislation abrogated the native authority. The 1950 Act was a mere adaptation of the British councillor system. It had a three-tier system comprising the county councils, urban or rural district councils and local councils.

The Eastern Region Local Government Law of 1955 retained the same structure and introduced democratic processes. Hence, it emphasized elective rather than appointive councils and broadened the council's functions considerably. That system was slightly modified by the Eastern Region Local Government Law of 1960.

The Nigerian Civil War (1967-1970) saw the Eastern Region as the main battlefield. Therefore, local government structures and administration was severely afflicted by the war time emergency situation.

The post-civil war programme of reconstruction, rehabilitation and reconciliation (the 3Rs), bore testimony to the local government structure in that part of the country. As was aptly opined by Professor Eme Awa:

> *The new arrangement introduced by the three states in the defunct Eastern Region all sought to coordinate the zeal of the local community for self help development and to reduce corruption in*

---

[2] Mike Adeleye, *Local Government Administration in Nigeria*, (Pure Language Communications Ltd., Lagos, 2001): 50.

local government by integrating the machinery of local
administration and that of the state government. [3]

The notable formula of the then East Central State offered a two-tiered system
known as 'divisional administration'. The thrust of this administrative system was
the replacement of local government councils by development councils. Thus,
community councils were created as the formative structure and divisional
councils as the upper setting.

Each community council selected a representative to the divisional council
which was controlled by a divisional officer, who was appointed by the state
government. The objective of the system was to achieve the active participation
of the local people in the general management of local development projects
through the supervision and guidance of the divisional council.

This design took cognizance of the town unions and age-grade networks
as the hub of community development, and coopted these organizations into the
administrative machinery in the community councils in conjunction with the state
government. The community councils were charged with the arduous
responsibility of providing services at the community level. The urban councils
were equally saddled with the task to provide advanced and specialized public
services required in the urban area. Each administrative division was accountable
to the Divisional Administration Department of the Cabinet Office in Enugu.

Western Region

The fiery zeal of the nationalist struggle, which was fanned by the Macpherson
Constitution of 1951, also found favour with the then Western Region. It was out
of the Western Region that the Mid-West Region was created in August,1963. In
Olubunmi A. Fayemi's striking words:

> *Soon after the constitution had been adopted, the then Eastern*
> *and Western Regions changed their Local Government system to*
> *reflect the ideology of independence at the time.* [4]

---

[3] E.O. Awa. *The Transformation of Rural Society: A study of rural development in the
Eastern States of Nigeria 1970-76* (Kuru NIPSS,1992): 64.

[4] Olubunmi A. Fayemi. Local Government Administration in Nigeria. (Pure Language
Communications, Lagos, 2001) p. 336.

In furtherance of the independence mission, the Western Region Local Government Law of 1952 came into force. It was crafted like that of the Eastern Region, on the broad-based British councillor system— a radical departure from the native authority system. This enactment introduced elective principles and distinguished the elected members from their traditional counterparts in the council. The 1957 Local Government Law of the Western Region was an improvement on the 1952 legislation. That 1957 law prevailed until the end of the First Republic in 1966.

The political crises, which started during the Western Region Elections in 1963 and culminated in the end of the First Republic through the coup of January 1966, impacted adversely on local government administration in the Western Region. The emergency government of the civil war opened the way for the adoption of an ad-hoc hybrid management system in the grassroots tier of government.

The sole administrator system was prevalent in the Western Region and the Mid-West during the civil war. It entailed the deployment of a senior civil servant, who was a non-indigene, to the area. The sole administrator was accountable to the state governor who appointed him.

The political and social upheaval generated by the Agbekoya riots of 1968-69 in the Western Region necessitated the demise of the sole administrator system. The council-manager system was introduced as the replacement initiative following the American model.

The council manager (chief executive and administrative officer of the council) was to be a qualified professional who could be hired from outside the particular local council of his operation. Thus, he need not necessarily be a civil servant. The administrative structure also provided for the supportive management committee, standing committee and area committees to aid the council manager in the discharge of his duties.

But the council manager, just like the sole administrator, was accountable to the state governor. The lack of autonomy of that tier of government, as reflected in the overbearing interference of the state government, frustrated the system. In the same vein, other systems such as development administration, divisional administrator system, caretaker committee, electoral college or cabinet system were experimented to no avail.

c. The Northern Region

The political culture of this region was compatible with the colonial policy of indirect rule and its attendant native authority system. Therefore, there was no remarkable resistance nor radical departure from that order as was the case in the Eastern and Western regions. Mike Adeleye's illuminating remark was:

> *The pattern of change in the North was more gradual, taking the form of a reform of existing structures as reflected in the Northern Region Native Authority Law of 1954.* [5]

In this sphere, the ruling political party in the region — the Northern Peoples Congress (NPC) had, as far back as 1950, desired a reform and an almost outright abolition of the native authorities. The same NPC, also requested the abolition of the House of Chiefs and its replacement by an advisory council of chiefs.

The military introduced some significant changes in the Northern Region that weakened the influence of the traditional rulers. The case of Kano State which was divided into eight administrative districts under the control of eight senior civil servants appointed by the military government was instructive.

These developments left Nigeria with different shades of local government structures and administrations. The salient feature was that local governments, from colonial era to independence   and until 1976, lacked legal personality. Therefore, they were not statutory bodies that could sue and be sued. This anomaly affected the operations of that tier of government and exposed it to wanton unconstitutional manipulation of the regional, state and central government. It then became a pliable political pawn in the hands of First Republic politicians, as well as subsequent military leaders.

The 1976 Local Government Reform

The parlous state of local government administration in Nigeria from independence to the 1970s, caught the attention of the 1974 Public Service Review Commission under the chairmanship of Chief Jerome Udoji. That review commission highlighted the fundamental problems of local government administration and proffered some germane remedial measures. The main plank of that review, was for a single tier structure and autonomous local administration with minimal interference of the state ministry of local government.

---

[5] Mike Adeleye, 50.

The emergence of the Mohammed/ Obasanjo regime in 1975, and their focal point of interest in local government as their launching pad for the return to civil rule, popularized that local government reform. Hence, the 1976 Federal Republic of Nigeria 'Guidelines for Local Government Reform', became an indelible landmark in the history of local government in the country. The 1976 reform was projected to stimulate development, sustain democratic self-govern-ment and encourage initiative and leadership potentials at the grassroots.

In the actualisation of the laudable policy of that reform, the guidelines were promulgated by all the states as their Local Government Edict. This reform was the first attempt to harmonize local government administration by a uniform standard throughout the whole country. The structure was for a single tier system known as the local government authority, with a population range of 150,000 to 800,000. The reform insisted that the membership of the local government council should be predominantly elected (75%) either through direct or indirect election from the communities. But that 25 per cent of the membership of each council may be nominated by the state governor. The aim of the reform was that the grassroots government will be autonomous with little or no interference in their internal operations. Thus, the state ministry of local government was reduced to the capacity of an advisor — to assist and guide — rather than control the local governments within their jurisdiction.

The new structure brought every local government council under the leadership of an elected chairman; the administrative arm was headed by a career administrator, known as the secretary to the local government. The reform also standardized operations through the departmentalization of every local gov-ernment.

Local government experience in the Second Republic (1979-1983)

The pertinent provisions of the 1976 Guidelines for Local Government Reforms were incorporated into the 1979 constitution. Hence, the constitution guaranteed a system of democratically elected local government and specifically listed the functions of that tier of government. That constitution also mandated the federal and state government to make direct financial grants to the local government.

But most regrettably, the Second Republic politicians resonated the disheartening experience of the First Republic through their unconstitutional politicization and illegal manipulation of local government affairs. Mike Adeleye summarized the situation:

> *... the gains made as a result of the 1976 local government*
> *reforms were however frittered away by the succeeding civilian*
> *government between 1979-83. Local government was turned into*
> *a political chess game. Each political party wanted to control the*
> *local government councils in the states where it controlled the*
> *executive power.* [6]

The democratic elections guaranteed by the constitution were never held at the grassroots level throughout the duration of that civilian era. The governors employed the unconstitutional tactics of handpicking local government chairmen and councillors. The depressing scenario deepened with their appointment of political party agents and loyalists as caretaker committees to run the affairs of the local governments.

The Second Republic saw the proliferation of local governments from 310 to 701.[11] These were largely created out of political and personal interests, while the state governments reigned with impunity over local government affairs. The other states also had to toe the same debilitating path.

The most outstanding problem of this grassroots tier, during the Second Republic, was the diversion of their constitutionally ordained ten per cent (10%) of the federal allocation by the state governments. The only notable exception to this unconstitutional anomaly was the then Lagos State government under Lateef Jakande. In short, the state governments assumed control of local government funds and relegated that tier to mere subsidiary accounting outposts. The net effect was captured in Dr. Kunle Awotokun's unmistakable remark that:

> *The local governments of this era were politically impotent and*
> *financially insolvent such that they could not pay their salaries let*
> *alone perform their statutory functions as contained in the 1979*
> *constitution.* [7]

---

[6] Adeleye, 51.

[7] Some notable examples, Oyo State increased from twenty four (24) to fifty six (56); Kaduna State from seventeen (17) to seventy (70); Lagos State from ten (10) to thirty (30) See: Kunle Awotokun, *Local Government Administration in Nigeria.* (Pure Language Communications, Lagos, 2001) p.45.

Buhari Regime and the Ibrahim Dasuki Panel Report 1984 - 1985

On December 31, 1983, Nigeria's Second Republic came to an end, with the emergence of the military in power under the leadership of Muhammadu Buhari. The overwhelming political problems of the country, which were reflected in the gloomy state of affairs in the local government, received the regime's urgent attention. The regime immediately proscribed all the politically motivated local governments established by the civilian administration between 1979 1983.

That regime also dissolved the unwholesome caretaker or management committees which the civilian administration bequeathed on the grassroots tier throughout the country. The remedial initiative of that regime was the appointment of senior state civil servants known as 'sole administrators' to take over the running of the local governments.

In May 1984, the Buhari administration inaugurated a 21-member committee under the chairmanship of Ibrahim Dasuki, (thus, the popular reference to the committee's report as Dasuki's Report). The committee was charged with, among other responsibilities, re-examining the existing structures, functions and financial resources available to local governments for the performance of its functions.

Incidentally, the Buhari administration was toppled by a palace coup in August 1985, before the submission of the committee's report. The committee remarked that the local governments had more of operational problems than structural problems.

But the committee's report was not fully adopted due to the unified command structure of the military administration. In this wise, the problem of the grassroots tier deepened as state governments continued their overbearing interference in the affairs of the local governments.

Babangida's reform and the introduction of the presidential system in local government

The Babangida regime embarked on a return to civil rule programme which entailed a comprehensive reform of the civil service and local government system. The genesis of the local government reform was the report from the Political Bureau of 1986. The 1988 civil service reform, which was aimed at changing the orientation of public bureaucracy towards the adoption of the American presidential democracy, was also reflected on the local government tier. The attendant blueprint being: The implementation *of Guidelines on the Application of the Civil Service Reforms in the Local Government Service* issued by the office of the then vice-president empowered the legislative arm of the local government with these functions:

    i.   Law-making, debating, passing local legislation;

    ii. Approving amending and possibly criticizing local government annual budget;

    iii. Vetting and monitoring the implementation of projects;

    iv. Examining and debating monthly statement of income and expenditure;

    v.   Advising, consulting and liaising with the local government chairman who is the chief executive in the local government system.

These electoral and presidential system improvements were targeted to enhance the executive capacity of the chairman and legislative efficiency of the council. In order to actualize that policy objective, the Basic Constitutional and Transitional Provisions Amendment Decree No. 10 of 1991 was promulgated. That enactment introduced the principle of separation of powers into the local government jurisdiction. Thus, the chairman and his executive aides ceased to be members of the council.

The presidential doctrine of separation of powers was consolidated and elaborated by the Local Government Constitutional and Transitional Amendment Decree No. 23 of 1991, which formally adopted the council as the legislative arm of that tier of government. Section 1(a) of that decree designated the elected 'leader' and 'deputy leader' from amongst the elected councilors to be at the helm of affairs of the local government legislature. The same decree of 1991 also increased the number of local government areas in the country to 593.

That administration's drive for local government autonomy resulted in these eloquent policy decisions:

----

[8] (Government Printer, Lagos October, 1988).

i.   The abolition of the ministry of local government in all the states of the federation and its replacement with the department of local government in the deputy governor's office.

ii. The abolition of local government service commissions in all the states, thus transferring personnel matters affecting the senior cadres of local governments to the local councils.

iii. The appointment of the secretary to the local government directly by the chairman without the interference of the state government.

iv. Increase in local governments share of the federation from 10% to 15% and later to 20%. Furthermore, this allocation was to go directly to the local governments without passing through the state governments as it used to be.

The state governments were mandated to remit 10% of their internally generated revenue to the local government.

But the implementation of the above initiative was easier said than done. It was a pathetic experiment that exposed the lack of capacity of that tier of government to operate efficiently on expected autonomous basis. The independence which the reform accorded the council chairman in the appointment of the secretary and senior personnel was wantonly abused and politicized. This frightening development resulted in floodgate of petitions and protests to the federal government for the reversal of that policy initiative. The federal government yielded to the outcry and protest from many interest groups, especially the senior council officials whose job security were threatened.

As a consequence, the federal government reverted back to the old local government system in June 1992. In this wise, local government service commissions were re-established and saddled with the responsibility of appointing the secretaries to local governments and to handle senior personnel matters. The ministry of local government was also resuscitated. The local government service commission was responsible for the recruitment, promotion, discipline and welfare of all local government officials from levels 07 and above. The junior staff from levels 01 - 06 were to be handled by the local government council.

Abacha era and local government affairs

This regime focused on restructuring the past local government reform measures. In furtherance thereof, it adopted these changes:

i. It reverted to the old order of the fusion of the legislative and executive functions of local government.

ii. The election of supervisory councillors, the chairman and the vice-chairmen, to constitute the executive council in each local government was reinstated.

iii. The deployment of the heads of department of local governments became the joint responsibility of the local government service commission in concert with the state department of local government and the local government chairman of that particular area.

iv. The empowerment of the head of state to remove any local government chairman who, in his view, is undermining the implementation of the transition programme.

The Abacha administration organized a local government election in 1997 and also increased the number of local government areas in the country to 768.

Abubakar's transition to democracy programme

The sudden and ignominious death of Sani Abacha in June 1998, ushered in the transitional government of Abdulsalami Abubakar. The primary focus of that regime was to return the country to civilian rule as soon as possible. This came to pass on May 29, 1999, after fifteen years of military dictatorship. In pursuit of that laudable goal, that government hitherto sacked all the local government officials elected under the Abacha regime in 1997, and dissolved its entire structure.

In Abubakar's spirited drive to create a new and conducive democratic culture, he hinged his transition formative base on local government elections. Hence, the enactment of the Basic Constitutional and Transitional Provisions) Decree No. 36 of 1998. That decree vide Section 18(i) provided that:

> . . . subject to the provision of subsection (1) of this section the chairman shall vacate his office at the expiration of a period of 3 years commencing from the date when in the case of a person first elected as chairman under this decree he took the oath of allegiance and the oath of office or the person last elected to that office took the oath of allegiance and the oath of office or would but for his death have taken those oath.

This decree proffered the legal basis for election into local government areas in 1999. Although the 1999 constitution had detailed provisions on local government, it made no mention of the tenure of the elected officers.

This critical constitutional lacuna has resulted to the unconstitutional operation of caretaker committees instead of elected local government officials. The existing local government and council areas as provided by section 3 (6) of the constitution is

> There shall be seven-hundred and sixty-eight local government areas in Nigeria as shown in the second column of Part I of the First Schedule to the constitution and six area councils as shown in Part II of that schedule.

But some states have specified the tenure of their elected local government officials through their local government laws.

Chapter 4

Constitutions: Sources and Functions

The constitution is an instrument of government under which laws are made and are not a mere Act or law, and the construction which the court will give to a constitutional provision must be such that will serve the interest of the constitution and best carry out its object and purpose and give effect to the intention of the framers.

Supreme Court in *AG Ondo State v.AG Federation* [1]

A constitution is a collection of the fundamental principles dealing with the organization of government, the distribution of power among the organs of government and the rights of the citizens of a state. These basic principles may be written or implied in the country's customs and conventions. A constitution is also a body of rules by which a society is governed and which serves as its legal charter.

K.C. Wheare [2] sees the constitution of a state as:

... the whole system of government of a country, the collection of rules which establish and regulate or govern the government.

As aptly held by the Supreme Court of Nigeria in the case of *PDP v. INEC*: [3]

---

[1] [2002] 9 NWRL Pt 722, p.242.

[2] KC Wheare, *Modern Constitutions*. 2 nd edition, Oxford University Press, 1966: 1.

[3] [1999] 1 NWLR Pt. 626.200 SC, p 205.

A constitution is the organic law or 'grundnorm' of the people.
While it seeks to provide the machinery of government it also
gives rights and imposes obligations on the people it is meant for.

Our apex court through the words of Uwaifo JSC in *Attorney General of Ondo State v. Attorney General of the Federation & Ors.* defined the constitution as:

... an organic instrument which confers powers and also creates rights and limitations. It is the supreme law in which certain first principles of fundamental nature are established. Once the powers, rights and limitations under the constitution are identified as having been enacted, their existence cannot be disputed in a court of law. But their extent and implications may be sought to be interpreted and explained by the court in cases properly brought before it. All agencies of government are organs of initiative whose powers are derived either directly from the constitution or from law enacted thereunder. They therefore stand in relationship to the constitution as it permits of their existence and functions.

There are numerous experiences and areas from which a state's fundamental laws and governing principles can be derived. These sources vary in terms of the historical engagement of a particular country. There are statutory, as well as non-statutory sources. These sources include:

i. Customary norms and laws

Cultural norms and values influence a society's mode of conflict resolution, thereby, dictating the trend of communal affairs. The societal way of life is an integral part of a constitution. The prominent constitutional recognition, which is accorded to customary and sharia courts in Nigeria is a case in point. The English experience that culminated in the Bill of Rights of 1689 was an outcome of the conflict of the Catholic Church and the Protestant Reformation.

ii. A country's historical experience

A constitution is a mirror of a state's political history. Nigeria's colonial experience under British rule, shaped her constitutional development from

---

[4] [2002] 7 MJSC. p. 18.

1900-1963. The fears of the minority groups in Nigeria led to the incorporation of the Fundamental Human Rights provisions in the independence Constitution of 1960. It then became the forerunner to the same measures as chapter four (IV) of the 1979 and 1999 Constitutions.

Similarly, the Magna Carta (1215), the Petition of Rights (1628), the Bill of Rights (1689) and others were English landmarks towards freedom from royal dictatorships. These fuelled democratic agitation and protests, which neutralized the absolute powers of the monarchs. The French testimony from the first to the fifth Republican Constitutions also support this point. The revolutionary struggles were in the quest of freedom.

The Supreme Court beautifully upheld this stance in the case of *Attorney General of the Federation v. Attorney General Abia State & 35 Others* where Justice Belgore stated that:

> *Our constitution is a product of our own circumstance, and the like of section 315 (supra) has lived with us all along. Similar provisions were in independence constitution of 1960 but the exercise of it was limited to only six months of its existence because it was under transitional provisions. The Republican constitution of 1963 limited it to three years. It is obviously now deliberate that Section 315 has no limited time. It must be pointed out that no two democratic constitutions are the same. Our own constitution has its peculiarities due to our historical circumstance.*

iii. *Constitutional conferences and constituent assemblies*

The contributions of eminent citizens elected or selected for the deliberation, review, and ratification of a country's draft constitution are vital. The composition determines the nature, scope, legitimacy and the acceptability of the country's constitution.

For instance, the historical effort of the founding fathers of the United States in the inauguration of the two Continental Congresses in Philadelphia is noteworthy. The outcome was the Declaration of Independence and Confederal Government in 1774 and 1775, respectively.

---

[5] [2003] 5 MJSC p.128 - 129; per Belgore JSC..

The United State's Constitutional Convention of 1789 was in the same vein. It produced the workable federal constitution with the guiding principles of separation of powers and bicameral legislature.

In a similar fashion, Nigeria since the 1950 Ibadan Conference, has witnessed constituent assemblies that deliberated over all her constitution-making processes up to 1994/1995. However, military regimes, as shown by the examples of the 1979, 1995 and 1999 constitution-making processes, tinkered with the final drafts. Such official military interference undermines salient representative input.

iv. Legal, political and social writings/ public opinion

The intellectual writings of prominent political thinkers, philosophers and jurists, have provided the beacon light for the framing of many constitutions. In this sphere, Baron de Montesquieu's (1689-1755) treatise on the separation of powers, A.V. Dicey's (1835 *Laws of the Constitution*) exposition on the rule of law, the American *Federalist Papers* (1788) and Professor B.O. Nwabueze's works on constitutional law must be appreciated. [6]

The opinions of citizens expressed in writing, debates and civil society activism contribute immensely in the framing of a constitution. The regional political debates that preceded the 1950 Ibadan conference in Nigeria provided a platform for popular participation. The public discourse held by the Professor Cookey-led Political Bureau (1985-1986) [7]and the debate on the 1999 Constitution under the Constitutional Debate Coordinating Committee (1998), served similar purposes.

It is equally remarkable that plebiscites and referendums have been applied favourably in securing public acceptability of many constitutions the world over.

v. The influence of successful foreign countries

The constitutions of the emergent developing countries of the world are often localized versions of the constitutions of the older successful democratic states.

---

[6] See A.V. Dicey *Laws of the Constitution* 19 edition, (Macmillan, London); B.O. Nwabueze, *Constitutional History of Nigeria*. (Christopher Hurst, London, 1982).

[7] However, the military regime was not sincere with respect to its 1992 programme to hand back power to a democratically elected government.

In this wise, the British Westminster and the American presidential system have become models for the drafting of the constitutions in many countries. Thus, encouraged by the glamour and stability of the American presidential system, Nigeria adopted the system in 1979. This replaced the former parliamentary system operated from 1960 to 1966.

The invaluable role of foreign-based non government organizations (NGOs) in the democratic project of many developing states is incontestable. Hence, NGO assistance and support programmes have contributed substantially to the making of some states' constitutions. This is common in states with protracted military rule, which has destroyed the democratic process and values.

Functions of a constitution

A constitution is an inevitable ingredient of any organized union or administrative body. The Court of Appeal affirmed that the constitution is vital to the citizens, the state and government machinery. In the case of *Abaribe v. Abia State House of Assembly*[8] it was held that:

> *A constitution is not a mere common legal document. It is essentially a document relating to and regulating the affairs of the nation state and stating the function and powers of the different components of the government as well as regulating the relationship between the citizens and the state. It equally makes provisions for the rights of the citizens within the compass of the state.*

The basic functions of a constitution include:

i. Acting as a country's mission statement

A general feature of most constitutions is that they state the objectives for the corporate existence of their countries, and set the means of achieving the projected goals. Hence, the inclusion of 'fundamental objectives' and 'directive principles of state policy' in most modern constitutions (Chapter II, 1999 Constitution, Sections 13-24). The reassuring provisions of Section 14 (1) of the 1999 Constitution is that: The Federal Republic of Nigeria shall be state based on the

---

[8] [2002] 14 NWLR (Pt 788) 466CA. p. 472.

principle of democracy and social justice. The constitution then becomes a country's political, social and legal compass.

ii. *Delimits governmental powers*

The systematic constitutional arrangement of government roles into legislative, executive and judicial powers eliminates confusion in governance. In the constitutional context, the above three co-equal and coordinated departments are sovereign within their allocated jurisdictions.

The principle of separation of powers as endorsed by sections 4, 5 and 6 of the 1999 Constitution, strongly confirms this point. Characteristically, article VIII of the Declaration of Rights of the Constitution of Maryland:

> That the legislative and judicial power of government ought to be
> forever separate and distinct from each other; and no person
> exercising the functions of one of the said departments shall
> assume or discharge the duties of any other.

iii. *Enhances the formulation and the execution of public policies*

A constitution creates the organizational ability and specialization in a nation state through specific allocation of governmental powers. As aptly remarked by Professor B.O. Nwabueze:

> *A constitution is a mode of organizing a state and its government.*
> *It is in other words, a body of fundamental principles according*
> *to which a state is organized.* [9]

Therefore, state projects and programmes will be initiated and executed in line with the constitutional guidelines.

iv. *Guarantees citizens' rights*

The age-long crusade for freedom and liberty of man was intensified by the Magna Carta, Petition of Rights, Bill of Rights, United Nations Declaration of the Universal Human Rights and similar charters. These declaration have found local expression through their embodiment in almost all constitutions as *fundamental*

---

[9] B.O. Nwabueze, *Constitutional History of Nigeria*. Christopher Hurst, London, 1982.

human rights. In unmistakable prose, the United States Declaration of Independence on 4 July 1776, avowed that:

> We hold these truths to be self-evident, that all men are created equal, that they are endowed by their creator with certain unalienable rights, that among these are life, liberty and the pursuit of happiness.

In line with this liberal spirit, the 1999 Constitution of Nigeria devoted chapters III and IV to citizenship and fundamental human rights.

Therefore, in the Second Republic case of the *Federal Minister of Internal Affairs and Ors v. Shugaba Darman*, [10] the court held that:

> *In cases involving an infraction of fundamental rights of a citizen, the court ought to award such damages as would serve as a deterrence against naked, arrogant, arbitrary and oppressive abuse of power as in this case.*

v. *Serving as an instrument of development*

A constitution as a living instrument grows along with the state as a corporate entity. This dynamic quality opens the constitution to review in the form of amendments and alterations in response to the increasing needs of the citizenry. Hilaire Barnett eloquently stated this organic quality of the constitution:

> *At the heart of this matter lies one simple fact: all constitutions — however defined and categorized — are dynamic organisms. They are dependent for much of their meaning and relevance on the societal framework which surrounds them.* [11]

It is undisputable that the Basic Law of the Federal Republic of Germany (constitution) was the principal instrument of that country's unification in 1990. It suitably incorporated the citizens from the former Eastern bloc into the democratic virtues of the Western bloc.

---

[10] [1982] 3NCLR 915.

[11] Hilaire Barnett, *Constitutional and Administrative Law*. 3rd edition, (Cavendish Publishing, London): 10.

Chapter 5

Constitutions: Nature and Type

The constitution can only set the standard – and provide a framework of law and order. It cannot solve specific problems directly.

Rom an H erzog

━━

C ountries can be categorized as unitary, federal and confederal states, based on the constitutional structure which they operate.

Constitutional structures

Unitary system (or unitarianism)

This is a constitutional arrangement in which political power and authority are concentrated in one central government. This central government can create and permit the existence of local authorities (provinces, states, districts, counties and sundry) to exercise political power only by delegation.

Hilaire Barnett appraised the British unitarianism in these words:

> *No power is given to the regions or to local government other than that decreed by Parliament. Regional parliaments and assemblies and local authorities are entirely creatures of Acts of Parliament, and any power given can subsequently – subject only to political acceptability to the electorate – be withdrawn.[1]*

───────────────────────────

[1] Hilaire Barnett. *Constitutional and Administrative Law.* 3rd edition. (Cavendish Publishing Limited; London. 2000):13.

Unitarianism is a manifestation of the principle of centralization. The British Local Government Act of 1985 detailed the central parliament's domineering influence in a unitary system. That Parliamentary Act statutorily abolished the Greater London Council and other Metropolitan Borough Councils in 1985.

Confederation (or confederalism)

A confederation is a loose association of sovereign (independent) states formed for the purpose of promoting and accomplishing certain common objectives. The spirit of the loose union, is to cooperate without relinquishing or sacrificing the sovereignty (governmental autonomy) of the individual member states.

Confederations included United Netherlands (1576-1746), United States of America (1771-1789), German confederation (1815-1867), East Africa Confederation of Kenya, Uganda and Tanzania and the defunct Sene-Gambia of Senegal and Gambia (1980-1989). The global drive towards regional economic and political unions, such as the European Economic Community (EEC), the Economic Community of West African States (ECOWAS) and others, manifest features of confederation.

Federal system (or federalism)

Federalism is a system of government in which powers are shared constitutionally between the central government and the individual regions, states, or provinces that constitute the federation. The power sharing arrangement usually ensures that each level or tier is independent or autonomous.

The central government represents the whole country in external and internal matters of common interest. Hence, matters of defence and state security are mostly the exclusive jurisdiction of the central government, while regional, state or provincial authorities exercise exclusive authority on planning and raising of local taxation. A federation typifies the principle of decentralization. The 1999 Constitution section 2(2) clearly states that:

> Nigeria shall be a federation consisting of states and a federal capital territory.

The above notion is in consonance with the verdict of the Supreme Court in *AG Lagos state v. AG Federation & 35 Ors,* in which it was stated that:[2]

> *By section 2(2) of the 1999 Constitution Nigeria shall be a federation and by the doctrine of the federalism, which Nigeria has adopted, the autonomy of each government, which pre-supposes its separate existence and its independence from the control of the other governments essential to federal arrangement. Therefore, each government exists not as appendage entity in the sense of being able to exercise its own will in the conduct of its affairs free from direction by another government.*

Federal states include the United States of America as from 1789, Switzerland from 1848, Dominicans of Canada (1867), Commonwealth of Australia (1900) and Nigeria since 1951, save under the military. Hilaire Barnett captures the basic features of federalism thus:

> *The common features of all federal states are the sharing of power between centre and region – each having an area of exclusive power, other powers being shared on some defined basis. Equally common to all federations is the idea that the written constitution is sovereign over government and legislature and that their respective powers are not only defined by the constitution but are also controlled by the constitution, which will be interpreted and upheld by a supreme court.*[3]

The above premise found favour with the submission of Professor B.O. Nwabueze as *amicius curiae* in the case of *AG of Ondo State v. AG of the Federation & Ors.*[4] This legal luminary opined that:

> ... *The three requirements of the autonomy of the state governments, which firstly carries the notion of equality of status*

---

[2][MJSC] 2003. 7 July, p.18.

[3] Hilaire Barnett, 106.

[4] [2002] 4 NWLR p.33 para FG).

as each government has, by virtue of its independent existence, an equal status as a government with the other governments and is entitled to an equal say, though not necessarily equal weight, in the common council of the Federal State. However, federalism accommodates a certain amount of inequality in power and financial resources between the national and regional governments, so long as any preponderance in favour of one is not such as to reduce the other to virtual impotence.

Secondly, the principle of autonomy in a federal system implies that neither the central government nor the regional government can confer functions or impose duties on the functionaries of the other without the consent of its chief executive as was expressly enacted in sections 99 and 100 of the constitution of the Federal Republic of Nigeria 1963.

Thirdly, the principle of autonomy prohibits one government, while keeping within its power, from exercising it in a way as, in its practical effect, impedes, burdens or interferes with the exercise of the power or the management of the affairs of another government.

The Supreme Court amplified the spirit of the Nigerian federalism in *AG of Ogun & Ors v. AG Federation*[5] when the court held that:

Neither the National Assembly nor the President has the constitutional power to regulate or interfere with the exercise by a state governor of his executive functions. It would also not be competent for a state assembly or a governor to regulate or interfere with the exercise by the president of his executive functions.

The apex court, based on the above premise, declared unconstitutional the President Shehu Shagari's Public Order Act. It is pertinent to remark that the term 'federal military government,' is a constitutional misnomer. The centralized military command structure contradicts the decentralized federal principle.

---

[5] [1982] 3 NCLR. p.166.

Therefore, the state military governors were appointed by the head of state and the ruling council, to whom they were absolutely accountable.

Unitary command culture: A legacy of military rule

The unitary command culture has had a lingering negative impact on Nigeria's federalism with the central government's undue domination of almost all areas of governance. Uwaifo JSC dealt with this issue in *AG Lagos State v. AG Federation and 35 Ors* (supra). There, he posited that:

> *Upon that lingering psyche, the Federal Military Government ought not to have extended its functions to conceive of an urban and regional planning scheme for Nigeria with the implications that it had intruded into the power of the state governments to decide the physical planning of their states for which they would bear the financial burden squarely and take full control for its implementation as envisaged in a federal system of government* . . [6]

thus, generating the ceaseless clamour for the introduction of true fiscal federalism to actualize the constitutional autonomy of the component states.

Professor B.O. Nwabueze bemoaned this crippling phenomenon that has plagued Nigerian federalism for ages thus:

> *An arrangement, such as existed in Nigeria under the military regime, which legally obliges one government to accept direction from another on the conduct of its affairs is not federalism in the true sense of the word.*[7]

It is most unfortunate, that this frustrating trend is still reflected in our public affairs during a civilian regime. The overwhelming and overbearing influence of the federal might in virtually every sector of our national life confirms this factor.

The central disposition of the ruling Peoples Democratic Party (PDP) in canvassing her interests further authenticates this argument. The constitutional role

---

[6] [2003]MJSC 7 July, p.18.

[7] B. O. Nwabueze: Federalism in Nigeria under the Presidential Constitution: Lagos State Ministry of Justice Law Review Series. 2003 p.1

of the National Judicial Council, in its role to oversee the role of state high court judges, testifies unreservedly to this puzzle of federalism. The jurisdiction of the anti-graft agencies of the federal government — the Economic and Financial Crimes Commission (EFCC) and the Independent Corrupt Practices Commission (ICPC) — which covers the field, neutralizes the fervency of Nigerian federalism. As sternly held by Nigeria's leading constitutional jurist, Professor Nwabueze:

> *Federalism presupposes that the national and regional governments should stand to each other in a relation of meaningful independence resting upon a balanced division of power and resources. Each must have power and resources sufficient to support the structure of a functioning government able to stand on its own against the other.*[8]

This worrisome pattern peaked when the then President Olusegun Obasanjo, without recourse to the court, ordered the seizure of money due to the Lagos State Government from the Federation Account on behalf of its local government councils. This despicable development was the subject matter of the case *Attorney General of Lagos State v. Attorney General of the Federation* It was most unfortunate, that a mere personal memo from the president to the minister of finance could stop the payment of constitutionally ordained fund to a state government. More so, the decision of the Supreme Court that the president had no constitutional power to stop the release of money due to Lagos State Government from the Federation Account on behalf of its local government councils, could not reverse that action. In short, the funds were finally and fully released to the Lagos State Government by President Umaru Musa Yar'Adua, Obasanjo's successor.

Most regrettably, however, the same president, Umaru Musa Yar'Adua resurrected the same issue when he threatened to stop the same subvention to Lagos State local governments in 2009. This unfortunate issue still hovers over the relationship between the two governments (October 2009).

---

[8] ibid, 2.

[9] [2004] 18 NWLR Pt. 904.1.

The scope of constitutions

The constitution prescribes the limits of the power of each organ of government and of the various tiers as well. This feature is most prominent in federal constitutions. Section 4(2) of the 1999 Constitution deals with this subject matter.

The delimitation of constitutional powers is usually in this order:

vi. The Exclusive Legislative List

This constitutional area is specifically and exclusively reserved for the central government legislation. The Supreme Court upheld this position in *AG Abia State v. AG Federation*,[10] where it was declared that:

> *By virtue of section 4(2) of the 1999 Constitution, the National Assembly is empowered to make laws with respect to any matter included in the Exclusive Legislative List set out in Part I of the 2nd schedule to the Constitution; and by section 4(4) the National Assembly has the power to make laws with respect to matters in the Concurrent Legislative List set out in Part II of the 2nd schedule to the Constitution.*

In further justification of the above statement, section 4(7)(a) of the Constitution clearly enjoined the House of Assembly of a state to legislate on any matter not included in the Exclusive Legislative List. This constitutional schedule contained 68 items. The profound wide powers of the National Assembly through the Exclusive Legislative List was emphasized vide items 67-68 to the effect that:

- Any other matter with respect to which the National Assembly has power to make laws in accordance with the provisions of this Constitution.

- Any matter incidental or supplementary to any matter mentioned elsewhere in this list.

The Supreme Court, speaking through Ogwuegbu JSC in the *Attorney General of Ondo State v. Attorney General of the Federation & Ors*,[11] declared that:

---

[10] [2002] 6 NWLR 264 SC. p.300.

[11] [2002] 4 NWLR p.12 .

The reference to incidental and supplementary matter on the exclusive legislative list underscores the well established principles of law that every grant of power includes by implication all such other powers as are reasonably incidental thereto and not expressly excluded.

It was on this plank of argument that the court ruled in that case Attorney General of Ondo State v. Attorney General of the Federation [12] that:

The National Assembly possesses both incidental and implied power to promulgate the Corrupt Practices and Other Related Offences Act 2000 in order to enable the state, i.e., the Federal Republic of Nigeria to implement the provisions of section 15(5) of the Constitution.

ii. Concurrent Legislative List

This constitutional subject-matter is held on the basis of partnership between the central government and the component units (states in Nigeria). In this constitutional domain, power is given to each level of government to make laws, but the overriding power is reserved for the central government. The Supreme Court illustrated the principle of this in *AG Abia State v. AG Federation* [13] (supra). The court held that:

The House of Assembly of a state has the power to make laws with respect to any matter not included in Exclusive Legislative List and any matter included in the Concurrent Legislative List.

The 1999 Constitution endorsed this device through sections 4(4)(a) and 4(7((b), to the extent that the component states share legislative powers with the National Assembly on items set out in the first column of Part II of the second schedule to the Constitution to the extent prescribed in the second column opposite thereto. The Constitution had 30 items within this area. It sets out, in some specific terms,

---

[12] Supra p.12 para 9.

[13] [2002] 6 NWLR 264 SC. p.305.

the limits of these co-existing powers, thereby reducing confusion and conflicts between the central and state governments.

This view, as affirmed by our constitutional law icon, B.O. Nwabueze, is that:

> *It is somewhat innovative in its approach in that, apart from enumerating the . . . matters, it also defines the respective extent of federal and state power in respect of these matters, with the aim of reducing possible conflict, especially through the application of the doctrine of covering the field. The result is that a concurrent matter no longer necessarily implies that both the federal and state governments are competent to act over its entire field. In respect of some matters in the list, their competence is respectively restricted to some aspects only of a so called concurrent matter, making such aspects exclusive to the one or the other.*[14]

The Supreme Court defined concurrent in *Olafisoye v. FRN.*[15] She held that:

> *The word 'concurrent' means existing together. What is meant therefore when a matter is said to be concurrent to Federal and State Governments is that their powers in respect of it exist side by side together. In other words, the powers of both governments in respect of the matter are co-existent, not mutually exclusive; the power of one does not exclude that of the other. Both governments can in theory at least, act on the matter. But their power need not necessarily be co-extensive in the sense of extending over the entire field of the matter: they may co-exist only in respect of some aspects of it.*

In the case of any conflict arising from the exercise of the powers within this jurisdiction, the central law shall prevail, and that of the state becomes void to the extent of its inconsistency [Section 4(5)]. The central government under the operation of the doctrine of *covering the field,* can easily erode the autonomy of

---

[14] Nwabueze, 40-41.

[15] [2004] 4NWLR. 864 580 SC. p. 603 para.14.

the component units on this subject matter. The Supreme Court recognized this doctrine in *AG Abia State v. AG Federation* (supra)by emphasizing that:

> *The doctrine of 'Covering the Field' also referred to as the doctrine of inconsistency means that when a state law, if valid, would alter, impair or detract from the operation of a Federal Law, then to that extent it is invalid.*[16]

This jurisdiction is usually a subject of contention between the central government and the federating states.

iii. Residual list

The residual list is traditionally the preserve of the component or federating states. The residual lists contains items that were neither listed in the exclusive nor concurrent list. The Supreme Court's supportive tone on this topic in *AG Abia State v. AG Federation* is:

> *And by virtue of section 4(7)(a) of the 1999 Constitution residual matters are for the state, and not the federal, to legislate upon.*[17]

The residual jurisdiction may be enumerated or not enumerated (implied as items outside the exclusive and concurrent lists). The 1999 Constitution does not categorize any other list beyond the exclusive and concurrent lists.

Types of constitutions

Constitutions are conventionally classified as *'written'* or *'unwritten'*, based on their manner of documentation. The procedure of their amendment or alteration further characterizes them into 'rigid' and 'flexible'.

i. Written constitution

This is where the basic laws and principles in relation to the organization of government, the distribution of powers, and the rights of the citizens are contained in one document or a series of documents. The United States of America, the

---

[16] Supra, 327.

[17] Supra, 305.

Republic of Germany and Nigeria are classic examples of countries with written constitutions.

ii. Unwritten constitutions

An unwritten constitution in contrast to a written one, is where the basic laws and principles guiding the state are not codified or expressly written as a document or series of documents. The British Constitution, drawn from diverse sources as far back as the 13th century to the present day, is an example of an unwritten constitution. It has become recognized over a long period of time and usage.

iii. Rigid constitutions

This term is applied to a constitution that requires a long and difficult process beyond ordinary law making procedures for its amendment or alteration. The framers of a written constitution usually focus on building a comprehensive legal framework for their country, which prevents the provisions of the constitution from frivolous and incessant amendments. Hence, they devise stringent procedures that must be complied with for the amendment or alteration of the constitution.

Nigeria's 1999 Constitution, Section 9(2) provides that the National Assembly on issues outside new states and boundary adjustment (Section 8) can amend the constitution. That amendment requires a proposal supported by the votes of not less than two-thirds majority of all the members of both houses and approved by a resolution of the houses of assembly of not less than two-thirds of all the states.

Furthermore, Section 9(3) of the same constitution added to the requirement for the National Assembly to be able to amend Section 8 (New States and Boundary Adjustment) and Chapter IV (Fundamental Rights). Here, the proposal must be approved by the votes of not less than four-fifths majority of all the members of each House of Assembly, of not less than two-thirds of all the states. The above-cited provisions highlight the rigidity of the 1999 Constitution.

iv. Flexible constitution

The flexibility of a constitution relates to where the method of amendment is the same as the ordinary law-making process. In Britain, which is a notable example of a flexible constitutional arrangement, amendment can be effected by mere parliamentary majorities. The traditional concept of parliamentary sovereignty aids constitutional flexibility because no court can hold an Act of Parliament to be void.

Alteration (amendment) of the constitution

Our current federal constitution categorized procedures for its alteration with two different requirements. This constitution accorded great importance to the creation of new states, boundary adjustments and fundamental human rights. The unique importance accorded these three items namely: (i) creation of new states, (ii) boundary adjustment, and (iii) human rights manifest the rigidity of the 1999 Constitution. It created strict and special requirements for their alteration or amendment.

Alteration of other provisions of the constitution

The constitution through Section 9(2) requires that an Act of the National Assembly seeking an alteration of any part of the constitution, save Section 8, can only be passed by either chamber of the National Assembly with the support of not less than a two-thirds majority of all the members and approved by a resolution of the houses of assembly of not less than two-thirds of all the states.

Alteration (amendment) of Section 8 and Chapter IV of the Constitution

Section 9(3) of the constitution specifically requires that a legislative proposal for the alteration of these two important portions of the constitution can only be passed by either house of the National Assembly with a support approved vote of not less than a four-fifths majority of all the members of each house, and also approved by a resolution of the Houses of Assembly of not less than two-thirds of all the states.

The significance of state creation was highlighted in Section 9(4) where it was stated that the number of members of each House of the National Assembly shall, not withstanding any vacancy, be deemed to be number of members specified in Sections 48 and 49 of the Constitution.

Chapter 6

Supremacy of the Nigerian Constitution and the Separation of Powers

It is relation of a superior to an inferior authority. The constitution is supreme over the legislature because it controls the legislature in the latter's law-making function.

Professor B.O . N w abueze, SA N

---

*T*he constitution is the supreme law of the land. It enjoys overriding superiority over all laws and institutions within its jurisdiction; all laws, policies and initiatives are subordinate to its prescribed limits and procedures. Hence, Section 1(1) of the 1999 Constitution emphatically states that:

> This constitution is supreme and its provisions shall have binding force on all authorities and persons throughout the Federal Republic of Nigeria.

The Supreme Court re-affirmed this status in *AG Abia State v. AG Federation*[1] in these words:

> *The constitution is the grundnorm and the fundamental law of the land. All other legislations take their hierarchy from the provisions of the constitution. The provisions of the constitution take precedence over any law enacted by the National Assembly even though the National Assembly has the power to amend the constitution itself. By the provisions of the constitution, the law*

---

[1] [2002] 6 NWLR.264SC. p.300.

> *made by the National Assembly comes next to the constitution,*
> *followed by those made by the House of Assembly.*[2]

The concept of the supremacy of the constitution means that any law, policy, initiative or procedure that is inconsistent with any provision of the constitution is to the extent of the inconsistency null and void. This supremacy is specifically spelt out in subsection 1(3) of the 1999 Constitution. Also, in the case of *INEC v. Musa*, 40[3] the Supreme Court, with a tone of finality, pronounced on the registration of more political parties that:

> *The legislative power of the legislature cannot be exercised*
> *inconsistently with the constitution. Where it is so exercised, it is*
> *invalid to the extent of its inconsistency.*

The legislature and supremacy of the constitution

The legislature is the law-making organ of the country and its federating units (the National Assembly and state houses of assembly) in accordance with the spirit and provisions of the constitution which subordinates the legislature to the constitution.

The Supreme Court affirmed this position in *AG Abia State* v. *AG Federation* (supra):

> *The National Assembly does not have any inherent power to make*
> *laws. It is a creation of the constitution and it can only exercise*
> *such power as conferred on it by the constitution.*[4]

In more uncompromising and emphatic language, the apex court, in *INEC v. Musa*[5] (supra), held that:

> *The supremacy of the National Assembly is subject to the overall*
> *supremacy of the constitution. Accordingly, the National*
> *Assembly, which derives its legislative power from the*

---

[2] [2002] 6 NWLR 264 SC. p.298-299.

[3] [2003] 3 NWLR pt. 806 p.109.

[4] Supra, 303.

[5] Supra.

constitution, cannot go outside or beyond the constitution. Where such a situation arises, the courts will, in an action by an aggrieved party, pronounce the act unconstitutional, null and void. [6]

This concept is evident in the fact that the constitution controls the legislature and prescribes its composition, quorum, practices and procedures. The legislature is bound to comply strictly with the provisions of the constitution, else, its enactments will be invalid.

Nigeria's attempts at establishing democracy since 1960 have produced landmark decisions in the Supreme Court in support of this doctrine. In the case of *Balewa v. Doherty*, [7] the Supreme Court of Nigeria voided the Commissions and Tribunal of Enquiry Act of 1961. Declaring the Act null and void, the Supreme Court held that the Act did not have jurisdiction to judge the regional competence of the Western Region to manage its own affairs and had no right to question the conduct of a civil servant in the Western Region, which was an independent unit with its own constitution.

Another landmark decision occurred during the Second Republic, in the celebrated case of *AG Bendel v. AG Federation*, [8] the Supreme Court's verdict rested on the premise:

That the Allocation of Revenue (Federation Account, etc) Bill 1980 did not pass through the legislative process laid down by the 1979 constitution and that, consequently, the Allocation of Revenue (Federation Account, etc) Act 1981 is not an Act of the National Assembly and its entire provisions are null and void and of no effect whatsoever.

---

[6] Supra, 114-115.

[7] [1961] IANLR 604 (SC).

[8] [1981] ANLR p.104 para.13.

The same spirit of judicial review and constitutionalism characterized the case of *AG Abia v.AG Federation* (supra), where, in a most eloquent tone, the Supreme Court declared that:

> *The provisions of Sections 119, 120, 121 and 122 of the Electoral Act 2001 do not deal with matters of procedure regulating elections to local government councils. Some of the provisions in Section 21 are, in fact, already in the Constitution. The National Assembly lacks the legislative power to enact these sections. They are unconstitutional, inoperative, null and void.*[9]

The supremacy of the constitution demands that the substantive and procedural requirements of the constitution must be strictly adhered to, otherwise, the emergent enactment or law will be declared void.

It is pertinent that most of the striking court decisions that have upheld the spirit of judicial review in the current dispensation were made in view of the concept of the supremacy of the constitution. The verdicts in *INEC v. Musa; AG Ondo v. AG Federation; AG Lagos v. AG Federation and 35 Ors; AG Abia v. AG Federation* (supra) corroborate the supremacy of the constitution as the beacon of democracy. This means that the legislature must comply strictly with the provisions of the constitution, even when it becomes necessary to alter or amend the constitution.

Doctrine of 'separation of powers'

The most popular exponent of the separation of powers was the French Jurist, Baron de Montesquieu (1689-1755), in the book, *The Spirit of the Law* (*Esprit des Lois*). Other political writers and thinkers such as John Locke, Aristotle, Blackstone, Harrington, Hegel and the American *Federalist* writers also dealt with the concept.

The doctrine of the separation of powers upholds the traditional three basic divisions of the organs of government and their functions. In this wise, law making (the legislature), execution (the executive), and adjudication (the judiciary) are distinguished and performed by three separate and independent organs of government.

---

[9] supra, p. 348.

By implication, there is to be a clear demarcation of functions between the legislature, the executive and the judiciary, in order to check abuse of power. Baron de Montesquieu's strict adherence to the independence of these organs is expressed as follows:

> *When the legislative and executive powers are united in the same person, or in the same body of magistrates, there can be no liberty . . . Again, there is no liberty if the power of judging is not separated from the legislature and executive. If it were joined with the legislature, the life and liberty of the subject would be exposed to arbitrary control; for the judge would then be the legislator. If it were joined to the executive power, the judge might behave with violence and oppression. There would be an end to everything, if the same man, or the same body, whether of the nobles or the people, were to exercise those three powers; that of enacting laws, that of executing public affairs, and that of trying crimes or individual causes.[10]*

In the case of *Ahmad v. Sokoto State House of Assembly*, the Court of Appeal stated three implications of the doctrine of separation of powers:

a. That the same person should not be part of more than one of these three arms or divisions of government.

b That one branch should not dominate or control another arm. This is particularly important in the relationship between the executive and the court.

c That one branch should not attempt to exercise the functions of the other; for example, a president, however powerful, ought not to make laws or indeed act, except in the execution of laws made by the legislature. Nor should the legislature make interpretative legislation; if it is in doubt, it should head for the court to seek an interpretation.[11]

---

[10] Appadorai, 516-517.

[11] [2003] 15 NWLR pt. 791, 538 CA p.545-546.

In accordance with this concept, the 1999 Constitution assigned specific roles to each of the three arms of government. Section 4 confers law-making powers on the National Assembly and the state houses of assembly. By virtue of Section 5, executive powers rest with the president, to be exercised by him directly, or through the vice-president and ministers of government or officers in the public service of the federation.

State governors also exercise executive powers directly or indirectly through deputy governors, commissioners and officers in the public service of the states. Likewise, Section 6 vests judicial powers in the courts.

The Supreme Court lucidly highlighted this political concept in *Attorney General of the Federation v. Attorney General of Abia State & 35 Ors*[12] by pronouncing that:

> *The principles behind the concept of separation of powers is that none of the three arms of government under the constitution should encroach into the powers of the other. Each arm – the executive, legislative and judicial is separate and equal and co-ordinate department and no arm can constitutionally take over the functions clearly assigned to the other. Thus the powers and functions constitutionally entrusted to each arm cannot be encroached by the other. The doctrine is to promote efficiency in governance by precluding the exercise of arbitrary power by all and thus prevent friction.*

Experience has shown, however, that the complete separation of powers is impossible. The term merely fulfills administrative convenience, because a rigid separation of powers frustrates government activities. Hood Philips has rightly observed that:

> *A complete separation of powers in the sense of a distribution of the three functions of government among three independent sets of organs, with no overlapping or coordination, would (even if theoretically possible) bring government to a standstill.*[13]

---

[12] supra.

[13] O. Hood Philips. *Constitutional and Administrative Law*. 16ᵗʰ edition. (ELBS Fletcher and Son. 1978), 14.

Concept of 'checks and balances'

It is only through the application of the complementary doctrine of checks and balances that the separation of powers can be realized in real life situations. The doctrine of checks and balances seeks to control and limit the power of one branch of government through the powers of another. In practice these distinguishable branches of government with definite functions, influence each other while exercising their constitutionally allotted powers.

The executive arm of government is acclaimed as the most prolific initiator of legislative bills in most democracies. The assent of the chief executive is required for the transformation of a bill passed by the legislature, into law. On the other hand, the legislature and the judiciary also perform roles that have executive complexion and that overlap each other's primary domains.

As rightly remarked by Professor B.O. Nwabueze:

The idea of checks and balances presupposes that a specific function is assigned primarily to a given organ subject to a power of limited interference by another organ to ensure that each organ keeps within the sphere delimited to it.[14]

It is on the above premise that the 'three month crisis' in the House of Representatives (2007) comes to the fore.[15] The stance of President Umaru Musa Yar'Adua was that, based on the principle of separation of powers, the executive arm of government lacked the jurisdiction to interfere in that crisis.

But since that legislative arm was inaugurated on the powers of the president by his proclamation vide Section 64 (3) of the constitution, the above cited position of the president is not convincing. In short, the dissolution of that legislature is equally subject to the president's proclamation under the same constitutional provision (Section 64 (3)).

This 'three month crisis' also resulted in the postponement of the president's presentation of his 2008 Appropriation Bill to the National Assembly,

---

[14] B.O. Nwabueze, *Constitutionalism in the Emergent States* (Christopher Hurst & Co. London, in association with Nwamife Publishers, Enugu, 1973), p. 20.

[15] This is the crisis that led to the removal of the Speaker of the House of Representatives, Mrs. Patricia Olubunmi Ette (see Chapter 7 for a fuller discussion).

which is matter of urgent national importance. The president, based on his constitutional Oath of Office and Oath of Allegiance to preserve, protect and defend the Constitution of the Federal Republic of Nigeria, should have made a national pronouncement on the issue. He could have used this crisis to caution the legislators and set a higher moral tone, more especially as the physical combat during the committee session and on the floor of the house was demeaning to the high offices these people hold.

The uneasy silence of the Senate and the state houses of assembly nationwide on this issue cannot be attributed to their duty to the concept of separation of powers. The complementary concept of checks and balances could have been applied proactively to redeem this national embarrassment.

Dr. Cornelius Ejimofor's poignant assessment of this stark reality was instructive:

> *In essence, the concept of separation of powers is incomplete without the concept of checks and balances. The latter supplements the former, and both concepts constitute a dual principle. Any system of government based on the principle of separation of powers that fails to incorporate some elements of the twin principle of checks and balances will lack coordination of the three branches of government and risk the possibility of partial tyranny in the form of isolated legislative, executive or judicial abuse. The system of checks and balances provides an overlapping of authority which makes it possible for each of the three branches of government to limit the excesses of the powers granted to the other two. It ensures that officials of the different branches of government would not exceed their powers or merge powers to rule tyrannically.*[16]

Modern government demands mutual coordination and the marriage of roles between all the arms of government. Public functionaries must, therefore, ensure that the expected advancement of their constituencies is guaranteed. The emphasis

---

[16] Dr Cornelius Ejimofor 'The Concept of the Separation of Powers' a paper presented at the legislative workshop for members of the Anambra State House of Assembly, Enugu, March 1981, p. 7-8.

should be on cooperation and respect between the various arms of government as a model for political stability.

Chapter 7

General Functions of the Legislature

Legislation is the formulation of laws by the appropriate organ of the state, in such a manner that the actual words used are themselves part of the law. The words not only contain the law, but in a sense they constitute the law.

O . H ood Philips & Paul Jackson

---

*T*he legislature is the branch of government charged with the responsibility of making, revising, amending and repealing laws for the advancement and well-being of the society. This primary role notwithstanding, the necessities and complexities of public administration have made it necessary for the legislature to perform some seemingly non-legislative duties, ie, engage in executive and judicial functions. These are aimed at checking the executive and shaping public policies for the benefit of the country. These functions are discussed below.

i. Approval of executive and judicial appointments

In many countries, the constitution requires that the chief executive (prime minister or president) submits the list of his nominations for members of his executive council and other government functionaries to the legislature. The legislature screens and approves such nominations before they are confirmed and announced. Likewise the Nigerian president is required by the constitution to submit the nominations for his cabinet (ministers and special advisers), federal judges, ambassadors, and some other public officials to the senate for approval.

ii. Adoption and ratification of treaties

In some countries, international agreements with international organizations cannot be recognized and enforced unless they are adopted by the country's legislature. This role is most evident in countries like Nigeria and the United States, which operate the principle of incorporation with regard to international law. In these countries, international treaties must be domesticated or localized by the legislature before they come into effect. Thus, international treaties must receive legislative approval and local enactment before they can be legitimized.

iii. Approval of public spending

As a rule in most democratic constitutions, public money cannot be raised or spent without legislative approval. Although the proposal for raising and spending public funds comes from the executive, it must receive legislative approval for it to be operational. Hence, annual estimates and budgets prepared by the executive are submitted to the legislature as appropriation bills. On approval by the legislature and after the chief executive's assent, they transform into appropriation laws or Acts for the running of the country within prescribed periods.

iv. Investigation and resolution of conflicts

The legislature also has the responsibility to register public opinion and grievances. This role has earned it the names: *'society's post office', 'errand boy', 'committee of grievances', 'congress of opinion'* and so on. In this wise, most of the nagging private and public problems of the citizenry, can be expressed through the legislature. Thus, protest marches, demonstrations and petitions in private and public capacities are directed towards the legislature. The Public Complaints Committee of the legislature reflects the mood of the populace. The constitutional powers of the legislature to investigate executive actions and private wrongdoings places it in a vital position of being the guardian of democracy and the protector of citizens' rights.

v. Electoral role

In some countries, the legislature, as the most representative arm of government, performs some electoral functions. In the United States, the Congress counts and checks the votes cast by the electoral college (the group of electors who choose the president and vice-president). If no candidate secures a majority of the votes by the electoral college, the responsibility for selecting a winner rests with the Congress. The House of Representatives chooses the president, while the Senate elects the vice president. Similarly, in Germany, the Bundestag elects the chancellor.

vi. Impeachment and judicial function

Impeachment entails a charge of serious misconduct against a public office holder. In some countries, the legislature is empowered to investigate an allegation of such misconduct. The outcome of such an investigation determines the continuance or the removal of the office holder in question.

In the United States, the House of Representatives is empowered to bring charges of impeachment against officials of the national government. If a particular charge attracts the majority of the votes in the House of Representatives, the Senate then sits as a court to it.

The United States Congress has exercised this power on two occasions since its inception in 1789. There have however, been some acquittals. In 1868, the House of Representatives voted to impeach President Andrew Johnson, but the Senate narrowly acquitted him. President Bill Clinton passed through the same fate in 1998. President Richard Nixon resigned in 1974 before the House of Representatives voted on the impeachment charges against him.

vii. Checks on the conduct of members

The legislature, in recognition of the onerous constitutional responsibilities placed in its hands, acts as a role model for the society. Thus, it can censure and administer punitive measures to erring members, such as suspension, fine, and expulsion for improper conduct.

In 1989, in the United States, James C. Wright Jr, as the Speaker of the House, resigned his seat after being accused of receiving a bribe and earning more income from outside sources than the House Rules permitted. In 1997, Newt Gingrich went on record as the first Speaker of the House of Representatives (in the US) to be reprimanded. He was fined $300,000 for using a tax-exempted donation for political purposes and for giving misleading information to the House Committee on Ethics.

viii. Authorizes taxation and fiscal policies

The legislature, in most democracies, is also saddled with the responsibility to collect taxes, duties, imports, excises and other levies, as will be dictated by her enactments.

The policy deliberation and decision mechanism of the parliament avails her of the opportunity to undertake tax reforms and other related revenue reviews. In this sphere, the executive arm of government and her agencies charged with this subject matter, yield constitutionally to the powers of the law-making body to attain tax review or reform. Thus, public interest represented by the legislators becomes paramount as the input of the citizenry in the eventual tax law or fiscal policy.

ix. Consents to the use of the armed forces and declaration of state of emergency

The liberal democratic standard the world over, is the constitutional check on the executive command and control of the armed forces through legislative approval. Therefore, the chief executive requires the confirmation of the parliament (legislature) before the armed forces could be deployed for external or domestic mission.

Similarly, the suspension of the ordained constitutional procedure by the declaration of a 'state of emergency' due to a natural disaster or a miscarriage of public policy also requires the consent of the legislature.

Therefore, there must be a measure of collective responsibility on broad-based decisions that will entail military action or the suspension of constitutional operations.

That collective deliberation and open resolution for recourse to such emergency option, accords transparency and legitimacy to the resultant government action. Hence, actualizing the democratic tenets of government of the people by the people for the people.

Types of legislature

There are two types of legislature depending on the number of the chambers: unicameral and bicameral.

i. Unicameral legislature (unicameralism)

This is a legislature with one chamber. State houses of assembly, as currently constituted in Nigeria (vide Section 4(6) of the constitution) are unicameral. The local government's lawmaking council is equally a unicameral legislature.

ii. Bicameral legislature (bicameralism)

This is a legislature which has two chambers. The first chamber is usually referred to as the *'lower house'*, while the second is called the *'upper house'*. It is customary in this arrangement for the upper chamber to embody more experienced men than the lower chamber. In addition, the membership of the upper chamber is usually smaller than the lower chamber. Alexis de Tocqueville aptly described the quality of the United States' Senate in these words:

> *Scarcely an individual is to be perceived in it who does not recall the ideal of an active and illustrious career; the Senate is composed of eloquent advocates, distinguished generals, wise magistrates, and statesmen of note, whose language could, at all times, do honour to the most remarkable parliamentary debates . . .* [17]

Presently, the National Assembly in Nigeria, which is composed of the Senate and the House of Representatives (Section 4(1) of the constitution) is a notable example of bicameralism. The Senate is the upper chamber, while the House of Representatives is the lower chamber. Other examples of bicameralism are: the British parliamentary system of the House of Lords and the House of Commons, the United States' Congress, comprising the Senate and the House of Representatives, Germany's Bundesrat and Bundestag, and the French National Assembly, comprising the Chamber of Deputies and the Senate.

---

[17] Alexis de Tocqueville, *Democracy in America.* Vol.1 (Alfred A. Knopf, New York, 1948), 204.

Blank

Chapter 8

Legislative Powers in the 1999 Constitution

Where the constitution sets the conditions for doing a thing, no legislation of the National Assembly or of a State House of Assembly can alter those conditions in any way, directly or indirectly, unless the constitution itself, as an attribute of its supremacy expressly so authorizes.

Suprem e C ourt in *INEC v. M usa* [1]

T he 1999 Constitution conferred the legislative powers of the federation on the National Assembly. Also, the legislative powers of the component states are conferred on the state houses of assembly. The Supreme Court affirmed this in *AG Ondo State v. AG Federation*, (supra) where it was stated that:

By virtue of Section 4(1) of the 1999 constitution, the power to legislate for the Federal Republic of Nigeria is vested in the National Assembly, to wit: The Senate and the House of Representatives. Section 4(2) empowers the National Assembly to make laws for the peace, order and good governance of the federation or any part thereof with respect to any matter included in the Exclusive Legislative List which is set out in part 1 of the 2nd schedule to the constitution. [2]

---

[1] [2003] 3 NWLR pt.806, p.109.

[2] [2002] 9 NWLR pt.722. p.242.

Similarly, Section 4(7) (a) – (c), deals with the source and extent of the legislative powers of a state house of assembly. In the performance of these roles, the National Assembly and the state houses of assembly have these duties.

i. Approval of executive and judicial appointments

The constitution empowers the Senate to approve the ministerial appointments by the president (vide Section 147(2)). This power, as conferred by Section 154(1) of the constitution, also extends to the appointment of chairmen and members (except ex-officio) of federal commissions and councils and other bodies (enumerated n Section 153(1)). Confirmation of ambassadorial appointments is contained in subsection 171(4).

Equally, the appointment of the Chief Justice of Nigeria and the justices of the Supreme Court, are subject to confirmation by the Senate (Section 231(1)-(2) of the constitution). Senate must also approve the appointment of the president of the Court of Appeal (Section238(1)) and that of the Chief Judge of the Federal High Court (Section 250(1)).

In the same vein, the state house of assembly is vested with the power to confirm the state nominees for the post of commissioner. [3]By virtue of Section 198 of the constitution, the state house of assembly also confirms the appointment of chairmen and members of bodies or commissions listed in Section 197(1) of the constitution. With regard to the judiciary, the state house of assembly is empowered to confirm the appointment of the chief judge of a state (Section 271(1)), the grand kadi of the sharia court of appeal of a state (Section 276(1)) and the president of a customary court of appeal (Section 281(1)).

ii. Approval of public spending

Nigeria subscribes to the general democratic principle that public monies cannot be raised or spent without legislative approval. Hence, Section 80(3)-(4) of the constitution clearly states that:

> No money shall be withdrawn from any public fund of the federation, other than the consolidated revenue fund of the federation, unless the

---

[3] Vide subsection 192(2) of the constitution.

issue of this money has been authorized by an Act of the National Assembly.

State houses of assembly derive their jurisdiction on expenditures similar to that of the National Assembly, by the provisions of Section 120(3)–(4) of the constitution.

iii. Impeachment check on the executive

The constitution provides formidable checks and balances to the actions of the executive arm of government through the impeachment instrument to be used by the legislature. The severity of an impeachable offence was affirmed by the court of appeal in *Abaribe v. Abia State House of Assembly* revealed that:

> *An impeachable offence is a gross misconduct which may mean a grave violation or breach of the constitution or a misconduct of such a nature as amounts in the opinion of the House of Assembly, to gross misconduct.*[4]

The National Assembly derives the power to remove the president or the vice-president from Section 143 of the constitution. A state house of assembly can express this power against the governor or the deputy governor of the state by virtue of Section 188. In *Abaribe v. Abia State House of Assembly* (supra), the Court of Appeal endorsed the judicial complexion of this power. It was held that:

> *When the House of Assembly is exercising its constitutional power in a matter relating to proceedings on impeachment, the House is performing a judicial function.*[5]

Nigeria has witnessed disturbing applications of this constitutional power on frivolous grounds since 1979. In the Second Republic, the Kaduna State House of Assembly removed Governor Balarabe Musa from office through a questionable application of this power. Prior to this, Balarabe Musa's nominees for

---

[4] [2002] 14 NWLR pt.788. 466 CA p.474.

[5] supra p.473.

commissioners for the state were rejected by the House on three occasions. Thus, he governed Kaduna State for twenty-one months without an executive council until his eventual removal.

In April 2000, Senator Arthur Nzeribe, without due process, introduced a motion in the Senate for the impeachment of President Olusegun Obasanjo. In a more brazen fashion, the House of Representatives arrogated to itself the constitutional prerogative of the Senate President under Section 143(2) (a) and that of the National Assembly under Section 143(4) by proceeding with impeachment charges against the president in 2002. This was repeated in May 2005, when some members of the House of Representatives again embarked on a plan to impeach the president.

The trend from the states since 1999 revealed that deputy governors became victims of this provision. It was a veritable instrument in the hands of governors to deal with uncooperative and disloyal deputies.[6]

This republic's impeachment drive, started with the Abia State House of Assembly's removal of Enyinnaya Abaribe as the state's deputy governor in 2000.

Iyiola Omisore, the deputy governor of Osun State was impeached in 2002. In 2003, the Anambra State House of Assembly impeached the state deputy governor, Dr. Okey Udeh. Akwa Ibom State followed suit with the impeachment of the state deputy governor, Christopher Stephen Ekpenyong on 23 June 2005. However, the House later reversed the decision as a result of intervention by the ruling Peoples Democratic Party (PDP) and reinstated Ekpenyong.[7]

In Ekiti State, Abiodun Aluko, the deputy governor, was impeached in 2005. On 14 February 2006, Abia State House of Assembly removed Dr. Chima Nwafor, deputy governor of the state.

The wind of impeachment also began to blow against the governors, starting with the hasty impeachment of Diepreye Alamieyeseigha, the governor of Bayelsa State, on 9 December 2005. Similarly, on 12 January 2006, 18 members of the 32-member Oyo State House of Assembly impeached Rashidi Ladoja, the chief executive of that state.

---

[6] supra.

[7] Ekpeyong, however, was *re*-impeached by the house later in the same year.

On 16 October 2006, amid political confusion and the dissenting pronouncements of two different impeachment panels of investigation, Ayo Fayose and Mrs Abiodun Olujimi were removed as governor and deputy governor, respectively, of Ekiti State. Anambra State also joined the impeachment drive when 21 lawmakers, at 5.30 a.m. on 2 November 2006, removed the state governor, Peter Obi from office. The worrisome impeachment wind also blew over Plateau State at 6.30 a.m. on 13 November 2006. There, a faction of six legislators out of a house of 24 members, brazenly impeached Joshua Dariye as governor of the state.

In June 2008, twenty members of the Adamawa House of Assembly served an impeachment notice on the State Governor Vice-Admiral Muritala Nyako, rtd. The ruling People's Democratic Party (PDP) intervened and resolved the matter as an internal party or 'family affair'.

On Thursday, August 13th 2009, the Bauchi State House of Assembly impeached the deputy governor of the state, Alhaji Muhammed Garba Gadi.

The House of Representatives also issued an impeachment threat to President Umaru Yar' Adua for his failure to implement the 2009 budget (July 2009).

iv. Checks on principal judicial officers

The National Assembly through the Senate and the State Houses of Assembly play vital role in the appointment and removal of judicial officers in both tiers of government.

These judicial appointments are subject to the recommendation of the National Judicial Council (NJC). Hence, by virtue of Section 231 (1) and (2) of the constitution, the chief justice of Nigeria and justices of the Supreme Court, will be appointed by the president based on the recommendation of the National Judicial Council (NJC) and subject to the confirmation of the Senate.

Similarly, the chief judge of a state and the judges of the state high court shall be appointed by the governor of the state based on the recommendation of the National Judicial Council and subject to the confirmation of the State house of assembly as ordained by Section 271 (1) and (2) of the Constitution.

It is the appointment of the head of the other federal courts that require Senate confirmation. The judges of these other courts are appointed by the president on the recommendation of the National Judicial Council.

See   Section 238   (1)-(2) Court of Appeal

         Section 250   (1)-(2) Federal High Court

         Section 261   (1)-(2) Sharia Court of Appeal of the Federal Capital Territory

         Section 266   (1)-(2) Customary Court of Appeal of the Federal Capital Territory

The state constitutional jurisdiction is also in accord with the above category as follows:

         Section 276   (1)-(2) Sharia Court of Appeal of a State.

         Section 281   (1)-(2) Customary Court of Appeal of a State.

The removal of these judicial officers as provided by section 292 (1) (a) (i) - (ii) demand vital parliamentary imput especially in respect of the presiding judicial officers at both layers of government.

Hence, the president acting on an address supported by two-thirds majority of the Senate can effect the removal of the presiding judicial officer of any of the federal courts – section 292 (1) (a) (i).

In the same vein, the state governor acting on an address supported by two-thirds majority of the house of assembly of the state can remove the presiding officer of any of the courts under the state jurisdiction – Section 292 (1) (a)(ii)

The other judicial officers apart from these presiding judicial officers of the afore stated courts can be removed by the president (federal jurisdiction) or the governor (state jurisdiction) based on the recommendation of the National Judicial Council. The reason for the removal shall be based on the inability to discharge the function of the office or appointment which arose from infirmity of mind or of body or for misconduct or contravention of the code of conduct – section 292 (1) (b).

v. Adoption and ratification of treaties

The National Assembly shares a constitutional responsibility with the president of the country in the actualization of international treaties or conventions entered into by Nigeria with other foreign states or international organizations. Nigeria operates the international law principle of incorporation of treaties. International agreements must therefore be domesticated or enacted as local laws before they can be enforceable and binding. The provision of section 12(1) of the 1999 Constitution highlights this principle thus:

> No treaty between the federation and any other country shall have the force of law except to the extent to which any such treaty has been enacted into law by the National Assembly.

The Supreme Court stressed this point in the case of *Abacha v.Fawehinmi,*[8] where it was held that:

> *An international treaty entered into by the Government of Nigeria does not become binding until enacted into law by the National Assembly. Before its enactment into law by the National Assembly, it has no such force of law as to make its provisions justifiable in our courts. This was the tenor of Section 12(1) of the 1979 constitution now re-enacted in Section 12(1) of the 1999 Constitution.*

The power to sign a treaty resides exclusively with the president. The constitution, however, requires the National Assembly to consent to its application as a local enactment. This stipulation has resulted in the non-utilization of many treaties, conventions and other forms of international agreements, which Nigeria subscribed to, because the National Assembly did not consent to make them local enactments.

vi. Electoral role

A simple majority of a joint session of the National Assembly, as required by section 136(1) of the constitution, can approve the appointment of the vice-president as president, in a situation where the president-elect dies or is unable to be sworn into office. In this situation, the vice-president elect assumes the office of the president. However, the consequent nominee for the

---

[8] [2000] 6 NWLR (Pt 660) 228 SC. p.246 para.3.

vice-presidency must be subjected to the vote of a joint session of the National Assembly.

Similarly, by a simple majority, a state house of assembly can approve the appointment of the deputy governor of the state as governor in a situation where the governor-elect dies or is unable to be sworn into office (see section 181(1) of the constitution). The contention in the case of *PDP v. INEC*[9] ran counter to the provision of the foregoing section. In this instance, Atiku Abubakar vacated his position as governor-elect of Adamawa State before he could be sworn in as vice-president.

In addition, the National Assembly can enact laws on the procedures for regulating elections. Similarly, the state houses of assembly can legislate on local government elections. The Supreme Court affirmed this when it declared in *AG Abia State v. AG Federation* (supra):

> *By virtue of item II on the concurrent legislative list in the 1999 Constitution, it is the National Assembly that has power to make laws with respect to the conduct of elections to a local government council. However, the house of assembly of a state is not precluded from making laws with respect to election to the local government council so long as such laws are not inconsistent with any law validly made by the National Assembly.*[10]

vii. Authorizes taxation and fiscal policies

The constitution appreciates governance as a collective enterprise. Hence, the citizenry's input, as their civic duty through their elected representatives in taxation and related levies, is guaranteed. This factor resonates the age-old dictum of 'no taxation without representation'. Thus, any bill or proposal to increase or decrease taxes or levies requires the passage by the National Assembly.

Likewise revenue allocation which aims at equitable distribution of the national wealth is covered by Section 163 of the constitution. The primary role of the National Assembly as upheld by Section 163 is:

---

[9] [1999] INWLR Pt 626 SC.

[10] supra, p. 322.

Where under an Act of the National Assembly, tax or duty is imposed in respect of any matters specified in item D of Part II of the second schedule to this constitution, the net proceeds of such tax or duty shall be distributed among the states on the basis of derivation and accordingly–

(a) where such tax or duty is collected by the government of a state or other authority of the State, the net proceeds shall be treated as part of the Consolidated Revenue Fund of that state;

(b) where such tax or duty is collected by the government of the federation or other authority of the federation, there shall be paid to each State at such times as the National Assembly may prescribe a sum equal to the proportion of the net proceeds of such tax or duty that are derived from that state.

It is obvious from the tenor of these constitutional provisions, that the social well-being of the citizenry is derived from their mandate to collect taxes and distribute this tax revenue equitably. That democratic power is expressed through their elected representatives in the National Assembly. The National Assembly legislation, in furtherance of the provisions under item 59 of the exclusive list and item 7 of the concurrent legislative list, upholds this point. The central legislature can, using the concurrent legislative list, prescribe the terms under which the state governments are empowered to raise money through taxes.

viii. *The use of the armed forces and the declaration of a state of emergency*

In the spirit of collective responsibility, the constitution charges the National Assembly with maintaining and equipping the armed forces through its legislation. The constitutional authority for this power is Section 217(2).

The constitution strictly subjects the power of the president to seek the consent of the National Assembly when deploying the armed forces domestically. Thus, according to Section 217 (2) (c) of the constitution:

Suppressing insurrection and acting in aid of civil authorities to restore order when called upon to do so by the president, but subject to such conditions as may be prescribed by an Act of the National Assembly.

Meanwhile, the president needs the support of the National Assembly for the declaration of war between the federation and another country. In short, no member of the armed forces shall be deployed on combat duty outside the country without a prior approval of the Senate. These conditions are as contained in Section 5 (4) (a) - (b) of the constitution that:

> . . . the president shall not declare a state of war between the Federation and another country except with the sanction of a resolution of both houses of the National Assembly sitting in a joint session; and except with the prior approval of the Senate, no member of the armed forces of the Federation shall be deployed on combat duty outside Nigeria.

Similarly, the consent of the National Assembly is a preceding condition for the president's declaration of a state of emergency as ordained by Section 305 of the constitution.

ix. Checks on the conduct of members

The constitution, through the 5th Schedule Part II emphatically lists legislators as public officers, hence the code of conduct for public officers applies to them. According to Section 3:

> The president and deputy president of the Senate, Speaker and deputy speaker of the House of Representatives and speakers and deputy speakers of the houses of assembly of the states, and all members and staff of the legislative houses [are classified as public officers].

The same responsibility is placed on the members of the National Assembly and the houses of assembly of the states by the Legislative House (Power and Privileges) Act Cap 12 of the Laws of the Federation of Nigeria 2004, and also, theCodeof Conduct Bureau and Tribunal Act (Cap C15 Laws of the Federation of Nigeria 2004). Irrespective of these legal provisions, however, the behaviour, contributions and official pronouncements of many legislators are irritating. The unwholesome behaviour of some members of the National Assembly since 1999 has been a problem. More significantly, the Senate has replaced its president and other principal officers several times following serious allegations and/or actual instances of impeachable conduct. Perhaps the climax was the bribery allegation of April/May 2005, which resulted in the resignation of Adolphus Wabara, the then Senate president.

The same upper chamber was embroiled in a ten-million naira scandal. The money was allegedly given to the chairman of the Health Standing Committee, Mrs. Iyabo Obasanjo-Bello. The money was the 'fallout' from the Ministry of Health's unspent 300 million naira, which had not been returned to the federal treasury as directed by the presidency at the end of the 2007.

House of Representatives crisis 2007

The lower chamber of the National Assembly (House of Representatives) was inaugurated on June 5, 2007. In the course of that inauguration session, Mrs. Patricia Olubunmi Etteh emerged as the first female Speaker in the history of our national parliament. But by August 20, 2007, that chamber had become the object of negative public scrutiny. The issue was a whooping 628 million naira renovation contract to repair the official residences of the Speaker and her deputy, then barely two months in office.

The controversy raged on with many worrisome rowdy sessions, that disrupted the conduct of the constitutional duties of that lower chamber. In the course of the crisis, the members were polarized into two groups (pro and anti-Etteh).

On September 5, 2007, the House resolved and inaugurated a nine-man probe panel led by David Idoko to investigate that contractscandal. That panel which consisted of six members of the ruling Peoples' Democratic Party (PDP) and three members of the minority parties (they were all members of the House of Representatives), started sitting on September 10, 2007. The panel interviewed principal officers of the House, the contractors engaged to do the renovation project, and other relevant persons and officials.

The probe panel while conducting its investigation in a committee room, degenerated into a shameless exchange of physical blows between some pro and anti Etteh lawmakers on September 20, 2007.

The David Idoko-led probe panel submitted its report on September 26, 2007. The report which was unanimously signed by the nine members, indicted the Speaker for the award of the controversial contract without recourse to due process.

That lower chamber witnessed a series of uneasy adjournments at the instance of the Speaker, this was protested by some members who were calling for a debate on the Idoko-led panel report. These rowdy sessions which culminated in a call for the Speaker's resignation (amid opposition by her supporters) climaxed on October 17, 2007. It was the day Dr. Aminu Safana, a pro-Etteh member of the House, collapsed and died during the unfortunate yelling and shouting episode on the floor of the house.

This disheartening climate of confusion and acrimony burdened and impeded the official activities of the House of Representatives for almost two weeks. On October 30, 2007, Mrs. Patricia Olubunmi Etteh and Alhaji Saidu Babangida Nguroye resigned their positions as Speaker and Deputy Speaker, respectively. The same day, (October 30, 2007), the House with a majority vote of 290 against 30, elected Terogu Tsegba as the pro-tempore or interim Speaker.

On November 1, 2007, the House of Representatives with overwhelming majority voted 304 for and 20 against, and elected Oladimeji Bankole as the new Speaker. Thus, bringing to an end, the disturbing and embarrassing three-month house renovation scandal that crippled that chamber's proceedings.

Chapter 9

Legislative Oversight, Supervision and Control of Administration under the 1999 Constitution

The proper office of the legislature is to watch and control the government; to throw the light of publicity on its acts, to compel a full exposition and justification of all of them, which anyone considers questionable and; if the men who compose the government abuse their trust ... to expel them from office.

John Stuart M ill

*T*he 1999 Constitution focuses attention on the principle of separation of powers and the twin concept of checks and balances. Thus, it empowers the National Assembly and state houses of assembly with control, supervision and oversight of the central and state executive arms.

Although the terms *'supervision'*, *'control'* and *'oversight of administration'* can be used interchangeably, they have different meanings in strict administrative law parlance. Walter J. Oleszek's [1] definitions are noteworthy:

- Supervision means a continuing concern on the part of the legislature with the details of administration and in particular, with specific content of administrative decisions.

---

[1] Walter J. Oleszek, Congressional Procedures and the Policy Process. *Washington DC Congressional Quarterly* (1978), 202-212.

- Control implies direction and less concern with the details and is centred on major rather than minor issues.
- Legislative oversight entails the continuing review by the legislature of the effectiveness of the executive in carrying out its mandate.

The following are some comprehensive provisions entrenched in the constitutions 0for the purpose of checking the executive—

i. *Legislative approval of the budget*

The 1999 Constitution upholds the trite principle that no money can be raised or spent without legislative approval. Hence, the president shall prepare and lay before the National Assembly, an appropriation bill at any time during the financial year, as required by Section 81(1)-(2) of the constitution. For state governors, a similar obligation to their respective houses of assembly is derived from Section 121(1)-(2) of the constitution. The legislature subjects the appropriation bill to severe scrutiny and review. The legislature has the power to reduce the funds allocated, but cannot increase or reallocate such independent funds to different departments.

ii. *Receipt and application of the auditor general's report*

The 1999 Constitution vide Section 85(2) places an onerous responsibility on the auditor-general of the federation. It charges him with the task of auditing all the public accounts of the federation and of all offices and courts of the federation and to submit his reports to the National Assembly. The National Assembly is equally entitled to the accountant-general's financial statement within ninety days of the auditor-general's receipt of the statement [Section 85 (5)].

The state houses of assembly are entitled to their respective auditors-general's reports and the accountants-general's statements similar to the National Assembly as provided for by Section 125(5) of the constitution.

Through this mechanism, the legislature can expose cases of mismanagement and abuse of public office and ensure strict transparency and accountability in public administration.

The controversy generated by the release of the auditor-general's report in 2002 is most regrettable. Although the National Assembly is mandated by the constitution to handle the issue, the president moved auditor's report to the federal executive council. The auditor's report which indicted all the arms of government, including the legislature, for financial recklessness was never acted upon with the expected legislative vigour and independence that should have been employed in addressing the queries raised by the report.

iii. *Confirmation of appointments*

Another platform from which the legislature exercises control oversight and supervisory powers is in the confirmation of certain high ranking appointments.

The legislature applies its power to confirm or reject appointments as an expression of its values, sense of equity and fairness in the running of public affairs. The nomination hearings offer the legislators the ample opportunity of probing and scrutinizing the qualifications, independence, capability, financial assets and physical health of the nominees. The position of the law in the case of *Governor of Kaduna State v. the Kaduna State House of Assembly*[2] is to the effect that:

> *Section 173 (1979) Constitution gives discretionary and uninhibited power to confirm or refuse to confirm the governor's nominations and particularly to bear in mind the fact that the house has not been directed by the constitution even by the remotest inference for its decisions.*

iv. *Power to conduct hearings and investigations*

An outstanding method of legislative control of administration is committee hearing and investigation into the executive branch's operations. The public trust of governance demands that legislators must monitor government programmes, policies and projects for proper implementation. Also, the performance of public administrative officers vis-à vis projected goals must be monitored.

Committee hearings offer legislators ample opportunity to acquaint themselves with and appraise the administrators' plan of action. They must also discover the usefulness of government policies to the citizenry whom they represent. In the truthful words of Onyekwere Nwankwo:

---

[2] [1981] 2 NCLR 722.

> *The power to investigate and expose is probably one of the most*
> *well known instruments through which legislators could supervise*
> *the administration.*[3]

The legislature is invested with the power to conduct investigations into any matter over which it has the right to make laws; and also over the conduct of affairs of any person, authority, ministry or govern ment department charged, or intended to be charged with the responsibility for executing or administering laws enacted by the legislature, and those disbursing or administering money appropriated by the legislature.

The National Assembly is vested with these powers by Section 88 of the constitution. The authority of the state houses of assembly on this subject matter is derived from Section 128 of the constitution. The purpose of this legislative power of investigation or inquiry as stated in Section 88(2) (b) of the constitution is to:

> Expose corruption, inefficiency or waste in the execution or
> administration of laws within its legislative competence and
> in the disbursement or administration of funds appropriated
> by it.

In furtherance of this very important legislative role, the legislature or a committee set up by it is empowered to procure evidence and examine those which may be material to the investigation.

The legislature has the power to issue a summons or warrants to compel the appearance of any person before it. The National Assembly derives this power from the provisions of Section 89 of the constitution, while for the state houses of assembly, it is Section 129. Nevertheless, the legislature must bear in mind the court's decision in *Adikwu & Ors v. Federal House of Representatives & Ors*[4] which stated that:

---

[3] G. Onyekwere Nwankwo. 'Legislative Supervision of the Administration'. A paper presented at the Workshop for Legislators. Anambra State House of Assembly, Enugu (1981) p.9.

[4] [1982] 3NCLR. p.394.

> *The exercise of the investigating powers of the legislature does not permit the legislature to compel a newsman to disclose his source of information except in grave and exceptional circumstances, eg, the security of the nation or state.*

v. *Control of public funds and monitoring the annual budget*

The fiscal powers or the power of the purse of the legislature, places her in a watchdog position over the public funds.

The eloquent letters and mandatory spirit of section 80 (3) and (4) of the constitution as well as section 120 (3) and (4) are instructive. These provisions categorically state that no moneys shall be withdrawn unless authorised by an Act of the National Assembly or law of the State House of Assembly. These sections strictly place the withdrawal of public funds as the sole right of the national and state houses of assembly.

Therefore, the oversight role of the legislature on public moneys goes beyond the approval of the annual or a supplementary budget. That control and supervisory role extends to strict adherence to the letter of the consequent legislation and due process. The United States Congress achieved this measure through the enactment of the Budget Control Law in 1974. That law forced the congress to compare total spending with total receipts and also curtailed the president's power to refuse to spend appropriated funds. The budget control law also created a series of deadlines by which the congress must abide for its action on the budget. Thereby, curtailing delay on the passage of appropriation bill.

The renewed zeal of the National Assembly in checking the executive spending of public funds towards the last quarter of 2007, is in line with this spirit. Thus, the Senate's stance on the 300 billion naira which some ministries and departments illegally lodged in some accounts. It resulted in the upper chamber's refusal to pass the 2008 Appropriation Bill unless the executive recalled that whopping 300 billion naira illegal lodgment.[5]

The National Assembly needs to employ her constitutional investigative or scrutinizing powers on this matter and subject the alleged officers involved to the full arm of the law. The recall of the amount involved and refusal to pass the

---

[5] *ThisDay* Newspaper: Senate in 2008 Budget Blues; Saturday December 22, 2007, p.52.

budget will not proffer adequate check nor deterrence for such blatant abuse of public office.

vi. *The power to establish and regulate authorities for the federation or any part thereof*

This legislative power which is ordained by item 60 of the second schedule to Part I of the Exclusive Legislative List and other provisions of the constitution is enviable. In furtherance of her constitutional roles, the legislature, especially the National Assembly exercises wide powers. The unmistakable provision of section 4(4) (b) is that the National Assembly shall have power to make laws with respect to:

> . . . any other matter with respect to which it is empowered to make laws in accordance with the provisions of this constitution.

The import of these legislative powers, enabled the National Assembly to establish via her Act, agencies like the Independent Corrupt Practices Commission (ICPC) and the Economic and Financial Crimes Commission (EFCC).

The legal action in contention for the enabling Act of the ICPC being the Corrupt Practices and Other Related Offences Act 2000 in the case of *AG of Ondo State v. AG of the Federation & Ors* [6] reveals this point. There, the Supreme Court speaking through Katsina Alu JSC, posited that:

> *It is also my view that item 60(a) of the Exclusive Legislative List read together with Section 4(2) of the 1999 constitution not only imposes a duty on the Federal Government to abolish all corrupt practices and abuse of power but also impose a duty of making a law through the National Assembly for that purpose. In addition, item 68 of Exclusive Legislative List gives the National Assembly power to make laws on any matter incidental or supplementary to any matter mentioned elsewhere in the Exclusive List.*

This power enables the National Assembly to create, alter or abolish executive agencies and even to change their functions. Thus, the enabling act of any agency

---

[6] [2002] 7 MJSC.

or authority created by the National Assembly, can be altered through amendments or reviewed for better performance. Therefore, the oversight role of the legislature becomes the hallmark of checks and balances.

vi. Receipt of statutory annual reports from commissioners

It is mandatory, that a statutory annual report of each ministry, commission or agency be presented to the house of assembly for consideration of the ministry's estimates. The ministry's failure to present this annual report must be explained officially to the House. The standing orders or rules of state houses of assembly also have laws which deal with this subject. Thereby officially keeping the legislature abreast of the duties and obligations of each ministry, as well as their performance rating and areas needing improvement.

Chapter 10

Legislative Houses: Powers and Privileges

The law and practice of privilege reveals the extent to which individual members and parliament as a body are free from outside pressure – whether from interest groups, sponsoring bodies and institutions or the media – a freedom which is central to ensure an independent parliament.

Hilaire Barnett

*E*very democratic legislature exercises certain powers and privileges, which are regarded as essential to its dignity and proper functioning. The legislature has certain privileges, which enhance their contributions as an independent arm of government and the elected representatives of the state. The purpose of the privileges is to protect the legislature and legislators against undue interference and distraction in the discharge of their constitutional duties. The Legislative Houses (Powers and Privileges) Act Cap L12 Laws of the Federation of Nigeria 2004 governs this subject-matter in Nigeria. The preamble to this Act specifically declares that it is:

> An Act to declare and define certain powers, privileges and immunities of the legislative houses established under the Constitution of the Federal Republic of Nigeria and of the members of such legislative houses; to regulate the conduct of members and other persons connected with the proceedings thereof and for matters concerned therewith.

The constitutional provisions, which mandate the National Assembly and the state houses of assembly to regulate their affairs, also empowers these law making bodies to create rules or orders on this subject matter. Hence, the contents of the standing orders and rules of the various legislative houses set out the privileges and immunities of the house collectively and that of the individual members.

More so, item 47 on the Exclusive Legislative List in the second schedule of the constitution categorically puts forth the:

> . . powers of the National Assembly and the privileges and immunities of its members.

It is evident that the National Assembly can make laws on this subject item on the Exclusive Legislative List. This important Act (Legislative Houses (Powers and Privileges) Act Cap L12) which regulates the operation of the legislature can be examined under four sub-headings.

This time honoured parliamentary concept was highlighted in the celebrated case of *Bradlaugh v. Gossett (1883-84)* There Lord Coleridge C.J. at page 275 held that:

> ....*equally well established, which seems to me decisive of the case before us: what is said or done within the walls of the parliament cannot be required into a court of law .... The jurisdiction of the Houses over their own members, their right to impose discipline within their walls, is absolute and exclusive.*

i. *Freedom of speech and debate in the legislature*

This freedom is an inherent attribute of every free legislature and is statutorily ordained under 'power and privileges'. Although the Legislative Houses Act deals specifically with freedom of speech, the provisions also cover debates within the legislature. Thus, Section 3 of the Act provides that:

> No civil or criminal proceedings may be instituted against any member of a legislative house:
>
> > a. in respect of words spoken before that house or a committee thereof or

---

[7] [1883-1884] 12 QBD 271.

b. in respect of words written in a report to the House or to any committee thereof or in any petition, bill, resolution, motion or questions brought or introduced by him therein.

This age-old tradition of the English parliament was also recognized by Article IX of the Bill of Rights (1689). This position was affirmed in the case of *Ezeoke* v. *Makarfi* [8] where the court's decision was that:

Members of the legislature are immune to proceedings in respect of words spoken before the legislative house and words written in report to the house or to a committee of the house.

Legislative powers and privileges under this subject also apply to the publication of reports of proceedings. Sections 24-25 of the Legislative Houses Act forbids the publication of any statement, whether in writing or otherwise, which defames a legislative house or any committee thereof.

ii. *Freedom from arrest or molestation*

This is the second individual privilege of the members of the legislature. Apart from the freedom of speech, the others are collective privileges of the parliament.

This aspect of privileges protects the members from arrest in all actions during the proceedings of the parliament. But this privilege shall not be allowed to interfere with the administration of criminal justice. Thus, it is not a shield for treason, felony and breach of the peace.

The objective of this privilege is to ensure the proper functioning of the legislature, by excluding the legislators from arrest in civil proceedings in the course of their legislative duties. This immunity is confined to civil suits. The true position is that a member, who is imprisoned by the order of a court of competent jurisdiction, has no special privilege.

The Act prescribes punishment on conviction or option of fine for the infringement of these powers and privileges. The Legislative Act also empowers and protects persons authorized by the legislature to publish reports, papers, minutes, votes or proceedings and shields such persons against any civil or

---

[8] [1982] 3 NCLR.p.663.

criminal proceedings. This immunity is provided for by Section26-27 of the Legislative Houses Act. These powers and privileges must, however, be exercised in strict compliance with the due process of law. The British case of *Stockdate* v. *Hansard*[9] established this point. It was held that an order from either house in Britain authorizing the publication of papers outside parliament did not, however, ensure that the publisher would be immune from charges of libel.

In a more emphatic tone, the court in *Adikwu & Ors* v. *Federal House of Representatives & Ors*[10] ruled that:

> *The investigating powers of the committee of the House of Representatives or such a body are subject to the provisions of the constitution and in particular the fundamental rights guaranteed under Chapter IV.*

The Court of Appeal in *El-Rufai* v. *House of Representatives*[11] elaborated on these issues thus:

> *The legislature has no general authority to invite citizens to appear before it save as provided under section 88(2) of the constitution. In the same vein, the court cannot assume jurisdiction on the internal proceedings of the legislature in respect of a mere invitation to citizens to appear before it. More so, where such invitation does not materially affect the civil rights of such citizens.*

iii. *The conduct of members*

The National Assembly and state houses of assembly and the legislative councils are generally esteemed as a group of honourable and great minds with impeccable character. Hence, the law sets a high ethical and moral standard for these men and women who hold political power in trust. The Legislative Houses Act stipulates

---

[9] [1839] 9 A & E.1.

[10] [1982] 3NCLR p.394.

[11] [2003] FWLR Pt 173.

civilized standards against unbecoming conduct such as bribery. Thus, section 20 provides that:

> Any member of a legislative house who accepts or agrees to accept or obtains or attempts to obtain for himself or for any other person any bribe, fee, compensation, reward or benefit of any kind for speaking, voting or acting or on account of his having so spoken, voted or acted or having so refrained shall be guilty of an offence and liable on conviction to a fine of hundred naira or to imprisonment for two years or to both such fine and imprisonment.

In 1994, in Britain, the *'cash-for questions'* scandal resulted in a public outcry and far-reaching punitive measures following serious allegations against members of the parliament (Tim Smith and Neil Hamilton) for accepting money from Mohamed Al Fayed for the tabling of parliamentary questions to ministers.[12]

This incident led to the setting up of the Lord Nolan Inquiry, which set the standards for public service and the report of the parliamentary commissioner on standards by Sir Gordon Downey. The outcome of the inquiry and report was the emergence of a code of conduct and guide to the rules relating to the conduct of members.

In May 2009, the British House of Commons erupted into the 'United Kingdom Parliamentary Expenses Scandal'. That controversy was ignited by a newspaper (*Daily Telegraph*) report detailing allegations of lavish expense claims by some members of the parliament.

The British public outcry resulted in instant repayment of the sums by some of the affected members, resignation, and apology to the nation at large by the party leaders.

The Prime Minister Gordon Brown's stance on the issue was:[13]

...repayment will not necessarily be sufficient sanction. Unacceptable behavior will be investigated and disciplined.

---

[12] See *Guardian* (20 October 1994) for details.

[13] 1-2 Guardian Newspaper: UK Parliamentary Expenses Scandal, Tuesday, May 19, 2009, p. 16-17.

The leader fo the British opposition conservative Party David Cameron also lend his own party's moral weight to the issue by declaring that:

> *Conservative MPS must repay any excessive expensive claims or*
> *face expulsion from the party.[14]*

In furtherance thereto, five cabinet members resigned from their ministerial positions. The Speaker Michael Martins also resigned as the presiding officer of the House of Commons. Thus, Michael Martins became the first Speaker in three hundred (300) years in British Parliamentary history to be ousted after Sir Trevor in 1695.

The public outcry also precipitated instant investigation of the scandal by the Metropolitan Police. Hence, provoking collective condemnation of the unwholesome attitude of elected public officers.

Regrettably in Nigeria, similar issues have not been treated with the deserved objectivity and transparency. Legislative houses in Nigeria have been reduced to theatres of physical combat, corruption and endless allegations of fraud.

There is a general misconception that there is a shield of immunity protecting every legislator in the house from punishment for wrongdoing. Therefore, the throwing of chairs and other acts of gross misconduct continue, while the lawmakers hide under parliamentary immunity. The true position of the law, however, as vividly stated in Section 21(1) of the Legislative Houses Act is that:

> Any member of a legislative house who being a member of a committee of the House, publishes to any person not being a member of such committee any evidence taken by the committee before it has been reported to the House; or
>
> iv. assaults or obstructs any officer of the legislative house within the chamber or precincts of the House; or
>
> v.assaults or obstructs any officer of the legislative house while in the execution of his duty; or

---

[14]1-2 Guardian Newspaper: UK Parliamentary Exdpenses Scandal, Tuesday, May 19, 2009, p. 16-17.

vi.is convicted of any offence under this Act, shall be guilty of contempt of the Legislative House.

Equally lucid is the provision of Section 21(4) that:

a. Nothing in this section contained shall be construed to preclude the bringing of proceedings, civil, or criminal, against any member in respect of any act or thing done contrary to paragraph (b) or (c) of subsection (1) of this section.

iv. *Contempt of the legislature*

The general impression is that the legislative house will be hallowed and sacrosanct. Therefore, any act or omission which obstructs or impedes either the house of parliament in the performance of its function or which obstructs or impedes any member or officer of such house in the discharge of his duty may be treated as contempt. Section 21 of the Act provides penalties for contempt of the legislative houses, including the suspension of an erring member, which can be effected by a house resolution. A suspended member shall not be entitled to his/her salary and allowances for the period of the suspension. He/she is not permitted to enter the chamber or the precincts of the house, and can otherwise be forcibly removed. Such a forcible removal cannot attract a court action(Section 22). The house cannot, however, suspend indefinitely any member based on the proviso to section 21(2) of the Legislative Houses Act. The court's decision in *Oloyo* v. *Alegbe*[15] is salient:

It is only the court and not the Speaker that can determine whether or not the seat of a member of a house of assembly has become vacant.

This topic brings to mind, the national embarrassment on September 20, 2007. The hot exchange of words and the subsequent physical blows by the members of the House of Representatives before the Idoko-led probe panel deserve official sanction from that chamber. That indefensible unwholesome behaviour, amounted to disorderly, contemptuous and disrespectful conduct in the presence of that

---

[15] [1982] 3 NCLR 647.

committee. Most regrettably, that manifest contempt of the lower chamber, was merely glossed over.

Moreover, since those members who threw decency to the winds by fighting shamelessly, were not members of the probe panel nor were they invited witnesses thereto, they must be considered as strangers.

In the same vein, the strong moral stance of the 'Integrity Group' in waving the national flag and chanting the national anthem and other songs, raised salient parliamentary contempt issues.

The parliamentary contempt standard refers to any act or omission which obstructs or impedes either house of parliament in the performance of its functions or which obstructs or impedes any member or officer of such house in the discharge of his or her duty or which has a tendency, direct or indirectly to produce such result will constitute contempt.

Therefore, the display of civil disobedience by the Integrity Group, although it might be seen as patriotic act and done in the interest of the public, also amounted to parliamentary contempt. The pith or substance of this submission, is that this noisy display was an undeniable obstruction of the then speaker Patricia Olubunmi Etteh's duty, hence, a violation of the house privilege.

Likewise, the pro-Etteh group was chanting songs and waving white handkerchiefs, vociferous and contemptuous. in support and solidarity to the Speaker, It is most disheartening that such a chilling degree of parliamentary sacrilege went unpunished, especially with reference to fighting.

v. Legislative houses and jurisdiction of the courts

The principle of the separation of powers, governs the relationship between the legislature and the judiciary. In appreciation of this concept, the Legislative Houses Act stipulates that when a member of the house is arrested, detained or imprisoned, the court shall as soon as practicable, inform the Senate president or the Speaker of that legislature (Section 29).

Meanwhile, the legislature is not subject to the jurisdiction of the court in exercise of the powers vested in it by the constitution, the Legislative Houses Act or the Standing Orders of the House as provided by Section 30. In the British case

of *R* v. *Commissioner for Standards and Privileges ex parte Al-Fayed.*[16] The
Court of Appeal upheld this stance. It ruled that the court had no jurisdiction to
review the decisions of the commissioner, since he was accountable to the
parliament. In short, Section 30 of the Legislative Houses Act places legislative
activities beyond the jurisdiction of the court. This position was upheld in *Senator
BC Okwu V. Senator Joseph Wayas & Ors*[17] where it was decided by Adefarasin
C.J. at 528 that:

> *With respect, this court (and if I may say so, any Court in*
> *Nigeria) cannot interfere in the internal proceedings of the*
> *legislature. Any such interference would amount to an arm of the*
> *government (on this case the judiciary) imposing its control in the*
> *house of another who is master there? The court has no power*
> *with regard to the Senate's internal procedure..... Although the*
> *Court has jurisdiction to protect the provisions of the constitution*
> *and the rights conferred thereon it will not intervene in any matter*
> *within the domestic competence of the legislature nor will it*
> *intervene to enforce any rule which the legislature may have laid*
> *down to guide its internal proceedings.*

In the same spirit of legislative independence, Section 31 of the Legislative
Houses Act prohibits the service or execution of any court process within the
chamber or precincts of a legislative house when the house is sitting.

Nnanemeka Agu JCA highlighted this point in Senate of the National
Assembly & Ors v. Momoh.[18] He ruled that:

> *The internal affairs and functions of the National Assembly are*
> *not intended to be under the jurisdiction of the courts. This is*
> *because powers are separated. To allow writs of courts run freely*
> *in the chamber and precincts of the Senate while it is in session*
> *will amount to an erosion of the separateness of the senate within*

---

[16] [1998] 1WLR p.669. CA.

[17] [1981] 2NCLR p.522.

[18] [1982] 2 FNR. p.307.

the scheme of separation of powers and in contravention of S. 31
of CAP 102.

vi. Conduct of strangers

The Legislative Houses Act similarly expects strangers or visitors to the legislature to conduct themselves respectably within the chamber and precincts of the House. The Speaker or the presiding officer of the house can order the forcible removal of any stranger from the chamber or precincts of the house (Section 18).

More importantly, any person who tries to influence a member of the house by offering a bribe, fee, compensation reward or benefit of any kind, shall be guilty of an offence and liable on conviction to a fine of four hundred naira or to imprisonment for two years or to both such a fine and imprisonment (Section 19).

In appraising the House of Representative's crisis of 2007, the presence of cameramen on the floor of the House in the course of some rowdy sessions must be mentioned. Although these were accredited media practitioners known officially to the National Assembly, their presence on the floor while the members were engaged in a rowdy confrontation also violated that chamber privilege.

The caution notice and subsequent protest march to the National Assembly by the Nigerian Labour Congress (NLC) was also interesting. The mission of the Labour Congress was to lend their support to the Integrity Group by storming the National Assembly to force Mrs. Patricia Olubunmi Etteh to resign as the speaker of the House.

The Labour Congress activists kept faith to their protest notice by trooping to the National Assembly. But they were refused access by law enforcement agents. The strict jurisdiction of the Privileges Act, extends beyond the chamber to the precincts of the house. Therefore, the protest march with vests captioned 'Etteh Must Go', can only be executed wit h the consent of the authorities of the National Assembly. The National Assembly is a public institution, but the laws guiding its activities and deliberations must be religiously adhered to.

Furthermore, the nomination, election and removal of a Speaker or deputy speaker of the House is strictly an internal business of the members of the House. In this wise, the labour congress can only muster subtle support through informal lobbying of the members.

The criminal aspect of that scandalous contract can be prosecuted through any of the anti-graft agencies or the code of conduct tribunal or even a court of competent jurisdiction. But the limits of political and moral campaign or crusade in the face of the law, must be appreciated by all and sundry.

The disquieting issue, however, was that a solidarity group in support of the then Speaker, Mrs. Patricia Olubunmi Etteh, was allowed into the premises of the National Assembly to support her stance, a few weeks before the NLC protest. Thereby, creating a disturbing impression that the personal interests of a principal officer can override the public interest and morality.

A similar scenario was unveiled in year 2000 in the Senate, during that chamber's contract controversy. The then President of the Senate, Chuba Okadigbo, had moral supporters in the chamber gallery yelling 'Oyi', 'Oyi', "Oyi"

The afore stated incidents were offensive to the letter and spirit of the Legislative Privileges Act. They equally negate the exalted orderly conduct of the parliament, its honourable members and decorous environment. These are outright breaches of the privileges of the legislature.

As a corollary to its powers of investigation and supervision, the legislature can issue a summons and warrant to compel appearance before it or one of its committees. The warrant will be executed by the police (Sections 5-7 of the Legislative Houses Act). These provisions cannot, however, serve as an ouster clause, since the court can only give up a case where it lacks jurisdiction. The privileges and powers of the legislature must therefore, be exercised in line with the spirit of the constitution and other laws of the land.

The Supreme Court took the most remarkable stand on this issue in *AG Bendel AG Federation*[75] where it held:

> *... that generally, the court would respect the independence of the legislature in the exercise of its legislative powers and refrain from pronouncing or determining the validity of the internal proceedings of the legislature or the mode of exercising its legislative powers: however, if the constitution makes provisions as to the mode of exercising its legislative powers, then the court is duty bound to exercise its jurisdiction to ensure that the legislature comply with the constitutional requirements.*

vii. Code of conduct for members of the legislature

The spate of corruption-related offences in the legislative houses since 1999 is most regrettable. Since 2000, the Senate has tried self-corrective measures, such as the setting up of probe committees. Most of the offences are criminal in nature and are, therefore, beyond the jurisdiction of the legislature. The Senate, instead of handing over such cases to the appropriate authorities for investigation and prosecution have simply forced the removal or resignation of the guilty public officers, without dealing with the criminal offence.

The 2005 scandal involving members of the Joint Education Committee and the former President of the Senate Adolphus Wabara, attracted criminal proceedings at the instance of the presidency and not the Senate. The lawsuit initiated by the presidency and the national broadcast on the issues, violated the principle of separation of powers.

Jolted by this unwholesome development, the Senate drew up a code of conduct for its members. Meanwhile, the constitutional provisions of the code of conduct for public officers also apply to legislators. Each legislator must declare his/her assets. Preferably, they should continue in the professions or jobs and serve as legislators on part-time basis, as is the case is in most parts of the world.

The arraignment of Senator Iyabo Obasanjo-Bello before a high court for the purported ten million naira received on behalf of the Health Standing Committee (2008) was at the instance of the Economic and Financial Crimes Commission (EFCC). In short, the upper chamber had already absolved her of that offence.[19]

On May 14, 2009, the Economic and Financial Crimes Commission (EFCC) arraigned members of the National Assembly Committees in respect of the Rural Electricity Authority (REA) in an Abuja High Court. The prominent members included chairman of the Senate Committee on power Nicholas Ugbone and his House of Representatives counterpart Ndudi Elumelu.[20]

---

[19] See: Senator IyaboObasanjo, Queen of Scandals,*The News* (10 April 2008) or: www.sahara reporters.com.

[20]Guardian Newspaper: Ugbane, Elumelu, eight others in EFCC custody, Friday, May 15, 2009, p. 1-2.

As the power committee controversy was raging, the special adviser to the president on petroleum, Dr. Emmanuel Egbogah heightened the National Assembly's discomfort. He alleged that members of the Senate Committee on Petroleum were compromised by oil companies to frustrate their consideration of the Petroleum Industry Bill (PIB).

The Senate instituted a probe panel to review the committee's retreat activities in Ghana, which was the venue of that allegation.[21] But that Panel's report is yet to be released (July, 2009).

Meanwhile, the electorate must ensure that they elect people of proven integrity into the public office. It is startling to note that even after the repeal of the Legislative Houses Act, the meagre penalty of four hundred naira (×400.00), which was employed in the Second Republic (19791983), is still in use.

In order to provoke a more serious and sincere commitment to this subject-matter, this amount must be reviewed upwards. It should not be less than four hundred thousand naira (×400,000.00).

The prescribed penalty can be the denial of one-month salary and allowance of any member of the house who violates any of these privileges. The strength of the offence will determine the severity of the sanction.

The legislature must come to terms with its right to direct the Attorney General to prosecute persons guilty of contempt of the house. We have highlighted offences at law, therefore, the persons accused of these offences must face the eventual consequences of their acts as stipulated by the law.

It is no longer tenable to gloss over criminal offences by leaning erroneously on legislative immunity and privileges. The precedents set by the current crop of legislators will dictate the pace and state of mind of their successors. The unholy seed of contract scandal, which was planted in the year 2000, governed the opening months of the 2007 National Assembly. It is by every estimation, a fundamental factor that requires uncompromising remedy.

---

[21] *ThisDay* Newspaper: Ghana Saga, Anger in Senate as Probe Begins, Tuesday, May 19, 2009, p. 20.

Chapter 11

The Declaration of a State of Emergency

The condition upon which God had given liberty to man is eternal vigilance; which condition if he break, servitude is at once the consequence of his crime and the punishment of his guilt.

John Philpot Curran, 10 July 1790

*T*he history and development of constitutions has appreciated the need for safety devices to contain emergency situations that stem from natural disasters or the miscarriage of public policy. Thus, most democratic constitutions provide emergency laws to cover situations beyond the existing laws and executive initiative in order to quickly arrest an emergency situation to safeguard the integrity of the state and prevent loss of life and property.

In order to effectively combat such emergencies, the constitution yields to the employment of extraordinary measures and undemocratic strategies to prevent the destruction of the state. Thereby, suspending the traditional law making processes and policy formulation and execution method while adopting the rescue mission initiative to preserve the country or its affected area. This plank of reasoning is anchored to the doctrine of civil necessity. The import of the doctrine is settled on the justification for an action which is unlawful, but is necessary to preserve the life of the state or any part thereof.

Nigeria's constitutional law icon Professor B.O. Nwabueze summed up this doctrine thus:

By this supreme law of necessity, therefore, the organs of the state are entitled, in the face of such an emergency, to take all appropriate actions, even in deviation from the express provisions

of the constitution, in order to safeguard law and order and
preserve the state and society.[1]

Section 305 of the 1999 Constitution details the conditions and procedures for the declaration of a state of emergency in the federation, and of any part thereof.

i. *Conditions for emergency*

The constitution clearly states those severe situations in which the president can issue a proclamation of a state of emergency under Section 305 (3). These include:

(a) the federation is at war;

(b) the federation is in imminent danger of invasion or involvement in a state of war;

(c) there is actual breakdown of public order and public safety in the federation or any part thereof to such extent as to require extraordinary measures to restore peace and security;

(d) there is a clear and present danger of an actual breakdown of public order and public safety in the federation or any part thereof requiring extra-ordinary measures to avert such danger;

(e) there is an occurrence or imminent danger, or the occurrence of any disaster or natural calamity, affecting the community or a section of the community in the federation;

(f) there is any other public danger which clearly constitutes a threat to the existence of the federation; or

(g) the president receives a request to do so in accordance with the provisions of subsection (4) of this section.

The provisions of Section 305 (4) is to the effect that the governor of a state, based on a resolution supported by two-thirds majority of the house of assembly,

---

[1] B.O. Nwabueze, *Constitutionalism in the Emergent States* (Christopher Hurst & Company, London with Nwamife Publishers, Enugu, 1977), p.181.

can request the president to issue a proclamation for a state of emergency in his state.

The request of the state governor, must be fulfilled by the existence of the conditions listed in section 305 (3) (c) (d) & (e) of the constitution. The state of emergency must not extend beyond the boundaries of that particular state.

The president shall not declare a state of emergency under Section 305 (4) or in relation to a state jurisdiction, unless the state governor failed within a reasonable time to formally request the president to issue such a proclamation as ordained by Section 305 (5).

ii. *The procedure for the declaration of a state of emergency*

By virtue of section 305 (1) of the constitution, the president may, by instrument published in the official gazette of the government of the federation issue a proclamation of a state of emergency in the federation or any part thereof.

The elaborate provision of section 305 (2) is to the effect that the president must immediately after the publication, transmit copies of the official gazette containing the proclamation with a detailed account of the emergency situation to the president of the Senate and the Speaker of the House of Representatives.

It is then, the responsibility of the presiding officers of the two chambers of the National Assembly to convene or arrange for a meeting of each of their respective chambers. The National Assembly owns the constitutional power to consider the situation and decide whether or not to approve the president's proclamation by a two-thirds resolution. This approval must be secured within two (2) days after the publication, when the assembly is in session, or within ten (10) days when the assembly is not in session under section 305 (6) (b).

It is appropriate to note that the proclamation of emergency shall cease to have effect in event of the conditions contained in Section 305 (6) (a) - (d). These include:

(a) If it is revoked by the president by instrument published in the official gazette of the federal government of the federation.

(b) If it affects the federation or any part thereof and within two days when the National Assembly is in session, or within ten days when the National Assembly is not in session, after its publication, there is no resolution supported by two-thirds majority of all the members of each House of the National Assembly approving the proclamation;

(c) after a period of six months has elapsed since it has been in force. This is subject to the proviso enabling the National Assembly to extend the period for the proclamation of the state of emergency to remain in force from time to time for a further period of six months by resolution;

(d) at any time after the approval referred to in paragraph (b) or the extension referred to in paragraph (c) of this sub-section, when each House of the National Assembly revoke the proclamation by a simple majority of all the members of each House.

Procedures on proclamation of a state of emergency

Rules 134-137 of the Senate, deal with this subject matter. The House of Representatives is also guided by similar provisions.

The president of the Senate shall brief the Senate in a closed session on the circumstances of the proclamation of the state of emergency. It is after the closed session, that the senators will be availed of the document from the presidency in relation to that situation. (Rule 136).

The Senate should then resolve into a committee of the whole house for the consideration of that proclamation. Although a unanimous decision can direct against resolving into a committee of the whole.

The ultimate decision will be based on the provisions of the constitution (See Rule 137).

Emergency rule in Nigeria

The political crisis in the Western Region in the First Republic peaked with the declaration of a state of emergency in that region by the Tafawa Balewa-led federal government in 1962.

Our current dispensation has witnessed the exercise of these extraordinary constitutional powers by the then Olusegun Obasanjo-led administration in Plateau State (from 18 May to 18 November 2004) and that of Ekiti State (from 19 October 2006 to 19 April 2007).

The attempt, by President Olusegun Obasanjo, to extend the emergency rule via a proclamation of 18 April 2007 did not receive the constitutional support of the National Assembly. Therefore, that emergency rule in Ekiti State ceased and Hon. Tope Ademiluyi became the acting governor of the state.

A close look at the past events (the 1962 state of emergency in the Western Region) and the current events in Plateau and Ekiti states show that the constitutional conditions for the declaration of emergency were not met.

Western Region 1962

In issue, was the intra-party conflict within the Action Group which was the ruling party in that region. The crisis deepened when the regional governor dismissed the regional premier, Ladoke Akintola, and appointed a new premier as replacement. The dismissed premier then instituted a legal action to challenge the validity of the dismissal *Akintola v. Aderemi* (1962)[2]

When the Western Regional House of Assembly convened to approve the newly appointed premier and his cabinet, the members who were in support of Ladoke Akintola objected furiously to that initiative. The situation degenerated to a violent clash within the chamber between the members of both factions.

It is this unfortunate incident on the floor of the then Western Region House of Assembly which the then federal government capitalized on and declared a state of emergency in the region. The dubious excuse of the federal government for that action, was that it had become impossible for the government of the Western Region to carry on after that episode. Hence, the declaration of a state of emergency in that region.

Professor B.O. Nwabueze ably summed up that abuse of emergency powers in these words:

> *It must be noted, first, that the disturbances in the chamber of the House were caused by only ten supporters of Chief Akintola out of a house of 117, and secondly, that apart from the event in the House, the entire region outside it remained peaceful and unaffected by the rather uncivilised behaviour of the parliamentarians. When the House was cleared and locked up by the*

---

[2] 1 ANLR. 440 SC, (1962) WNLR. 185 SC 205 PC.

police, the members, returned to their respective homes, and
there was no sign of any attempt or intention to carry the affray
outside the chamber.[3]

Plateau State 2004

Emergency rule in Plateau State was anchored on the state of emergency (Plateau State) Proclamation 2004. The preamble to the proclamation claimed that there was a breakdown of public order and public safety in Plateau State, which led to a massive loss of life and property and created a serious humanitarian calamity within and outside the state.

An adjoining preamble also stated that there was a clear and present danger of the crisis in Plateau State spreading beyond the boundaries of the state to other states of the federation.

A further recital to that preamble, claimed that the government of Plateau State has been incapable of managing the situation. And thereby, came to the conclusion that the state had collapsed and there was no guarantee of public order or public safety in the state.

Based on the above cited proclamations and reasons canvassed therein, the National Assembly consented to a declaration of a state of emergency in Plateau State.

But a critical and unbiased appraisal of the political trends of that period in the state's history will likely paint another picture.

Plateau State has a land area of 26,899 square kilometers with seventeen local government areas and estimated population of between 2-3.5 million[4] If a political crisis of the dimension and gravity conveyed by the federal government's proclamations had actually erupted, the entire Middle Belt would have been engulfed by the disaster. In short, the consequent calamity would have attracted international attention due to the large number of displaced persons and human refugee traffic that can be associated with a social upheaval of such magnitude.

---

[3] B.O. Nwabueze, 175.

[4] Plateau State land area 26,899 square kilometer population estimate 2005 – 3,553,440 en-wikipedia.org; population 2,959,588, land area 26,899 sq kilometers – plateaustategov.com.

The evidence adduced by the then Speaker of the Plateau State House of Assembly, Hon. Simon Lalong, seemed tenable. The averment in his sworn affidavit is to the effect that:

> ... *the disturbances in the state were confined to just a small part of the state, the area in and around Shendam, which is just one of the 17 local government areas in the state.*[5]

There is no doubt, from the foregoing, that the specified conditions in the constitution for the declaration of state of emergency were not met. The disheartening scenario, confirmed Professor Nwabueze's summation that:

> *It was a perversion of power nearly as grievous as the declaration of an emergency over the entire Western Nigeria in 1962 on the strength of an affray in the chamber of the regional House of Assembly between its members but which did not affect the rest of the Region outside the House of Assembly building.*[6]

Ekiti State 2006 - 2007

In the course of the impeachment confusion that afflicted this state in 2006, the then President Olusegun Obasanjo, declared emergency rule in the state, via a national broadcast on October 19, 2006.

The State House of Assembly impeachment proceedings against the then State Governor Ayo Fayose and his deputy Mrs.Biodun Olujimi, paved the way for that depressing regime of confusion. The then Speaker of the state house of assembly, Hon. Friday Aderemi's bid to ascend the governorship seat, also deepened the worrisome situation.

The frightening political milieu, threw up a rivalry for the governorship of the state between Hon. Friday Aderemi and Mrs. Biodun Olujimi. Although Ayo Fayose also laid claim that he was still the governor of the state irrespective of the house of assembly impeachment exercise which procedure was massively criticized.

---

[5] Ben Nwabueze, *How President Obasanjo subverted Nigeria's Federal System*; (Gold Press Limited, Ibadan, 2007), p.201.

[6] ibid, 202.

The underlying import for the declaration of that state of emergency by the federal government, was that the confusion posed a grave danger to the existence of the state.

The commanding tone of President Obasanjo's broadcast was: *We now have a sad and ridiculous but unacceptable situation where there are three purported governors in the state.*

The supporters of the above reasoning held to the argument that the civil servants were thrown into confusion by the rival governments and thus, law and order as well as public safety were impaired.

But the two visible contenders to the governorship position Hon. Friday Aderemi who operated from the newly built governor's office and Mrs. Biodun Olujimi who functioned from the old governor's office, had reasonable presence of armed mobile policemen. The policemen were federal government officials and the Economic and Financial Crimes Commission (EFCC) which facilitated the impeachment proceedings, was also a federal government agency. In short, the impeachment motion and processes, were based on the EFCC's report against Governor Ayo Fayose.

It is pertinent to note, that Mrs. Biodun Olujimi, based her reason to assume governorship position of that state, on the fact that she was not indicted by the EFCC report. Therefore, the averment of the then Attorney General of Ekiti State, Owoseni Ajayi, in challenging the constitutionality of the emergency rule held sway. He averred that:

> *There was no imminent danger or any disaster at all or danger to the public or breakdown of law and order or public safety as every citizen in Ekiti State were [was]going about his/her normal business.*[7]

The two uses of state of emergency in respect of Plateau and Ekiti states were an abuse of power and instigated for political reasons and did not conform to the spirit and letter of the law. Likewise, Balewa's earlier declaration of the a state of emergency in the Western Region was purely political and there was no real justification for the declaration.

---

[7] ibid., 293.

Chapter 12

Elections and Election Petition Tribunals

Any electoral enactment which specifies a time constraint on the court to determine an election petition ... is to say the least very absurd and indeed defeats the intention of the constitution and the Electoral Act itself, which is to enable an aggrieved candidate to an election to seek redress in court.

U w ais JSC , in U nongo v.A ku 1983[1]

*O*ne basic tenet of democracy is the conduct of free and fair elections by an independent electoral body. In defense of this vital ingredient of democracy, the 1999 Constitution highlights the requirements for eligibility of representatives who will constitute the legislature. The organisation of elections in Nigeria is the responsibility of the Independent National Electoral Commission (INEC). The constitution provides for the direct election of single candidate constituency based on the simple majority system as prescribed by the Electoral Act.

Qualification for membership in the National Assembly

The 1999 Constitution, through the provisions of Section 65, upholds the following criteria for the membership of the Senate and the House of Representatives:

a. The Senate – citizenship of Nigeria and a minimum age of thirty-five

b. House of Representatives – citizenship of Nigeria and a minimum age of thirty

---

[1][1983] NSCC vol. 14, 565.

By virtue of Section 65(2)

> a. minimum of School Certificate or its equivalent
>
> b. membership of and sponsorship by a political party.

Similarly, the constitution outlines the same conditions for the disqualification of a person from election into the National Assembly in section 66. Meanwhile, Sections 106(1) (c) and 318 of the constitution provide for the educational qualification of members of the National Assembly and state houses of assembly.

Qualification for membership in the House of Assembly

The 1999 Constitution, in Section 106, highlights the following requirements for election as a member of a house of assembly:

a citizenship of Nigeria

> a. a minimum age of thirty
>
> b. minimum of secondary school certificate or its equivalent
>
> c. membership of, and sponsorship by a political party

As held in the case of *Bayo v. Njidda*:[2]

> *A close consideration of Sections 106 and 107 of the 1999 Constitution shows that any candidate who fails to meet the minimum constitutional requirements can be disqualified from contesting election by an Electoral Tribunal and such constitutional requirements have been recognized as valid questions that could form ground or grounds of an election petition by Section 134(1) of the Electoral Act.*

The constitution also specifies the conditions that would disqualify a person from being elected to a house of assembly through Section 107. Whoever has voluntarily acquired the citizenship of another country; adjudged to be a lunatic or declared to be of unsound mind; is under a sentence of death or imprisonment or fine for an offence involving dishonesty or fraud, imposed by any competent court of law or tribunal; has been convicted and sentenced for an offence

---

[2] [2004] 8 NWLR.

involving dishonesty and contravention of the Code of Conduct; has been declared bankrupt under the law in force in Nigeria; is employed in the public service, and does not resign before thirty days to the date of the election; is a member of any secret society; has been indicted for embezzlement or fraud by a judicial commission of injury or an administrative panel of inquiry; has presented a forged certificate to the Independent National Electoral Commission; is therefore disqualified by the constitutional provision.

Qualification for membership in the legislative council of local government

This is provided for by Section 109 of the Electoral Act 2006. A person shall be qualified for election if he/she:

    a. is a citizen of Nigeria

    b. is registered as a voter

    c. has attained the age of 25 years

    d. is educated up to at least the secondary school certificate level or its equivalent

    e. is a member of a political party and sponsored by that party.

The same conditions for disqualification of members of the state houses of assembly applies to of the legislative council of local governments.

Nomination of candidates

The constitution accords registered political parties the exclusive responsibility to nominate candidates for election. Thus, the inescapable constitutional requirement is that a candidate for an elective office must be a member of a political party and be sponsored by that political party. Therefore, there is no room for an independent candidate without the sponsorship of a political party under our current democratic dispensation.

    The glaring provision of Section 221 of the constitution is:

> No association, other than a political party, shall canvass for votes for any candidate at any election or contribute to the funds of any political party or to the election expenses of any candidate at an election.

In the actualisation of the above requirement, the political parties nominate and forward their eligible candidates to the Independent National Electoral Commission. Section 32(1) of the Electoral Act 2006, confirmed this stance by stating that:

> Every political party shall not later than 120 days before the date appointed for a general election under the provisions of this Act, submit to the Commission in the prescribed forms the list of the candidates the party proposes to sponsor at the elections.

The court of Appeal speaking through the words of Muhammed JCA in the case of *Isolo v. Yahaya*[3] declared that:

> *Nomination is the act of suggesting or proposing a person by name to an elective office. This certainly forms the part of the preliminary matters before the actual election is contested. The person nominated has not yet come to occupy that office.*

But this responsibility and function of the political parties, to nominate and sponsor candidates for elective offices, is not an unfettered right. It is a responsibility that is strictly subjected to the 'rule of law'. Hence, it cannot be transformed into a license to advance personal or parochial political interests at the expense of collective public purpose.

In order to check unbridled tactics of multiple nomination and the attendant confusion by political interest groups, Section 33 (2) of the Electoral Act 2006 vividly states that:

> No person shall nominate more than one person for an election to the same office.

> In the same corrective tone against multiple nomination, Section 33 (3) of the Electoral Act 2006 sets a penalty of a fine of x50,000 (fifty thousand naira) or three months imprisonment or both for whoever nominates more than one person for an election to the same office.

---

[3] [1999] 4 NWLR. 657 at p. 671-672.

The liberalism and flexibility of the law as an instrument of change and circumstances, was also upheld by the Electoral Act. In this wise, the political parties
were also empowered to substitute or change any of their nominated and
sponsored candidate before the date of the election. But the Act also set salient
conditions for the political parties to enforce this responsibility. Section 34 (1) and
(2) of the Electoral Act 2006 settled this subject matter thus:

> (1) A political party intending to change any of its candidates for
> any election shall inform the commission of such change in
> writing not latter than 60 days to the election.
>
> (2) Any application made pursuant to subsection (1) of this
> Section shall give cogent and verifiable reasons.

This subject matter was the major bone of contention in these cases: *Ugwu v.
INEC* [4] and *Amechi v. INEC* [5]

In *Amaechi v. INEC*[6] Rotimi Amaechi contested and overwhelmingly won
the governorship primaries conducted in Rivers State by the Peoples Democratic
Party (PDP) in December, 2006. The party submitted Rotimi Amaechi's name to
INEC as their candidate for governor for Rivers State on December 14, 2006 in
compliance with the provisions of Section 32 (1) and (2) of the Electoral Act
2006.

Rotimi Amaechi later filed a suit at the Federal High Court, Abuja, to stop
INEC from substituting his name or disqualifying him from participating in the
gubernatorial elections except in accordance with the provisions of Electoral Act
2006. But on February 2, 2007, the PDP forwarded the name of Celestine Omehia
in substitution of Rotimi Amaechi.

The Supreme Court in its decision on the case through Oguntade JSC held
that:

> *Amaechi vied in the primaries for the office. He won
> overwhelmingly. Amaechi's name was sent to INEC as PDP's*

---

[4] [2007] 6 SC Pt 1, 88.

[5] [2008] 1 SC Pt 1, 36.

[6] The Amaechi case was reported on p. 20-21 *ThisDay Newspaper*, January 23, 2008.

candidate. There is no doubt that PDP having previously sent Amaechi's name to INEC by a letter on 26/12/2006 could only validly remove the name or withdraw it if it complied with Section 34(2) of the Electoral Act 2006. But as it did not comply with the only method laid down by the law to effect the change, the consequence in law is that the said change was never effected. In the eyes of the law, Amaechi's name earlier sent to INEC was never removed or withdrawn.

It was on this basis, that the apex court ordered Rotimi Amaechi to assume the governorship seat of Rivers State. The standard of 'cogent and verifiable reasons' as provided by Section 34 (2) of the Electoral Act 2006 also held sway in the Supreme Court's decision in *Ugwu v. INEC* (supra). The striking words of Niki Tobi JSC in the lead judgment were:

I declare that there are no cogent and verifiable reasons for the 2nd and 3rd respondents to change or entertain the change of the name of the 1st respondent as candidate of the 3rd respondent for April 14, 2007 state governorship Election in Imo State.

The activist positivist posture of the Supreme Court has also established that INEC has no constitutional powers to disqualify any candidate nominated validly and forwarded to her by a political party. This is the import of the verdict of the apex court in *Action Congress & Anor. v. INEC* [7] There, section 182(1)(i) of the 1999 Constitution received judicial interpretation of the apex court when she held that:

An indictment is no more than an accusation, that the judicial powers of Nigeria are by virtue of 1999 Constitution vested in the court established under the constitution, and that INEC does not now possess the power to disqualify any candidate. The power it had to do so under the Electoral Act 2002 has been repealed.

---

[7] [2007] 12 NWLR (Pt 1048) P. 270 at 275.

Election tribunals

The 1999 Constitution and the Electoral Act 2006, offer aggrieved contestants for political offices the opportunity to legally challenge and, if possible, reverse unfair election results. The medium for the actualization of such redress is the election tribunal.

Hence, Section 285(1) of the 1999 Constitution provides for the establishment of one or more election tribunals by the National Assembly. These tribunals shall, to the exclusion of any court or tribunal, have original jurisdiction to hear and determine petitions as to whether:

    a. any person has been validly elected as a member of the National Assembly;

    b. a person's term of office under the constitution has expired;

    c. the seat of a member of the Senate or the House of Representatives has become vacant; and

    d. a question or petition brought before the election tribunal has been properly or improperly brought.

The composition of these election tribunals are set out in the sixth schedule to the constitution.

The Electoral Act 2006 (vide Section 144(1)) allows an aggrieved person to proceed with his petition to the tribunal within thirty (30) days of the declaration of the election result. The Electoral Act 2006 through section 144(1) stipulates that only a candidate in an election and a political party, which participated in an election can bring a petition before an election tribunal.

According to Section 145(1)(a)-(d) of the Electoral Act 2006, an election may be questioned on the grounds:

    a. that the person whose election is questioned was at the time of the election not qualified to contest the election;

    b. that the election was invalid by reason of corrupt practices or non-compliance with the provisions of the Act;

    c. that the respondent was not duly elected by a majority of lawful votes cast during the election; or

    d. that the petitioner or its candidate was unlawfully excluded from the election.

Meanwhile, by virtue of Section 144(2)

> an electoral or presiding officer whose conduct is the subject of
> a complaint, can also be joined as a respondent.

The position of the Electoral Act in line with Section 170 is that the tribunal shall
declare as elected, the candidate who has the highest number of valid votes cast
in the election.

Section 246(1)(6) of the 1999 Constitution clearly states that an appeal to the
Court of Appeal shall lie as of right from decisions of the National Assembly
Election Tribunals and Governor and Legislative Houses Election Tribunals on
any questions as to whether:

1. any person has been validly elected as a member of the
   National Assembly or of a House of Assembly of a state
   under this constitution.

2. the term of office of any person has ceased or the seat of
   any such person has become vacant.

Moreover, Section 246(3) of the 1999 Constitution makes it abundantly clear
that: The decision of the Court of Appeal in respect of appeals arising from
election petitions shall be final.[8]

The Electoral Act of 2006, in ensuring stability, provides in section
149(1)-(2) that a legislator shall remain in office for 21 days pending the
determination of the appeal. It is pertinent to note that the Electoral Act of 2006
by the provisions of Section 148 and, in conformity with Section 294(1) of the
1999 Constitution, demands for accelerated hearing of these election petitions. It
emphatically demands that election petitions have precedence over all other cases
or matters before the tribunal or court.

This innovation was to remedy the disturbing instances occasioned by the
Electoral Act of 2002, where election petitions, especially those of governorship
and presidential contestants, were not concluded, even long after the 2003 general

---

[8] This applies to all election petitions except those affecting the President and Vice
President; such cases start in the Court of Appeal then move onto the Supreme Court for final
decision.

elections. This situation negates the spirit of the constitution and smacks of unfairness, inequity, injustice and lack of good conscience.

The governorship election in Anambra State in 2003 makes the resolution of this issue more urgent. Dr. Chris Ngige governed the state from 29 May 2003 until 15 March 2006, when the Court of Appeal affirmed the decision of the lower tribunal in August 2005, which declared Peter Obi the actual winner of the election. Unfortunately, however, Dr. Chris Ngige enjoyed a 34 month tenure before the court's declaration which left the duly-elected candidate a mere 14-month tenure.

It was a worrisome development which Omokri JCA in that decisive judgment in *Ngige v. Obi*[9] highlighted thus:

> *Secondly, there are lessons to be learnt from the facts of this appeal. This petition that was filed on 16/5/03 following the result of the gubernatorial elections conducted on 19/4/03; it hung in the balance until 12/8/05 when judgment was delivered by the lower tribunal. This appeal came up for hearing on the 23/1/06 and judgment was delivered today. It has taken all of 35 months for the 1ˢᵗ respondent to receive justice in a court of law. 35 months is a very considerable portion of a 4 years term of office.*

The Supreme Court bravely remedied the above cited pathetic scenario in her judgment in *Obi v. INEC*[10] There, while speaking through Aderemi JSC in p.42, para D-E, the apex court declared that:

> *It was after the judgment of the Court of Appeal on the 16ᵗʰ of March 2006, and by force of law, that the Appellant (Peter Obi) took his oath of Allegiance and Oath of Office on the 17ᵗʰ of March, 2006. Applying the provisions of section 180(2) (a) of the constitution to facts of this case, which are not in dispute, the four year term of office of Peter Obi, as Governor of Anambra State would start running from the 17ᵗʰ March 2006 only to terminate on the 17ᵗʰ of March 2010. To interpret the provisions of section*

---

[9] [2006] 14 NWLR (pt. 999).

[10] [2007] 9 MJSC.

180(2)(a) otherwise will be to read into that subsection what the legislators never intended. The duty of a judex is to expound the law and not to expand it.

The Election Tribunal and Court Practice Directions 2007 and amendment thereto issued by the president of the Court of Appeal were in furtherance of this laudable objective. The Practice Directions was fashioned after the Lagos State High Court Civil Procedure Rules 2004 and Abuja Civil Procedure Rules 2004. The underlining objective of the Lagos High Court Rules which informed the Practice Directions as well, is:

> the application of these rules shall be directed towards the achievement of a just efficient and speedy dispensation of justice.

In pursuit of that purpose, the Practice Directions also introduced the procedure method of 'front loading'. This practice procedure entails that all petitions shall be accompanied with written statements disclosing the number of witnesses that each petitioner intends to call.

The written statements on oath, and documents, which the parties intend to be relied on at the hearing of the petition, must also be annexed to the petition. This fast tracking 'front loading' procedure also makes mandatory, a pre-hearing session where all interlocutory applications must be concluded. The Practice Directions also stipulate the time limit for the attainment of its objective of timely achievement of substantial justice.

Joshua E. Alobo affirmed the striking innovation of the Practice Directions in these glowing words:

> *The Practice Directions will therefore ensure justice to litigants and above all, the people whose mandate is desecrated by delay tactics employed by counsel and litigants, thereby ensuring the doing of substantial justice to parties and the preservation of the people's mandate.[11]*

---

[11] Joshua E. Alobo: *Election Petition in Nigeria* (cases and materials) (Josim Publishing House, Abuja 2007), p.30.

The pertinent innovations of the Practice Directions have yielded some historic dividends when compared with past election tribunal experiences of 1999 and 2003. The conclusion of the findings of the various election tribunals and their verdicts within six to eight months of their inauguration is heartwarming. Thus, Enugu, Adamawa, Kogi, Yobe, Bayelsa, Sokoto and Kebbi (and others) have had their governorship, National Assembly and state house of assembly election petitions decided by the tribunals.

The case for electoral reform

The aforestated impressive innovation of the Electoral Act 2006 and the Practice Directions notwithstanding, the electoral institution and machinery need a holistic review. The agonizing controversies that trailed the 2007 general elections and attendant crippling effects it has unleashed on our polity are reprehensible. The unwholesome conduct of local government elections in some states, after the 2007 episode, suggests that a drastic overhaul of the current structure is needed to redeem our democratic project from the disheartening electoral malpractice plague.

A critical appraisal of the content of the constitution, the Electoral Act of 2006 and the Practice Directions will reveal that an unhealthy culture of deliberate delay tactics is still obvious. The uncensored truth is that most of the election petitions are yet to be decided. The Practice Directions clearly and unequivocally reveals that election petitions must be answered in six months or less after the inauguration of the tribunal.

The provision of paragraph 3 (9) of the Practice Directions is incontestable where it stipulates that within 30 days of commencement of hearing by the tribunal, the pre-hearing session must have been completed, while interlocutory issues and applications must have been treated. In the same fast tracking target, paragraph 4(3) of the Directions requires no oral examination of a witness during his/her evidence-in-chief, except to lead the witness to adopt his written deposition which is tendered in evidence, along with all disputed documents or other exhibits referred to in the deposition.

It is therefore startling that some of these petitions are still within 'hearing session' for thirty-one (31) months after April 2007 election (August 2009). In short, the Osun and Ogun States governorship election petitions are yet to be decided at the tribunal stages. It was only on September 29 (2009) that the Supreme

Court ordered the Court of Appeal to expeditiously hear the appeal brought by the governorship candidate of the All Progressive Grand Alliance (APGA) for Imo State in the April 14, 2007 polls, Chief Martins Agbaso. This is 32 months after the election.

The presiding justice of the apex court in the case Dahiru Musdapher re-echoed the displeasure of INEC's worrisome frustrating practices, thus:

> . . . *the interlocutory appeal suggestive of a ploy by the governor*
> *and INEC to frustrate the hearing of the appeal filed by Agbaso at*
> *the Court of Appeal.* [12]

It is, therefore, startling that these petitions are still within 'hearing session', over a year after the April 2007 general elections. The unavoidable circumstances of public holidays, strikes by judicial staff and other logistic issues are also relevant with reference to the delay of these hearings.

The import of the Supreme Court decision in *Obi V. INEC* (supra) exposes the polity to the uneasy vacuum of illegitimate or unstable governance until the petitions are finally resolved and the validly elected candidate takes his oath of allegiance and oath of office. This precedent is a source of political anxiety in the affected constituency until verdict is given by the election tribunal.

The tenure of office of the governors of some states where elections were re-run, has become contentious issues that are now before the courts. The rowdy, non-transparent and unstable electoral system, has produced worrisome unpredictable results. Hence, frivolous court actions to determine the precise tenure of state chief executives due to inconclusive and unsatisfactory electoral process, has become the new trend.

Remedial measures

Democratic success is anchored on periodic free and fair elections organized by independent electoral commissions. As aptly reasoned by Kunle Adelowo:

> *Periodic elections, at which the people confer mandate on leaders*
> *or withdrew it, are an important building block of democracy.*
> *They epitomize choice, without which voting is a callous mockery*
> *of the supremacy of popular will. Electoral reform is the vehicle*

---

[12] *The Guardian* Wednesday, September 30, 2009, 3.

to that destination whereby people will file out to vote, and feel
secure in the belief that they are helping to reshape the republic.[13]

Hence, these measures are suggested:

i. *Restructuring of INEC*

The appointment of the chairman and members of INEC by the president and
confirmation by the Senate, as ordained by section 154(1) of the constitution, calls
for an urgent review. The experience, most especially with the 2007 general
elections, suggests the electoral commission as the agent of the president and his
ruling party — in this case, *Amaechi v. INEC & the Peoples' Democratic Party*
(PDP). In 2007 elections, the independence, impartially and neutrality standard
of INEC was severely impaired.

It is pertinent to note that, in almost all the states where the elections were
nullified, INEC was held culpable in collaboration with the PDP for frustrating
the citizens' mandate. The Supreme Court voi3ced out this unfortunate trend in
*Amaechi v. INEC (*supra) when in the lead judgment, Oguntade JSC stated that:

> *In this case, the PDP did not live up to that standard. It did*
> *everything possible to subvert the rule of law, frustrate Amaechi*
> *and hold the court before the general public as supine and*
> *irrelevant. Sadly, INEC and Omehia also did the same.*[14]

The sensitivity and relevance of the commission and its role requires a preliminary
screening process by a competent advisory body before the Senate confirmation.
The names of the prospective candidates, especially for chairmanship position of
the commission, must be disclosed to the public for collective contribution and
assessment.

This view fortifies the recommendation of the Electoral Reform
Commission that the appointment of the INEC chairman should cease to be a
presidential prerogative. Thus, the president can no longer appoint the INEC

---

[13] Kunle Adelowo, Imperative of electoral reform, not lynching. *The Nation* Newspaper
February 8, 2008, 6.

[14] *ThisDay Newspaper* January 23, 2008, 20.

chairman subject to Senate confirmation. This point can be strengthened through independent funding of the commission on first line charge from the Consolidated Revenue Fund of the Federation Account.

ii. Amendment of the Electoral Act

The disturbing culture of electoral malpractice and its attendant unbridled quest for power by our political class can only be checked by our reversal to the 1979-1983 procedure. Thus, no candidate will be sworn in as the president of the country or governor of a state until the determination of the election petitions. This will considerably curb the overwhelming abuse of the Practice Directions by respondents who employ public funds and the electoral commission's influence to frustrate their political opponents in the tribunals.

Therefore, elections must be held and election petition tribunals inaugurated four months to the end of the tenure of the incumbent administration.

iii. Political re-orientation and creation of a new political culture

Nigeria is still governed by the despicable and unhealthy political culture of winning a political contest by any means. There is no standard in our politics, and as such, the political parties are mere gatherings of all sorts of characters driven by the sole purpose of securing public office for personal interest.

More than a decade of democracy has not produced any viable political ideology nor identifiable political platform for nation building. The compelling motive has been the looting of the public treasury with impunity through the employment of inconceivable illegal tactics. The resultant effect has been a frightening rate of political, economic and social epidemics as defined by appalling corruption in all sectors.

There is an urgent need to change this mind set by engaging credible characters in political party affairs. The target must be on the mobilization of reputable citizens into political party affairs from neighbourhood settings. The current political mentality can only yield negative results. Hence, the need for a radical political paradigm shift.

iv. Pressure groups and civil society activism

The unbridled selfish interests of political parties can only be effectively curbed by the selfless public interest of pressure groups. This is imperative in our current dispensation where there is basically no political opposition in all the three tiers of government.

The robust presence of these civil rights groups, with their civic education and public enlightenment projects, will surely reactivate the docile political culture that has pervaded this country since 1999. The employment of civil disobedience, public rallies, peaceful demonstrations, court actions and publicity strategies of various dimensions will rekindle the populace and keep the ruling parties and functionaries within the ambit of the law.

v. *The establishment of parliamentary and leadership institutes*

The sophisticated demands of modern governance makes the presence of reliable public leadership institutions inevitable. The presence of such institutions and their resourceful input will considerably aid capacity building for all the tiers and arms of government, by exposing them to basic democratic tenets and practice procedures.

The exchange programme of these leadership training centres will allow for a promising interchange of ideas, human and material resources between Nigeria and other developed democracies and economies of the world.

The conducive training and capacity building facilities will upgrade and enrich the output of our current and future political leaders, to meet the civilized practices and conduct in well established democracies.

vi. *Special concessions for election tribunals*

The election tribunal and staff must be exempted from public holidays and strike actions until the completion of their responsibilities. It is a special national assignment that deserves special concessions. This requirement must be a conspicuous clause of the Electoral Act (2006).

There is need to retain the service of a unit of the tribunal in each geo-political zone on permanent basis. This special concession will deflate the seeming spate of apparent politically motivated public holidays which this countrywitnessed en route to the 2007 general elections. In many quarters, these public holidays were meant to frustrate the court pronouncements on some candidates that sued INEC and the ruling Peoples Democratic Party. Such inimical manipulation can easily be avoided by granting special status to election tribunals.

Chapter 13

Causes of Executive / Legislature Conflicts

Unless these departments of government be so far connected and blended, as to give each a constitutional control over others, the degree of separation which the maxim requires as essential to a free government can never be in practice maintained.

James Madison

---

*I*n most democracies, including Nigeria, the legislature is often perceived by the executive as overstepping her constitutional boundaries in the performance of her oversight duties. In short, the legislature is viewed as a meddling body whose activities hinder the government from speedily meeting the needs of the public. In turn, the legislature, being the constitutionally ordained watchdog of the people, views the frustration of her investigative role, as a direct affront to the *people's mandate*. Indeed, the legislature sees the executive's uncooperative attitude as a denial of the citizenry's *right to know*.

This cycle of mutual suspicion usually degenerates into a frosty relationship between both arms of government. The experience in most countries has established three identifiable patterns:

Polarized relationship

In this pattern, the legislature is unmistakeably antagonistic to the executive. The experience of Balarabe Musa's government in Kaduna State before his eventual impeachment provides an extreme instance of this pattern of relationship. The Senate under the leadership of Chuba Okadigbo (2000-2001), the House of Representatives under Ghali Umar Na'aba (1999-2003) and the conclusive phase of the Senate leadership under Anyim Pius Anyim typified this pattern of relationship at the National Assembly level. This worrisome pattern of

125

executive-legislative relationship was in the fore in Anambra State. The disquieting antagonism of the Speaker Michael Balonwu-led faction of the legislature against Governor Peter Obi from 2006 to 2007 was a case in point. Ogun State House of Assembly since the removal of Honourable Titi Oseni as the Speaker and her replacement with Honourable Tunji Egbetokun typifies this pattern.

Cordial relationship

In this pattern, executive-legislature disagreements over policies are resolved through healthy consultation and understanding. The Senate during Evan Enwerem's leadership and the initial stage of Anyim Pius Anyim's regime is an example of a cordial relationship.

The kind of relationship between the Senate and the executive since 2003, before the seeming uneasy aftermath of the attempted constitutional amendment to elongate the president's tenure in 2006, typifies this pattern. The relationship between most state houses of assembly and their governors from 2003 up to 2007 is in line with this spirit.

This development is an outcome of the 2003 general elections where the governors as party leaders, controlled the party primaries and the selection of candidates. In short, most of the assemblies have lost their constitutional oversight role to the overwhelming influence of the executive, thereby hampering the necessary checks and balances which should aid the social, economic and political well-being of the masses.

This trend is still prevalent in most states based on the general outcome of the 2007 general elections and verdicts of the election petition tribunals, so far.

The cautious leadership style of President Umaru Yar'Adua and his seeming non interference policy with the National Assembly affairs confirm this position. The tactical approach of the National Assembly, in gradually assuming her constitutional oversight responsibilities, also lays credence to this point. Thus, the insistence of the lawmakers on upward review of the oil price benchmark for the 2008 budget against the president's proposed estimate. The National Assembly's discovery of the illegal accounts containing a whopping sum of ₦300 billion (three hundred billion naira) by government departments and ministries is in tandem with this position. The painstaking diligence of the National Assembly in waiting for ministerial and departmental details before their passage of the 2008 budget, strengthens this factor.

Mild hostility

This pattern reveals a relationship of mild and inconsistent hostility short of outright antagonism between the executive and the legislature. This has been the trend of the relationship between the House of Representatives and the presidency from 1999 to 2007.

It is pertinent to note that the spate of impeachments witnessed in some of the states, was initiated by the external influence of the Economic and Financial Crime Commission (EFCC). The removal from office of Diepreye Alamieyeseigha (Bayelsa State), Ayo Fayose (Ekiti State) and Joshua Dariye (Plateau State) were executed on the strength of the EFCC.

Reasons for legislative-executive conflicts

There are various factors that shape the relationship of the executive and legislative arms of government. In appraising the inevitable conflicts between the executive and the legislative arms, the following reasons can be adduced:

i. *Nigeria's long years of military dictatorship*

Nigeria's experience of military dictatorship for almost three decades has made a political culture of unitary command ingrained in the executive arm. This is contradictory to the expected culture of *democratic bargaining* and the consultative negotiating mechanism of civilian rule.

Hence, the existence of the legislature as a check on the executive becomes a new inconveniencing experience in our political system. The general ignorance about the basic democratic and constitutional tenets, equally widen the gulf of confusion and suspicion between the legislature and the executive.

The legislature was in abeyance throughout the military era. This has led to the influx of mostly new members into the national, state and local government parliaments without any knowledge in democratic law-making processes and tenets. The predicaments of these new and inexperienced legislators are compounded by lack of funds and necessary facilities. This may, therefore, explaintheir seemingly standard antagonistic response towards the executive at the slightest provocation.

An unbiased appraisal of the eight years rule of President Olusegun Obasanjo in Nigeria from 1999 - 2007 will reveal his absolute military command culture. In short, that unitary command mentality nearly blurred the federal complexion of the 1999 constitution. As summed up by Professor B. Nwabueze:

His attitude towards the state governors as his subordinates, rather than as heads of autonomous governments – a carry over from the days of his tenure as the Head of the FMG from 1976 to 1979 – is reflected in his insistence that state governors must inform him, or perhaps even obtain his permission, before travelling abroad, implying a relation of subordination, the subjection of the Governors to his authority. They now also require the permission of the Economic and Financial Crimes Commission (EFCC), a Federal Government Agency, before travelling out of the country.[1]

ii. *Executive hegemony (managerial, financial and technical resources)*

The vast financial, technical and managerial resources placed in the hands of the executive through the civil service and other establishments naturally gives her overwhelming leverage over the other government arms. This executive hegemony is manifest in the occasional trickle of funds from the executive to the legislature.

The true position is that the executive regards the legislature as a mere extension of its domain. This attitude is reflected in highly condemnable actions such as federal ministers, state commissioners and other principal officers shunning official invitations to appear before the legislature. This violation of the rule of law often happens in Nigeria.

The legislature evidently lacks the technical and managerial skills as well as the personnel and facilities to efficiently perform her constitutional duties. In the face of these palpable handicaps and frustrations, any form of disagreement with the executive can degenerate into a serious conflict.

iii. *Performance of the legislature*

National and state assemblies in Nigeria have not performed up to the expectations of the electorate. The first phase of our current dispensation (1999 - 2003) was characterised by allegations of mismanagement of funds, removal of presiding officers and even factionalization of the legislative houses, such as the case in Abia and Enugu states. Oyo State followed suit as from September 2005, Anambra and Plateau states, up to 29 May 2007.

---

[1] Ben Nwabueze: *How President Obasanjo Subverted Nigeria's Federal System*, (Gold Press Limtied Ibadan, 2007). p. xxvii.

The disquieting outcome of the National Assembly Joint Committee Constitution Review exercise, especially the inaugural outing in Minna, Niger State in May 2009 is most regrettable. In the face of such a vital national assignment, the rift between both chambers of the National Assembly recorded an embarrassing outburst. Thus, the contention for the chairmanship and deputy chairmanship positions, resulted in the abandonment of the joint committee effort by elected representatives of the country. Hence, both chambers inaugurated separate committees for the review of the country's constitution. This worrisome situation reoccurred when President Umaru Musa Yar'Adua could not present the 2010 budget to the joint seating of the National Assembly (19 November 2009), because of the flimsy rift between both chambers over the venue of the joint seating.

The Speaker of the Kano State House of Assembly was once removed on the allegation of bleaching his body. Currently, the assemblies are viewed as a docile rubber-stamp of the executive arm of government with no independent thrust.

It should be noted that one decade of parliamentary democracy from 1999 - 2009, has not produced prominent member- cum- privately sponsored federal bill nor a state bill in response to our overwhelming national challenges. The agonizing perils of our energy sector, the pathetic conditions of our federal and state road networks and other issues are yet to be addressed through our law making processes.

Furthermore, in the wake of the unbridled looting of the public treasury by chief executives, as the on-going trials of past state governors have shown, the national and state assemblies have not fashioned out a transparent remedy through public legislation.

iv. *Executive interference*

There is sufficient reason to consider the influence of the executive arm of government as the source of the various conflicts in the legislature. The chief executives as party leaders and unofficial financiers of the ruling party under their jurisdiction, exercise domineering influence. In turn, they dictate the election and removal of the presiding officers of the legislature.

In the public's estimation, the presidency under the Olusegun Obasanjo regime has had tacit influence in the selection of all the Senate presidents since 1999, save Chuba Okadigbo and Ken Nnamani.

In the bold words of Nwabueze:

> *Since the inception of the so-called democratic dispensation in May 1999 there have been five Presidents of the Senate in the choice or removal of all of whom the President has played a major part, if he was not the principal architect senators Evan Enwerem, Chuba Okadigbo, Pius Anyim, Adolphus Wabara and Ken Nnamani. He not only manipulated their choice or removal, he was able to get them to do his biding for a good deal of the time while they were there as senate presidents, enticing them with favours and blandishments of various kinds. And anyone of them refusing to do his biding and so incurring his displeasure did so at his peril.[2]*

v. Zoning of political offices

The ruling political parties tend to balance the influence of the presiding legislative officers and other notable officials with the appointments by the executive arm. Hence, the appointments of these public officeholders reflect the geo-political diversity of the areas covered by their operations. This consideration compromises merit and adversely affects legislative procedure and efficiency.

The 2007 House of Representatives crisis, must be viewed in this perspective. It is an established fact, that the ruling Peoples Democratic Party selected Mrs. Patricia Olubunmi Etteh as their own choice as the Speaker of the House.

The same PDP's solidarity for the then first lady Speaker of that House prolonged the crisis, until most of the members abandoned their party-lineage and toed the integrity path of transparency.

The political party hegemony, as attested to by the all conquering ruling party syndrome in local government elections in most parts of the country, tallies with this notion. The unfortunate mind-set is that the party in power is also the government in power.

The way forward

The democratic experience world over reveals that executive-legislative conflicts are inevitable. The public's interest must, however, be of uppermost concern in

---

[2] ibid, 138-139.

the mind of the legislative and the executive officials in the performance of their duties. Undue legislative interference in the administrative process can easily destroy the public service. On the other hand, if the legislature sleeps on her constitutional duties, such abdication can ultimately result in executive tyranny. This is the very antithesis of democracy.

There must, therefore, be a viable balance of influence among these arms of government in order to preserve the well being of the society whose mandate produced these officials. Moreover, measures should be put in place to ensure mutual understanding and co-existence between these arms of government.

i. *Interactive fora and enlightenment programmes*

Democracy demands social relationships outside the tense official setting of the public service. Retreats, seminars and workshops involving officials from both arms of government and interactive sessions will, therefore, greatly help to create confidence between both arms of government.

The collective responsibility and popular investment for the nurturing and growth of democracy demands the establishment of parliamentary institutes, leadership institutes and civic development centres. The presence of such democratic and citizenry training centres, especially by non-state actors, will enliven the political consciousness of the populace and prepare them adequately to undertake their political and social rights and obligations.

The establishment of such facilitators of democratic tenets and responsibilities will proffer a necessary societal watchdog role that will secure and protect the social contract demands on our political office holders.

The exchange programme of such centres with similar institutions in advanced democracies world over will also upgrade the legislative advocacy and practices locally to meet the prevalent international standards.

ii. *Transparent and accountable policies/ projects*

The current political situation in Nigeria reveals a worrisome uncompromising stance of both arms of government at the centre and state levels. The contention generally hinges on the failure or deliberate refusal to account for public funds approved and allocated for specific projects. In short, lack of prudence, financial indiscipline and a clear departure from established standards of accountability is at the root of most of these controversies. Adherence to appropriate financial accounting standards would resolve these issues. Hence, periodic audit checks and financial reports of all government statutory corporations, commissions, authorities, agencies and all persons and bodies listed in Section 85(4) of the constitution is paramount.

The constitutional oversight role of the legislature must be actualized through a well-spirited effort to check government departments, agencies, corporations and organizations at every level.

The sudden re-awakening to this constitutional role by the National Assembly must be sustained, even up to the state and local government levels. This initiative will only bear deserved fruits when the culprits are brought to book by the law of the land through courts of competent jurisdiction.

The implementation of the annual budget by the executive arm of governments especially the federal government has remained a thorny national issue since 1999. The unwholesome departure or disregard of the Appropriation Act for one decade of the country's representative democracy, has placed the executive and legislature arms on war path. Thus, the House of Representatives threat to impeach President Umaru Yar'Adua for his failure to implement the 2009 budget.[3]

The bleak truth, is that the deserved transparency and budgetary discipline and accompanying tenets are still very far away from the deplorable Nigerian practice.

It smacks of legislative indolence that public corporations, agencies, and organizations will be run for years without audited accounts and no official reprimand from the national and state assemblies.

iii. *Application of cooperative governance*

The practical experience of successful democracies strongly suggests that no arm of government can operate independently of the others. In short, absolute separation of powers is a political illusion. Ronald Reagan's administration in the United States employed this method fruitfully in securing approval for the Intermediate-Range Nuclear Forces (INF) Treaty in 1987.

Reagan invited senators to participate in the negotiation for the treaty. The senators' objections were highlighted and resolved before the presentation of the treaty to the US Congress. The treaty enjoyed smooth sailing and immediate approval of the congress due to the senators' initial involvement.

---

[3]*The Guardian Newspaper* – Editorial Budget 2009, Federal Government and the House of Representatives, Friday, July 24, 2009 p.14.

iv. *Political tolerance*

Political parties in Nigeria, especially the ruling parties, in all tiers of government have the obligation to provide political education for Nigerians and the inculcation of basic values into their members. There is urgent need to inculcate basic ethics and ideological direction into the polity. The political culture and socialization process should emphasize tolerance, maturity and patience. These values are not observable in our legislative and executive officials. Hence, issues that can be resolved amicably generally degenerate into unending controversies.

The temperament of the political parties and their actions in running public affairs suggest a frightening mentality of intolerance. The overture of ruling party supremacy, which is exhibited by all the political parties in their jurisdiction, is unwholesome. It is a deliberate design to decimate the opposition parties in all tiers.

The ruling parties in all the states held ruthlessly to their control of the electoral process in conducting local government elections. The boycott of the elections in most of the states, amidst public outcry, fell on the deaf ears of the ruling majority parties, who literarily won the chairmanships of all the local government contests in almost every state.

v. *Adequate funding of the legislature*

The legislature needs adequate and reasonable funding to be able to discharge her constitutional duties. Therefore, there is need to resuscitate the constitutional roles. The poor funding, facilities and inadequate personnel who are now running most of our legislative establishments cannot deliver the constitutional expectations for this arm of government.

The trend in which legislative allocations are released in expectation of an easy approval of a pending Executive Bill in the legislature is disturbing. The legislature must be financially independent to guarantee the actualization of the expectation on this most representative arm of govern ment. The legislature must also ensure financial prudence, accountability and due process in carrying out her responsibilities.

vi. *The presence of active civil society organizations*

These non-government organizations, which champion public causes, are inevitable platforms for the growth and development of democratic governance. They mobilize the populace and also articulate policy measures that will uplift the lives of their various societal catchment areas.

It is worrisome that meaningful civil society actions in Nigeria, dwindled with the demise of military rule in May 1999. The only collective voice in protest to govern ment's obnoxious policies is the Nigerian Labour Congress.

The inescapable import of the civil society in our current dispensation was highlighted by Professor B.O. Nwabueze. He stated that:

> *Civil society does more than act as a cheek, a counter force,*
> *against the abuse of power by government it also contributes in*
> *improving the quality of governance.*[4]

Therefore, there is need to resuscitate the civil activism of the Campaign for Democracy (CD) era in Nigeria, which exposed the military dictatorship of General Ibrahim Babangida and the late Sani Abacha to the world community. The focus of this new agenda will be on political education of the populace and collective watchdog role on public office holders. This measure, will surely curb the unremitting menace of senseless looting of our public treasury by our political leaders.

---

[4]Ben Nwabueze, *How President Obasanjo Subverted the Rule of Law*, xxxiii.

Chapter 14

Administrative Structure of the Legislature

Therefore, members must know the views of the voters and be guided by those views when considering proposed laws. Being a member of congress also means answering citizens' letters, appearing at local events, and having local offices to handle people's problems with the government.

Roger H . D avidson

---

*T*he National Assembly and state houses of assembly are assisted in their operations through an administrative structure which has been laid down in the Constitution. Section 51 of the 1999 Constitution describes the details of the administrative structure of the National Assembly under the Office of the Clerk and other staff.

Similarly, the office of the Clerk to the House of Assembly is dealt with in Section 93 of the constitution. The National Assembly Service Commission Act prescribes the method of the appointment of the Clerk and other staff of the National Assembly. The Constitutional provision is effected by the National Assembly Service Commission Act Cap No. 7 *Laws of the Federation of Nigeria* (LFN) 2004. Section 7(b) of the Act provides for the offices of:

    i.   the Clerk to the National Assembly
    ii.   the Deputy Clerk to the National Assembly
    iii.   the Clerk of the Senate
    iv.   the Clerk of the House of Representatives
    v.   the Deputy Clerk of the Senate
    vi.   the Deputy Clerk of the House of Representatives
    vii.   all other offices in the service of the National Assembly

The second schedule of the National Assembly Service Commission Act provides for the following departments:

i.   Personnel
ii.   Finance and supplies
iii.   Legislative budget and planning
iv.   Library, research and computer services
v.   Information and publication
vi.   Legal service
vii.   Estate and works

i. *Office of the Clerk to the National Assembly*

This office handles the administrative and professional affairs of the National Assembly. The staff are accountable to the Clerk as the administrative coordinator of the day-to-day running of the assembly. The Office of the Clerk is the management hub, the central administrative office of the assembly. The internal audit, liaison office, protocol, and sundry are within the domain of this office.

According to Section 10 of the National Assembly Service Commission Act, no person shall 'act' in the Office of the Clerk for a period exceeding six months, except by a resolution of each House of the National Assembly. The holder of the office, can be removed by a simple majority of each House of the National Assembly in line with Section 11 of the Act.

ii. *Personnel Department*

This department is responsible for the recruitment, appointment, promotion, training, discipline and general welfare of the staff of the National Assembly. The administrative coordination of the day-to-day running of the assembly lies with this department.

iii. *Finance and Supplies Department*

This unit manages the financial affairs of the assembly. It handles the funds, salaries and other financial needs of the assembly. It also prepares the accounting records of the revenue and expenditure of the assembly.

iv. *Legislative Budget and Planning Department*

This department prepares the annual estimates and financial projections, with regard to the assembly's set objectives. The strategic analysis and financial back-up of the assembly falls within the jurisdiction of this department.

v. Library, Research and Computer Services Department

The department studies and scrutinizes the proposals of the legislators. This is done with reference to existing laws and prevailing circumstances. It verifies data, authenticates relevant submissions, researches facts and scrutinizes proposals to meet the expectations of the electorate.

A modern library, with information technology facilities, is an important component of a modern legislature. It is the 'intellectual think tank' of the assembly. The neglect of this vital department in our national and state assemblies is worrisome. The need for a credible database for statistical records and national planning can never be overemphasised in modern law making processes.

vi. Information and Publication Department

The information and publication department is responsible for producing the daily verbatim reports on the votes and proceedings of the assembly (Hansard) and other official publications. It is usually headed by a specialist reporter, known as the editor or the director of publications.

vii. Legal Services Department

This department comprises of the legal drafting, litigation and counselling units. In legal drafting, the political thoughts and proposals of legislators are translated into law. This department ensures that the intentions of political sponsors of bills in the assembly conform strictly with the statutory requirements of law-making processes and procedures. Furthermore, contentious legal issues affecting the assembly are usually referred to this department for legal opinion and advice.

viii. Estate and Works Department

The responsibility of this department is to maintain the buildings, furniture and transport system of the assembly. This is the technical unit that manages the assembly's infrastructure and other fixed assets.

Business Instruments of a Legislature

The legislature uses numerous technical terms as working instruments of law-making. These include:

i. *Quorum*

A quorum for the meetings of the national or state houses of assemblies is formed by the presence of one-third of all the members of the house. Section 54(1) of the Constitution deals with the quorum for the National Assembly, while Section 96(1) covers the quorum for a state house of assembly. The quorum for a joint sitting of the Senate and the House of Representatives is formed by one-third of all the members of both houses (see Section 54(2).

As provided by Order 9(1) of the Standing Orders of Bayelsa State House of Assembly:

> The quorum of the House shall not be less than one third of all the members of the House.

The standard practice as set out by Order 9 (2), is that if a member brings to the notice of the Speaker that a quorum of the House is not present, the Speaker shall act swiftly. He shall direct all strangers to withdraw and order for a division of the members. If the House fails to attain the required quorum after two minutes of the withdrawal of strangers and the Speaker's count, the House shall be adjourned for lack of quorum.

ii. *Language*

Section 55 of the constitution provides that the business of the National Assembly shall be conducted in English language, and also in Hausa, Ibo and Yoruba, where adequate arrangements have been made for translation. Also, the business of the state house of assembly shall be conducted in English language. A state house of assembly may, however, conduct its affairs in one (or more) languages which are spoken in the state, as the house may, by resolution, approve (see Section 97).

Similarly the standing orders of the state houses of assembly concur that the proceedings and debates of the house shall be conducted in English, but the house may, by resolution, approve in addition to English, conduct the business of the house in one or more other languages spoken in the state when adequate arrangements have been made thereof.

A member may, however, present a petition in any other language if the petition be accompanied by an English translation certified to be correct by the member presenting the petition.

iii. *Voting*

Section 56(1) and (2) of the constitution states that decision- making in the National Assembly is done by voting. The voting process is decided by a simple majority of the members present. Similarly, Section 98(1) and (2) covers this subject for state houses of assembly. The presiding officer (Senate President or Speaker) can only cast his vote when there is a tie.

Recent voting irregularities

The interpretation of a simple majority has had some interesting results recently. For instance, Enugu and Abia states had two factions of the legislature between 2002 and 2003; Oyo State witnessed the same dilemma in 2005/ May 2007. In Enugu State, sixteen of the state legislators were in exile in Abuja while eight of them deliberated and passed bills in Enugu. The Abuja faction also passed bills whenever they were in Enugu, also using the state legislative building (see the case of *Asogwa v. Chukwu)[1]*. Anambra and Plateau states had the same uneasy development from 2006 till May 2007. In short, the removal of the governors of both states were effected by a faction of each house of assembly.

In Oyo, the thirty-two members of the State House of Assembly broke into two opposing factions, with eighteen of them against the state governor, Rashidi Ladoja, while fourteen supported him. The eighteen initiated impeachment proceedings against the state governor and, ultimately, removed him from office. Perhaps they did not remember how to calculate their fractions as the required two-thirds majority of the total membership of the house was not achieved.

One of the contentious issues in these stories was that some of the sessions were held in hotel complexes. This gross abuse of power was been settled in favour of Governor Ladoja by decisions at the Court of Appeal and Supreme Court in *Adeleke & Ors* v *Inakoju & Ors.[2]*

---

[1] [2003] 4 NWLR (pt. 811) p. 540.

[2] *The Nation* newspaper, 3 November 2006, p. 43-44.

In Plateau State, eight remaining members of the State House of Assembly after the declaration of the vacancy of the seats of their colleagues, initiated impeachment proceedings against the state governor, Joshua Dariye in 2006. The Supreme Court nullified that impeachment since they failed to constitute the required constitutional quorum out of the entire membership of twenty four members (see *Dapianlong v. Dariye*).[3]

The constitution requires a four-fifths majority of all the members for the alteration of provisions relating to fundamental rights (Section 9(3)) and a two-thirds majority in some other matters. In respect of impeachment, the quorum required is that two-thirds of all the elected members of the house of assembly be present (see chapter 24 which deals with impeachment proceedings).

iv. Standing Orders or Rules

These are the standard regulations governing the procedures and conduct of a legislature. Orders 1(a) and (b) of the Standing Orders of the Bayelsa State House of Assembly state that:

> (a) The proceedings in the Bayelsa State House of Assembly and in all Committees of the House shall be conducted according to the following Standing Orders.

> (b) In all cases not provided for hereinafter, or by sessional or other orders or practices of the House, resort shall be had to the practice of the British House of Commons in force for the time being which shall be allowed as far as it can be applied.

Upon the inauguration of the legislature, it is customary for the house to direct its 'rules and business committee' to produce rules or orders that will guide the conduct of the house. The mandate can equally be for the review of an old standing order inherited by the new legislature. Hence, the old standing order or rule will be reviewed to suit the needs of the current assembly. After the committee submits its findings to the house, a resolution of the whole house adopts the document as the standing orders or rules of the house. This exercise is in line with Section 60 and 101 of the Constitution which mandates the National Assembly and state houses of assembly to regulate their procedures.

---

[3] [2007] 4 SC Pt 3.

v. **Order paper**

This is the printed business schedule of a legislature for a particular day. It is the programme of the house that contains motions, bills and even committee meetings and other matters fixed for some particular dates. According to Order 39(1) of the Standing Orders of the Bayelsa State House of Assembly:

> An order of the day is a Bill or other matter which the House has ordered to be taken into consideration on a particular day. An earlier day order cannot be substituted for the day so appointed.

The order of the day shall be treated with precedence to their listing on the order paper. Hence, item **i** must be treated before items **ii** and **iii**. An order of the day can be postponed by a motion-without-notice of a sponsor or by another member, at his request. The Rules and Business Committee determines the date for the treatment of an order of the day which was not dealt with before the end of the sitting or was fixed for a day the House did not sit.

It is the responsibility of the Clerk to ensure the circulation of the order paper to each member of the house at the opening of each day's proceedings. The order paper, sets forth the business of the day. The order paper serves as the agenda of the house for a particular day, as scheduled by the business and rules committee.

vi. **The mace**

The mace is the symbol of authority of the legislature. The legislature cannot embark on any legitimate business in the chamber without the mace. In the British parliamentary tradition where it originated, it was both a weapon and an emblem of office for the sergeant-at-arms. The authority of the presiding officer (president of the Senate or Speaker of the House of Representatives, Speaker of a state house of assembly and leader of the local government legislative council) and his officiating role are inextricably linked to the mace as a revered instrument of the house. The arrival of the presiding officer for any official business of the house is heralded by the sergeant-at-arms, bearing the mace. The sergeant-at-arms is followed closely by the Clerk to the house and the presiding officer.

The placing of the mace on the table, before the Clerk at the centre of the chamber, signifies the readiness of the house to officially commence business. The lowering of the mace from the dais to the bracket, a hook beneath the table, immediately constitutes the house into a *Committee of the Whole House*. Thereafter, the Speaker is referred to as *chairman*.

Symbolically, the raising of the mace back to its place on the table, restores the Speaker and the house to their original status and roles. The lifting of the mace by the sergeant-at-arms and his consequent leading of the Clerk and the presiding officer out of the chamber, signals the official end of legislative proceedings. The coat of arms is represented on the mace at the head of a heavily gilded silver handle.

Consequently, the unwholesome action of breaking into opposing factions, whereby one faction claims the mace, or even steals or conceals the mace, and carries it to another venue and deliberates using the mace to constitute the group as a legal authority, is a gross abuse of that historically sacred instrument. Such unruly and undemocratic behaviour is totally out of place in the houses of assembly.

vii. Hansard/ Votes and Proceedings

The Hansard bears the assent of the Speaker and the Clerk to the house, as defined in 1907 by a select committee in England:

> *[This] is the official Report which though not strictly verbatim, is substantially the verbatim report with repetitions and redundancies omitted along with obvious mistakes but which, on the other hand, leaves out nothing that adds to the meaning of the speech or elucidates the argument.*

The origin of the Hansard dates back to the position of Luke Hansard as printer for the British government. In 1829, Luke Hansard's son, Thomas Curson, requested that the report bear the name 'Hansard'. That tradition has stuck and has also spread to many countries of the world as an emblem of parliamentary reports.

The National Assembly in Nigeria prints the daily reports of proceedings in each house, known as the 'National Assembly Debates'. Each house adopts the previous day's business. These reports are different from the Hansard, which is signed officially by the Speaker or Senate President and the Clerk to the assembly. Some state houses of assembly print official reports and the votes and proceedings.

As confirmed by Order 29 (3) of the Standing Orders of the Bayelsa State House of Assembly:

The Clerk shall keep minutes of the proceedings of the House and of the committee of the whole House and shall circulate a copy of such minutes to be known as the votes and proceedings, on the day following each sitting of the House, or as soon as possible thereafter.

viii. *Petition*

This medium enables interest groups (communities, organizations) and even private citizens to express their support or disapproval of a particular legislation. The common forms of petitions are complaints by members of the public, aggrieved groups or individuals seeking redress or help from the legislature. It is usually addressed to the petitioner(s) representative in the legislature who will formally present it to the house for consideration.

A petition may only be presented to the House by a member, who shall affix his name at the top of the document. The member who presents a petition shall confine himself to a brief statement of the parties from whom it originates, the number of signatures attached to it, and the material allegations contained in it.

ix. *A Bill*

A Bill is a draft or proposed law used by the legislature in the making of laws. A Bill is a potential law. This is because, the satisfaction of the constitutional provisions and the standing order requirements by the prescribed majority of the members along with the chief executive's assent, transforms it into law. The Constitution upholds the passing of Bills as the exercise of the power of national and state assemblies to make laws vide Section 58(1) and Section 100(1) respectively.

There are three types of Bills:

(a) *Public Bills* – These are Bills that command general application. Such a Bill affects every member of the catchment group or target group of such proposal. A sanitation law of a state, for example, concerns every person in that state.

(b) *Private Bills* – These are Bills for the particular interest or benefit of some persons or body of persons — The Medical Practitioners Act will affect only those in that medical field.

(c) *Hybrid Bills* – These are public Bills which also covers the private interests of particular persons or corporate bodies.

x. Motion

A motion is a request by a legislator(s) to the house or the executive arm of government for the immediate solution of an important issue. The object of the motion may arise within the constituency, the state, region or the entire country. A motion represents the collective expression of the populace through their representatives in the legislature on a matter of utmost importance.

xi. Resolution

A resolution is a formal declaration decided by vote and expressing the opinion of the house on a matter. It is required for the removal of the presiding officer of a state house of assembly (Section 92(2) (c) the House of Representatives and the Senate (Section 50 (2)(c)). A resolution can be simple, concurrent or joint in nature.

a. Simple resolution

This pertains to the decision of one legislature which demonstrates its stance on an issue it accords prominence.

b. Concurrent resolution

This type of resolution occurs mostly in constitutional spheres and involves the state and the National Assembly. It is used in the amendment of the Constitution or national issues of paramount importance like the adjustment of state boundaries and creation of states. Before the National Assembly can alter the Constitution a two-thirds majority of the state houses of assembly must concur (see Section 9(2) and 9(3) of the Constitution)

c. Joint resolution

A joint resolution is a declaration by the Senate and the House of Representatives on a particular issue of national interest. It is mostly employed in addressing matters of urgent national significance. For example, the National Assembly's joint resolution is provided for in Sections 64(2) and 105(2) of the 1999 Constitution to extend the periods of holding an election position beyond four years during a period of war as adjudged by the president of the federation.

Similarly, the declaration of a state of emergency by the president of the federation requires the resolution of each house of the National Assembly as contained in Section 305 (2) of the 1999 Constitution.

Chapter 15

Local Government Legislative Councils and Bye-laws

It was the firm belief of the federal government that an effective local government system would ensure that the human and material resources of the country are effectively mobilized and harnessed, that an unbroken chain of communication is maintained between the rulers and the ruled, and that the principle of participatory democracy and political responsibility is enshrined in the minds of the people.

Brigadier Shehu M usa Y ar'A dua

Foreword to *Local Government Reform*, Kaduna, 1976

A local government area is, by law, a legislative agency under the jurisdiction of a state government. In this wise, its legislative competence and will is manifested and expressed through a subordinate legislation that is traditionally known as 'bye-laws'. The source of the authority and validity of local government bye-laws is not directly derived from the Constitution, rather each state passes enabling laws which demarcate the responsibilities for the local governments.[1]

The enabling laws or acts specify the scope and content of the organizational structure of the local government area, as well as the bye-laws.

---

[1] An exception to this is the Federal Capital Territory which derives its power to make bye-laws from an Act of the National Assembly.

The 1999 Constitution enjoins every state government to ensure that each local government is democratically elected [vide section 7(1)]. That constitutional provision was fulfilled by the enactment of local government enabling laws by every state in 1999. For example, the states are expected to enact laws governing the organization and running of laws for the local governments within their jurisdiction. [2]

The Supreme Court was in support of state government's position, when it held in *AG Abia State v. AG Federation*[3] that:

> *It is the house of assembly of a state, and not the National Assembly, which has the powers to make laws with respect to matters relating to or connected with elections to the office of chairman or vice chairman of a local government council in that state or to the office of councillors therein.*[4]

The financial dependence of the local government councils on the state government was also highlighted in the case of *AG Lagos State v. AG Federation*, (supra) where the apex court stated that:

> *In the case of the local government, their allocations do not go to them directly. They are required in Section 162 (5) to be paid to the states for the benefit of their local government councils on such terms and such manner as may be prescribed by the National Assembly.*

Creation of a new local government

This subject mater is provided in Section 8 (3), (5) and (6) of the 1999 Constitution. The process of the creation of a new local government is detailed by Section 8 (3).

The house of assembly of a state is empowered vide Section 8 (3) to create new local governments by the passage of a bill that must satisfy these conditions:

---

[2] For example, see the Bayelsa State Local Government Creation and Transitions Provisions 1999.

[3] [2004]11-12SC.

[4] [2002] 6 NWLR 264 SC p.321 para.20.

The request for the creation of the new local government must be supported by at least a two-thirds majority of the members of the House of Assembly representing the area demanding the creation of the new local government area (Section 8 (3) (a) (i)).

In addition, at least a two-thirds majority of the members in the existing local government legislative councils in respect of the area (Section 8 (3) (a) (ii)). This mandatory request with specified majority support must be received by the state house of assembly.

This request will be democratically strengthened by a proposal for the creation of the new local government that will be approved in a referendum by at least two-thirds majority of the people of the local government area, where the demand for the proposed local government area originated (Section 8 (3) (b)).

The result of the referendum has to be approved by a simple majority of the members in each local government council in a majority of all the local government councils in the state (Section 8 (3) (c)).

In furtherance thereto, the result of the referendum will be approved by a resolution passed by two-thirds majority of members of the House of Assembly (Section 8 (3) (d)).

The constitution requires an input of the National Assembly in this process. Thus, an Act of the National Assembly shall make consequential provisions with respect to the names and headquarters of states or local government areas as provided in Section 3 and in Parts I and II of the First Schedule of the Constitution (Section 8 (5)).

The House of assembly is also required, after the creation of more local government areas pursuant to subsection (3), to make adequate returns to each house of the National Assembly. These mandatory returns will enable the National Assembly to exercise the powers conferred upon it by subsection (5) (Section 8 (6)).

The case of creation of a local government in Lagos State

The Lagos State House of Assembly in an exercise of its constitutional powers conferred upon the assembly by Section 8 (3), enacted the Local Government Area Law No. 5 of 2002. In March 27, 2004, the Lagos State Government conducted elections in 57 local government areas created by the said law (Local Government Area Law No. 5 of 2002).

On April 8, 2004, the President of Nigeria, Olusegun Obadanjo wrote a letter to the Minister of State in the Federal Ministry of Finance, Mrs. Nenadi E. Usman, highlighting the perceived unconstitutional creation of new local governments by Ebonyi, Katsina, Lagos, Nassarawa and Niger States.

On April 19, 2004, Mrs. Nenadi E. Usman, issued a circular to all the state governors and all the local government chairmen in the country, based on the President's memo of April 8, 2004. In the opinion of the President, these new local government areas were irregular, and the import of the circular was that no allocation from the Federation Account should be released to the local government councils of Lagos State and other states which similarly created new local government areas.

The Lagos State Government swiftly vide an originating summons, instituted an action against the federal government — the case of *AG of Lagos State v. AG of the Federation.*[5] While the case was pending at the Supreme Court, the Lagos State House of Assembly enacted the Creation of Local Government Areas (Amendment) Law 2004.

The Supreme Court upheld the constitutional powers of the state to create new local government areas through laws enacted by the house of assembly. The apex court speaking through Uwais CJN (*AG Lagos v. AG Federation*[6] posited that:

> *What follows from this is that the laws enacted by Lagos State that is Law No. 5 of 2002 and the 2004 law are both valid laws since the House of Assembly of Lagos State has the power under Section 4 subsections (6) and (7), 7 subsection (1) and 8 Subsection (3) of the Constitution to legislate in respect of the creation of new local government areas and local government councils which are one and the same for the purpose of Section 162 subsection (3) and (5) of the Constitution.*

---

[5] [2004] 11–12 SC Pt. 85.

[6] supra at page 113, para 25-30.

It was also the stance of the Supreme Court that the President of the Federal Republic of Nigeria has no power to authorize the withholding of the statutory allocation payable to Lagos State. In the emphatic words of Kutigi JSC at page 122 - 123, para 40:

> *It appears to me that nowhere in the Constitution is the President expressly or impliedly authorised to suspend or withhold the Statutory Allocation payable to Lagos State pursuant to Section 162 (5) of the Constitution on the ground of the complaints made against Lagos State by the Federal Government in this action or any ground at all. If the President has any grievance against any tier of government, he should go to court.*

The controversy that trailed that judgement, emerged from the reasoning of the majority of the members of the panel on the role of the Act of the National Assembly as ordained by subsection (5) and (6) of Section 8. In that mind-set, most of the Supreme Court justices found favour with the submission of the defence counsel Afe Babalola (SAN), that the state law will remain inchoate and unenforceable until the enactment of an Act of the National Assembly. In Tobi JSC's estimation at page 554, para 25-30:

> *It is my opinion that Law No. 5 of 2002 can only become constitutional if the National Assembly enacts the Act under Section 8 (5). And until that event happens, Law No. 5 of 2002 is inchoate and unenforceable. I think Chief Babalola SAN, got the point correct or right when he submitted that the claim against the law is that it is inchoate and therefore not enforceable in its present form. I entirely agree with that submission. In order to be enforceable, Law No. 5 of 2002 ought to have passed through the procedure laid down in Section 8 (6) of the Constitution.*

But the striking and inciting dissenting judgement of Uwaifo JSC and Akintan JSC, bore undeniable testimony to the true spirit of federalism as intended by the constitution. In Akintan JSC's lucid words in page 170, para 5-15:

> *It is therefore not correct to say that the process of creating the new local government councils by Lagos State was incomplete or*

> *inchoate until the National Assembly carries out its role under Section 8 (5) of the constitution. Similarly, I also hold that in the absence of any Act of the National Assembly passed under Section 162 (5) and 162 (7) restricting or prohibiting the newly created local government councils from benefitting from the revenue accruing from the Federation Account. It will be totally unconstitutional to withhold such fund from the newly created local government councils.*

It is most unfortunate, that the National Assembly has not taken the desired constitutional steps required by the constitution since 2004 (five years ago) after the enactment of the Lagos State Law. The threat by the federal government in July 2009 to sanction Lagos State government due to this issue also deepened our national ignorance.

The creation of local government as rightly held by the above cited judgment is entirely a state government affair. The consequential provisions cannot override the primary constitutional subject matter. Therefore, these local government areas of Lagos State, created through valid laws in line with constitutional provisions, are legal and constitutional. The democratic and legally ordained route for the resolution of any controversy thereto, is through a court of competent jurisdiction.

Functions of the local government

The constitution reposed salient responsibilities aimed at the advancement of the citizenry and their well being on the local government council. Hence, section 7 (3) provides that:

> It shall be the duty of a local government council within the state to participate in economic planning and development of the area referred to in subsection (2) of this section and to this end an economic planning board shall be established by a law enacted by the House of Assembly of the State.

In furtherance, section 7 (5) highlights that the functions to be conferred by law upon local government councils shall include those set out in the Fourth Schedule to this Constitution. The main functions of a local government council (Fourth Schedule) are as follows:

    (a) The consideration and the making of recommendations to a state commission on economic planning or any similar body on:

        i. the economic development of the state particularly in so far as the areas of authority of the council and of the state are affected, and

        ii. proposals made by the said commission or body;

    (b) collection of rates, radio and television licences;

    (c) establishment and maintenance of cemeteries, burial grounds and homes for the destitute or infirm;

    (d) licensing of bicycles, trucks (other than mechanically propelled trucks) canoes, wheel barrows and carts;

    (e) establishment, maintenance and regulation of slaughter houses, slaughter slabs, markets, motor parks and public conveniences;

    (f) construction and maintenance of roads, streets, street lightings, drains and other public highways, parks, gardens, open spaces or such public facilities as may be prescribed from time to time by the House of Assembly of a state;

    (g) naming of roads, and streets and numbering of houses;

    (h) provision and maintenance of public conveniences, sewage and refuse disposal;

    (i) registration of births, deaths and marriages;

    (j) assessment of privately owned houses or tenements for the purpose of levying such rates as may be prescribed by the House of Assembly of a state; and

    (k) control and regulation of:

        i. outdoor advertising and hoarding,

        ii. movement and keeping of pets of all descriptions;

        iii. shops and kiosks;

iv.   restaurants, bakeries and other places for sale of food
to the public;

v.   laundries, and

vi.   licensing, regulation and control of the sale of liquor.

The functions of a local government council shall include participation of such councils in the government of a state with respect to the following matters:

(a) the provision and maintenance of primary, adult and vocational education;

(b) the development of agriculture and natural resources, other than the exploitation of minerals;

(c) the provision and maintenance of health services; and

(d) such other functions as may be conferred on a local government council by the House of Assembly of the state.

The constitutional legislative and executive authority conferred on the local government councils cannot be restricted by the state government or any other arm. In short, the state legislature cannot validly or competently legislate to restrict or deprive the local government councils from exercising the executive and legislative authorities implicit in the above cited constitutional functions.

Hence, in the case of *Bamidele v. Commissioner for Local Government*[7] the Court of Appeal (through Uwaifo JCA) stated that:

> *. . . incidentally, Section 7(5) of the 1979 Constitution provides for the functions of Local Government Councils in the 4th Schedule to the Constitution, among which, as stated in paragraph 1 (e) thereof, is the establishment, maintenance and regulation of markets, motor parks and public conveniences. It will be unconstitutional for any other person or authority to purport to exercise that function on the state of the law. The function has been given to the Local Government. It has the duty to perform it.*

---

[7] [1994] 2 NWLR Pt 328 at p.574.

It may do so directly or by lawful delegation. It cannot be deprived of it nor can it surrender it. Any person who shows sufficient interest can take action to ensure that only the Local Government and no other continues to do or take responsibility for that duty.

This same basic reasoning guided the Court of Appeal in the case of *Knight, Frank & Rutley v. Attorney General Kano State*[8] where it was held that:

Once the state promulgates a legislation assigning the function of valuation of tenement rates to the Local Government as the 1979 Constitution had directed only the Local Government Council has the power to deal with the subject matter. Consequently, the state government has no power to deal with the matter and the local government council cannot, even if it wants to, divest itself of the power vested in it.

The Legislative Council

The legislative power of the local government resides in the 'legislative council'. The council is composed of all the elected councillors from every ward within a local government area, the Clerk and the support staff appointed by the Local Government Service Commission of the state.

The council has the power to debate and approve or amend the annual budget of the local government area presented by the chairman. The legislative arm also vets and monitors the implementation of projects and programmes approved by it in the budget of the local government area. It is also within the jurisdiction of the council to examine and debate monthly statements of income and expenditure submitted to her by the local government chairman.

The local government law-making body also advises, consults and liaises with the chairman of the local government area to perform such other functions as may be assigned to it by any law enacted by the State House of Assembly. The council also bears the legislative responsibility of the impeachment of the

---

[8] (1990) 4 NWLR Pt 143 at p. 211-212.

chairman and vice-chairman of the local government area in cases of gross misconduct as will be prescribed by the enabling law.

Leader and Deputy Leader

The Leader and Deputy Leader of the council will be elected to head this legislative arm by their fellow elected councillors at the inauguration of the council. Hence the Leader and in his absence, the Deputy Leader, presides over the sitting of the local government council.

There is also room for pro-tempore leader, whereby the councillors will elect one of their members to preside in the absence of the leader and the deputy leader. The office of the Leader and the Deputy Leader is similar to the customary position and role of the Speaker and the Deputy Speaker in any parliament or assembly. The leader or the deputy leader will vacate their offices under any of these conditions:

a.   If he ceases to be a councillor in that local government area

b.   When the council first sits after any dissolution of the council; or

c.   If he is removed from office by a resolution of the council by the votes of not less than two-thirds majority of the councillors in the council.

It is important to note that these officials act on behalf of the local government and not in their individual capacity in discharging their duties. Therefore, the local government will be held vicariously liable for their actions. The Court of Appeal affirmed this position in the case of *Jimoh* v. *Olawoye* where it was stated that:

> *The respondent's reliefs are against the Local Government and not the individuals who clearly acted on its behalf. In the circumstance, the non-joinder of Ifelodun Local Government is fatal to the case of the respondent and it ought to have been struck out by the trial court.*[9]

---

[9] [2003] 10 NWLR Pt.828.307 at p.320.

Procedures for making a bye-law

The traditional law-making procedures which govern the National Assembly and the state houses of assembly also guide the local government council. The National Assembly or a state houses of assembly can empower a local government to make a subsidiary law designated as 'a regulation', 'a rule' or by any other name so called. In the same fashion, it can also prescribe a form and procedure that will be different from the usual law-making process.

The prescribed form must be mandatorily or imperatively adhered to, since failure to strictly abide by it, will result in the invalidation of the subsidiary law so made. A local government bye-law may originate from an executive draft (the chairman and his personnel), members draft (from any of the councillors) and private draft (from any source outside the chairman and council ie, pressure group and general public).

The operative procedure is that every draft bye-law must be channelled to the council through the leader. It is the responsibility of the leader to reproduce and circulate the draft bye-law to every member of the council before the commencement of the legislative process.

In the same fashion with the act of the National Assembly and the laws of the state houses of assembly, a local government bye-law draft goes through the normal legislative route of first reading, second reading, committee stage, third reading and assent by the local government chairman.

The first reading entails the reading aloud of the short title of the bye-law draft by the Clerk to the council. There is opportunity for public presentation after the first reading. Hence, the proposed bye-law draft will be pasted on the council's notice board at the local government headquarters as well as in the area and district offices. This notice will be for a specified duration to enable the members of the public to contribute, if need be, in the proposed bye-law.

The Clerk to the council will then cause the draft bye-law to be read a second time at the expiration of the public notice. The collective reaction in terms of objections, comments and views are very important in according legitimacy to grassroots enactment. The second reading is achieved through the detailed analysis and debate on the demerits and merits of the proposed bye-law draft.

The next is the dispatch of the approved draft by required majority of councillors to the committee of the whole house or special committee for more scrutiny and final ratification. The third reading is the conclusive review of the entire piece of the proposed subsidiary legislation by the council. If the draft secures the approval of the required majority of the councillors, a clean copy will be produced. That final copy will then be sent to the chairman of the local government area for his assent.

If the chairman of the local government refuses or withholds his assent, he must notify the council within 30 days and send back the draft. If the draft is represented and approved by the required two-thirds majority of council members, it will become a bye-law without the chairman's assent. These procedures and processes are subject to the enabling laws and rules of the various local government areas.

Quorum

A local government requires a quorum of one-third of its members in order to conduct business during a normal sitting.

Political apathy at the local government level

It is most regrettable that this important seedbed of democratic rules and practices has not been given the attention it deserves. The general political apathy and overbearing influence of state governments constitute a frustrating hurdle to the growth of local government administration. Thus, the ordained democratic tenets and practice standards are hardly seen or felt in our local government affairs.

It is pertinent to note that we have no uniform rules or regulations that cover local governments. Therefore, each state's enabling law controls the grassroots affairs within its jurisdiction. Some states have not conducted local government elections since the inception of this democratic regime in 1999. In short, the local government administration and funds have been unconstitutionally relegated to being mere service units of the state governments. The various reports of the Economic and Financial Crimes Commission (EFCC) on most states confirm this negative development. The spate of caretaker committees inaugurated by some state chief executives in the place of democratically elected local government councils strengthens this worrisome departure from consti-tutionalism.

Problems of local government

This vital formative strata of our governance is overwhelmed with many problems. The numerous reforms and reviews have not yielded tangible results. The grassroots tier problems are as follows:

i. *The autonomy question*

Local government is an administrative agency of the state government. In this wise, it is viewed as an administrative subunit of the state government. The age-long unitary tradition of the military era, also reflects the suppression of this third tier of government by the state and federal government.

Thus, the dependence of local government on the state and federal governments, especially for revenue, affects it adversely. This worrisome development is reflected in the operation of caretaker committees in many states, against the constitutional directive for democratically elected local government councils.

The constitution must be amended to grant and ensure financial independence to local governments. The current revenue allocation of 20.60 per cent of federal revenue to local governments will reflect in LG projects and programmes if that tier is independent.

The virtual monopoly of the ruling political party in each state in the organization and conduct of local government elections, strengthens this point. This alarming trend, has resulted in the boycotting of elections by opposition political parties in most states, as the ruling party sweeps the polls.

The collateral effect, has been a local government instituted by the state government with neither political nor financial autonomy.

ii. *Illegal deductions and the subversion of statutory funds of local government*

This ugly trend that started in the First Republic has continued unabated from the military era up to the current dispensation. In short, the federal and state tiers, regard local government as mere subsidiary outposts for settlement of collective financial obligations.

Hence, for Nigeria's participation in the 1994 World Cup, each local government was forced to make a donation of two hundred and fifty thousand naira (₦250,000).

These unbridled tactics, peaked with Olusegun Obasanjo's regime from 1999- 2007. That regime embarked on monthly deductions from the council's Federation Account to pay primary school teachers. Moreover, the federal government in collusion with the Association of Local Government Chairmen of Nigeria (ALGON) in year 2000 purchased Toyota Prado jeeps for police divisions in all the councils of the federation by deducting from source from the Federation Account money designated to local government councils. The same government made deductions from the local governments federally and monthly allocated revenue to service the external debt.

This unconstitutional malaise climaxed with that administration's refusal to release the monthly council allocation from the Federation Accounts due to the Lagos State local government councils for many months. The Supreme Court's verdict stating the unconstitutionality of the action yielded half measure release of the funds that was finally released in full by the successor administration of Yar'Adua. The same pathetic testimony, revealed the deduction from source from the local government monthly allocation for the National Integrated Power Project (NIPP). This was revealed in course of the House of Representatives Committee investigation on the Energy Sector (March - April) 2008.

These financial anomalies frustrate local government administration, since the councils are hardly left with any fund with which to embark on grassroots-oriented projects after payment of staff salary.

iii. Poor performance and low calibre personnel

The overall performance of the local government council system throughout the country since May 29, 1999 is disheartening, as reflected in the words of F.A. Olasupo:

> *In the volumes of petitions by individuals to the Senate committee*
> *on state and local government matters which are currently*
> *reviewing the performance of the 774 local government councils*
> *in the country, not less than 80 council chairmen have been*
> *referred to the police for theft of council funds and other gross*
> *financial improprieties ranging from contract inflation, diversion*

> *of council fund to acceptance of kickbacks on contracts awarded*
> *by them since the inception of the current civilian administration*
> *on May 29, 1999.*[10]

This tier is also plagued with the capacity problem of unprofessional and unskilled personnel who can hardly deliver the expected objectives of the populace. The modern facilities and training schedules to upgrade this cadre, go far beyond the depth of the current local government financial purse.

iv. Democratization and constitutionalism problems

Local government administration in Nigeria, has not been conditioned to the basic tenets of democracy and the rule of law. It has remained an isolated platform for the advancement of the political interests of the state ruling party actors. This grassroots tier which should have the vehicle to drive community development and enshrine democratic values at the local level has become unorganized and disturbingly rowdy and a mere puppet dancing to the tune of highhanded state government.

Most of the local government councils have not seen an election since the 1999 transition election conducted by the military. The conduct of the elections in most states, by the State Independent Electoral Commissions has become a mockery of free and fair elections. The constitutional oversight role reposed on the state houses of assembly in order to create a conducive democratic environment has been abused in most states.

v. Unwholesome accounting processes and lack of transparency

The collateral damage done to the third tier of government in Nigeria, is reflected mostly in the wanton lack of transparency in her operations throughout the country. Statutory allocations have been severely subverted in most states while the internally generated revenue seems to be an informal conduit pipe of the officials and their unskilled collection agents.

The considerable increase in allocation to this tier, especially from the Federation Account, has not been reflected in any rural or even urban development project since 1999. The expected civic and constitutional accounting responsibility of publishing annual audited accounts of the councils has been

---

[10] Olasupo, 27.

observed more in the breach. The report of auditor general of local government has also remained a mirage in most states in the country.

Improvement measures for local government areas

This vital formative strata of our governance is overwhelmed with many problems. The various reforms and reviews since the colonial days have not yielded tangible results. Hence the following remedial measures are suggested.

i. Constitutional amendments for direct funding

The current practice of joint-state account vide section 162 (5) of the Constitution, subordinates the local government financially to state governments. The financial independence of this tier of government, will open the door for rural development and grassroots turn around.

ii. Creation of a local government revenue board

The spate of irregular collection of tolls and rates within the local government areas (LGAs) nationwide is frightening. There is a strong need to establish an administrative agency to harmonize and account for these informal collections. The LGA revenue board will be saddled with the responsibility of publishing annual, quarterly and monthly accounts of every LGA in the state.

iii. The need for an office of auditor-general of local government

The establishment of this office in some states has been overlooked for many years. The appalling state of local government accounts and the administrative malaise, makes this office imperative in every LGA. It is pathetic that the large sums of money that have accrued to the local governments since 1999, cannot be genuinely accounted for. The internally generated fees, levies and rates have also followed the same non-accounting path. The truth, is that our LGAs have been run for decades without audited accounts.

iv. Introduction of enhanced status and professionalism

The current calibre of local government officials cannot deliver the expectations of a modern grassroots development programme. Hence the need to employ technocrats to man this tier of government is imperative. The trend world over, is the transformation of this tier with urban and regional experts, as well as social development and rural administration experts.

v. Collaboration with international agencies and academic institutions

The experience and professional contributions of renowned agencies whose objectives border on urban and rural development are important. The output of these agencies when combined with that of our educational institutions, will progressively create the mental shift required to salvage this grassroots administration. Ultimately, the expected orientation and framing of professional urban and rural technocrats to replace this moribund cadre will be realized.

Chapter 16

Inauguration of the National Assembly

*What is government more than the management of the affairs of
a nation? It is not, and from its nature, cannot be the property of
any particular man or family, but the whole community.*

Thom as Paine (*Rights of M an*, 1791)

---

*T*he general elections held every four years herald the birth of a new
session of the National Assembly. The provisions of the Constitution, the
Standing Rules of the Senate and the Standing Orders of the House of
Representatives dictate the procedures of the opening session of each chamber.

i. *Constitutional authority for legislation*

The National Assembly is conferred with legislative powers of the federation vide
Section 4(2-3) of the 1999 Constitution. That power extends to section 4 (2, a-b)
which covers the concurrent legislative list. The legislative powers of the Federal
Republic of Nigeria shall be vested in a National Assembly for the Federation
which shall consist of a senate and house of representatives.

> (2) The National Assembly shall have power to make laws for the
> peace, order and good government of the Federation or any part
> thereof with respect to any matter included in the Exclusive
> Legislative List set out in Part I of the Second Schedule to this
> Constitution.

> (3) The power of the National Assembly to make laws for the peace,
> order and good government of the Federation with respect to any
> matter included in the Exclusive Legislative List shall, save as
> otherwise provided in this constitution, be to the exclusion of the
> Houses of Assembly of States.

ii. Clerk to the National Assembly opening address

The Clerk to the National Assembly, whose office is created by Section 51 of the Constitution as the chief administrator of the parliament, facilitates the first sitting of each chamber of the National Assembly. Thus, he makes the opening remarks and welcomes the newly elected National Assembly members as a preparatory stage to a new parliamentary era.

The Clerk to the National Assembly then assumes the responsibility to preside over that inaugural session with the assistance of other principal staff of the National Assembly. The procedure is that the newly elected members of the National Assembly shall assemble at their respective chambers at the time officially appointed for the first sitting.

iii. The President's proclamation

The Constitution vide Section 64(3) empowers the person elected as President to issue a proclamation for the holding of the first session of the National Assembly. As held by that provision:

> Subject to the provisions of this Constitution, the person elected as the President shall have power to issue a proclamation for the holding of the first session of the National Assembly immediately after his being sworn in, or for its dissolution as provided in this Section.

The president exercises this constitutional power through an official memorandum addressed to the Clerk to the National Assembly. The president's opening remarks and goodwill message to the newly elected members of the National Assembly are traditionally read by the Clerk to the National Assembly.

The Standing Rules of the Senate 2003 affirm this constitutional provision through Rule 2(2)(a) where:

> Senators-elect having assembled, the Clerk to the National Assembly shall: Read the proclamation for the holding of the first session of the Senate.

Similarly, the Standing Orders of the House of Representatives (17th May, 2007) vide Order II, Rule (2) (a) endorses the reading of the proclamation by the Clerk to the National Assembly for the holding of the first session of the House conducted according to the Standing Orders.

iv. *Roll call and return of writs*

The Clerk to the National Assembly will then proceed on the roll call of all the newly elected senators (in the Senate chamber) and the newly elected members of the House of Representatives (in the House of Representatives chamber). This roll call is usually in alphabetical order.

In response, thereto, each senator-elect shall present the writ of election and also the receipt for the declaration of assets and liabilities to the clerk to the National Assembly. The Clerk to the National Assembly shall in turn, confirm the writs of election and the assets and liabilities of each of the senator-elect and lay same on the Table of the Senate.

Senate Rules 2(2) (6) and 2(3) graphically illustrate this process in stating that the Clerk to the National Assembly shall after reading of the president's proclamation:

> Call the Senate to order and proceed to the roll call and confirmation of writs of election as well as declaration of assets and liabilities of senators – elect in alphabetical order.
>
> 2(3) Each senator-elect called shall present the writ of election and the receipt for the declaration of assets and liabilities which shall be laid upon the Table by the Clerk.

The same procedures and processes govern the lower chamber as ordained by Order II, Rule (2) (b) and (3) of the House of Representative's Standing Orders.

The confirmation of the authenticated writ of election issued by the Independent National Electoral Commission (INEC) is very important. Hence, it becomes a prima facie evidence of the electoral success of the senator-elect or member-elect of the National Assembly. The certificate of return duly authenticated by the INEC, forms the basis for the enlistment and swearing in of the named candidate as a member of the Senate or the House of Representatives.

v. Call for the nomination of the President of the Senate and his Deputy

The Clerk to the National Assembly is the presiding officer for the election of the President of the Senate and the Deputy President of the Senate. He will then call for the nomination from the senators-elect for both principal offices. This call is in line with the provision of Section 50(1) (a) of the Constitution.

The Standing Rules of the Senate capture this requirement in Rule 3(2) (a):

> A senator-elect, addressing the Clerk, shall propose another senator-elect to the Senate to be President of the Senate and shall move that such a senator-elect
>
> Do take the chair of the Senate as President of the Senate:

In response to the Clerk's call for nominations, any interested senator-elect can rise and propose to the Senate, his choice of candidate for the office of the president of the upper chamber. That proposal must be seconded by another senator-elect.

The nominee for the position of the President of the Senate, in line with the letters and spirit of the Senate Standing Rules, must accept and acknowledge his nomination. Rule 3(2) (b) categorically provides that:

> A senator-elect when nominated and seconded shall inform the Senate whether he or she accepts the nomination. He may then proceed to address the Senate.

The nominee's address is typically to canvass for the support of his fellow senators-elect based on his personal qualities and peculiar subject area of interest to the Senate and Nigerian public.

It is incumbent upon the Clerk to ask for further nominations. It is only when there is no further nomination that nominations will be formally declared closed. The relevance of this procedure is underlined by Rule 3(2) (d) which explicitly holds that:

> If more than one senator-elect is proposed as President of the Senate, the Clerk shall after the second nomination ask:
>
> 'Are there any further nominations?'
>
> And if there are no further nominations, the Clerk shall say,
>
> 'I declare the nominations closed.'

vi. *Call for the nomination of the Speaker and Deputy Speaker of the House of Representatives*

The Clerk to the National Assembly on the floor of the House of Representatives will, similarly, in line with Section 50 (1) (b) of the Constitution, call for the nomination of candidates for the office of the Speaker and Deputy Speaker from amongst the members-elect.

In affirmation, the Standing Orders of the House of Representatives vide Order II, Rule 3 (a) upholds that:

> A member-elect, addressing the Clerk, shall propose another member-elect with legislative experience as member of the National Assembly to the House to be Speaker and shall move that such member-elect, 'Do take the chair of the House as Speaker of the House of Representatives'.

The Clerk's call for nominations will attract the response of any member-elect to propose his choice for the position of the Speaker of the House of Representatives. That nomination must be seconded by another member-elect.

On the same tone with the Senate Rules in highlighting the importance of this exercise, Order II, Rule 3(e) posits that:

> If more than one member-elect is proposed as Speaker, the Clerk shall after the second nomination and after each subsequent nomination, if any is made and seconded, ask:
>
> 'Are there any further nominations?'

And if there are no further nominations the Clerk shall say:

> 'I declare the nominations closed.'

vii. *Election of the president of the Senate and Deputy*

The provision of the Standing Rules of the Senate is to the effect that if only one senator-elect is proposed and seconded at the close of nomination by the Clerk, that senator-elect shall be declared the president of the Senate. As graphically detailed by the Standing Rules 3(2) (c):

> . . . The Clerk shall then declare the senator-elect so proposed and seconded as president of the Senate such senator-elect shall

be conducted to the chair by the proposer and seconder of the motion, and shall take the chair of the president of the Senate.

But, whereby virtue of Rule 3(2) (d) there are more than one senators-elect who are proposed and seconded for the position of the President of the Senate, election will be inevitable at the closure of nomination.

When the contest is between two senators-elect who were duly nominated and seconded, the provisions of Rules 3(2) (e)(i) and (ii) will suffice. Hence, the Senate shall divide with the nominees, proposers and seconders serving as the election tellers. The election shall be conducted by the Clerks-at-the-Table making use of the Division List of the Senate under the supervisory eyes of the tellers. The Clerk of the Senate as the returning officer, shall submit the result of the consequent division to the Clerk of the National Assembly who is the presiding officer.

In a situation where there are more than two senators-elect vying for the office of the president of the Senate, the same voting division procedure will be adopted as upheld by Rule 3 (2) (f). In this vein, the senator-elect who received a majority of the votes, shall ascend the chair as the President of the Senate.

Where no senator-elect receives a majority of the votes in the division, then, the names of the candidates who received the smallest number of votes shall be excluded from subsequent imperative division(s) as ordained by the same Rule 3(2) (f).

In accordance with Rules 3(2)(g) - (h), once there is an equality of votes, the Clerk shall cause a further division to be held. This division shall continue until a candidate emerges as the eventual President of the Senate through a majority of the votes.

On the same premise, Rules 3(2)(i) creates room for the withdrawal of a contestant at anytime after the first division has been declared. The candidate must withdraw before the commencement of the second or consequent division. The Senate will proceed with the election with the mind set that the withdrawn candidate was never nominated.

If the withdrawal of a contestant leaves the Senate with only one candidate running for that exalted office, that only remaining candidate shall without further division, be declared elected as president of the Senate.

The election of the president of the Senate is considered a very important issue that forbids debate and takes precedence over any other business of the Senate as ordained by Rule 3(2)(c). It overrides all other business of the Senate to the extent that no motion for adjournment nor any other form of motion can be entertained by that chamber until its conclusion. It also sets in abeyance, the standing or special order of the Senate and permits the extension of the ordinary daily schedule of that upper chamber until the emergence of the president of the Senate.

The same nomination and voting procedures govern the election of the Deputy President, as evidenced by Rule 4.

viii. Election of the Speaker and Deputy Speaker of the House of Representatives

The House of Representatives operates almost the same procedure with the Senate in the election of her presiding officers:

The notable issues of slight difference lie in Order II, Rule 3(c) which states that:

> The member-elect so nominated may address the House for a maximum period of 5 minutes.

Furthermore, Order II, Rule 3(f) (i) created the option of electronic voting.

Therefore, if the House of Representatives Speaker emerges through the nomination of only one member-elect at the declaration of the closure of nominations by the Clerk to the National Assembly vide Order II, Rule 3(d), then is no need to vote and the person so nominated becomes the Speaker

On the other hand, the presence of two nominated and seconded members-elect will subject the House to voting. Here, the Clerks-at-the-Table will conduct the election and the proposers serving as tellers vide Order II, Rule 3 (f) (ii).

Similarly, the Clerk of the House of Representatives shall submit the result of the voting to the Clerk to the National Assembly. It is the Clerk to the National Assembly who will declare the member-elect who polled the highest number of votes as the Speaker-elect (Order II, Rule 3(f) (iii).

Where there are more than two members -elect nominated and seconded for the position of the Speaker of the House of Representatives, the provision of

Order II, Rule 3(g) is that there will be division and the member-elect with more than one half of the votes shall be the Speaker-elect.

But if no member-elect polls more than one half of the votes, the member-elect who had the smallest number of the votes shall be excluded from subsequent division and further voting.

The provision is that the voting will continue until a member-elect emerges as the Speaker by the support of the majority of the members.

Similarly, if there is an equality of votes, the Clerk shall proceed with further voting as held by Order II, Rule 3(h).

There is also provision for the withdrawal of candidates before the commencement of a second or subsequent voting (Order II, Rule 3(i)).

The election of the Speaker is a vital business that permits no debate (Order 2 Rule 3(j). It takes precedence over all other business of the House (Order II, Rule 3(l). The same procedure governs the election of the Deputy Speaker (Order II, Rule 4).

ix. *Oath of office, allegiance and membership of the president and Deputy President of the Senate and the Speaker and Deputy Speaker of the House of Representatives*

The Constitution, vide Section 52(2), makes it imperative that the aforestated presiding officers of the National Assembly shall declare their assets and liabilities, take and subscribe the Oath of Allegiance and the Oath of Membership as prescribed in the seventh schedule to the Constitution. This must be performed before the Clerk to the National Assembly.

This constitutional provision is affirmed by Rule 5 of the Standing Rules of the Senate and Order II, Rule 5 of the Standing Orders of the House of Representatives.

x. *President of the Senate and Speaker of the House of Representatives take the chair*

The Oath of Allegiance and membership niceties of the president of the Senate and his Deputy as well as that of the Speaker of the House of Representatives and the Deputy Speaker will be followed by the taking of their respective chairs.

These presiding officers — president of the Senate and the Speaker of the House of Representatives — will acknowledge the support of their fellow legislators in conferring them with such unique honour and responsibility.

Rule 6 of the Standing Rules of the Senate and Order II, Rule 6 of the House of Representatives detail this stage of the first sitting.

Thus, the president of the Senate will mount the exalted chair of that upper chamber and the mace will 'rise' (be lifted from the bracket below the table and be laid upon the table). The same symbolic lifting of the mace, as the symbol of authority in the House of Representative will herald the Speaker's taking of the chair in the lower chamber.

xi. *Oath of membership and allegiance of the other members of the National Assembly*

The constitution endorses the power and authority of the presiding officers of the National Assembly. Hence, Section 52(1) upholds that:

> Every member of the Senate or House of Representatives shall before taking his seat, declare his assets and liabilities as prescribed in this Constitution and subsequently take and subscribe to the Oath of Allegiance and the Oath of Membership as prescribed in the Seventh Schedule to this Constitution before the President of the Senate or, as the case may be, the Speaker of the House of Representatives . . .

The Standing Rules of the Senate (Rule 8) accords suitably with the provisions of the constitution. But Order II, Rule 7 of the House of Representatives elevates the status of the Speaker by requiring every member-elect to submit his or her certificate of election to the Speaker.

It is pertinent to note, that the constitution appreciates all members-elect to be on the same footage. Hence, every member-elect can aspire to contest and if possible, be elected by fellow members-elect as the president of the Senate or Speaker of the House of Representatives. Therefore, any provision in the Standing Rules or Orders that categorizes members-elect based on legislative experience is unconstitutional. It is on this premise, that Order II, Rule 3(a) of the House of Representatives offends the constitutional provision. It provides that:

> A member-elect, addressing the Clerk, shall propose another member-elect with *legislative experience* as member of the National Assembly to the House to be Speaker and shall move that such member-elect, 'Do take the chair of the House as Speaker of the House of Representatives'.

This categorization or 'ranking' can only be enforced at the subsequent election of a presiding officer after the inaugural session whenever a vacancy is declared. But in the course of the inaugural session after a general election, every member-elect is eligible to vote and be voted for as the presiding officer of any chamber of the National Assembly where he/she is duly elected as a member.

xii Motion for adjournment

Both chambers of the National Assembly, having successfully held their first sittings and elected their respective presiding officers and deputies, will conclude its business.

It is customary at this juncture for any member to move for the adjournment of the House. This will in turn be seconded by another member. The motion opens the way for few other members to take their turn to congratulate their newly elected presiding officers.

This brief heartwarming remarks and exchange of hilarious speeches will then be concluded by the presiding officer putting the motion for adjournment to question, vote and then, the closure of the session.

Chapter 17

Inauguration of a State House of Assembly

Prospects for the survival of parliamentary democracy in Nigeria are favourable, provided she learns lessons which the experience of other countries can teach her. The diversity of the ethnic groups, each with its distinctive qualities, can be a source of strength and stability, in a democratic society.

Chief H .O . Davies, 1961

*O*ur federal constitution vested the legislative powers of the various states in their respective houses of assembly. In this wise, the general election ushers in new members for these unicameral law-making bodies in the 36 states of the federation. The constitution and the various standing orders of each of these houses of assembly guide the procedures of their opening sessions.

(i) *Constitutional authority for legislation*

Sections 4(6) and (7) (a) - (c) provide that:

> The legislative powers of a state of the Federation shall be vested in the House of Assembly of the State.

> The house of assembly of a state shall have the power to make laws for the peace, order and good government of that state or any part thereof with respect to the following matters, that is to say:

> (a) any matter not included in the Exclusive Legislative List set out in Part I of the second schedule to this Constitution;

> (b) any matter included in the Concurrent Legislative List set out

175

in the first column of Part II of the second schedule to this Constitution, to the extent prescribed in the second column opposite thereto; and

(c) any matter with respect to which it is empowered to make laws in accordance with the provisions of this Constitution.

ii. *Opening address of the Clerk to the House*

The Clerk of the House of assembly, whose office is created by Section 93 of the Constitution and Order 29 of the Bayelsa State Standing Orders, is saddled with the responsibilities of the proceedings of the House, until the election of the Speaker and the Deputy Speaker. The Clerk renders the welcome address, and with the assistance of his other principal staff, lays the schedule for the inaugural session of the House.

As provided by Order 2(1) of the Standing Orders of the Bayelsa State House of Assembly:

> On the first day of the meeting of a new Assembly, pursuant to the proclamation of the Governor of Bayelsa State of Nigeria, members shall assemble at the time and place so appointed.

Governor's proclamation
iii.

The Constitution, subject to the provision of Section 105 (3), empowers the person elected as the governor of a state to issue a proclamation for the holding of the first session of the State House of Assembly. As provided by that section:

> Subject to the provisions of this Constitution, the person elected as the Governor of a State shall have power to issue a proclamation for the holding of the first session of the House of Assembly of the State concerned immediately after his being sworn in, or for its dissolution as provided in this section.

The state governor exercises this constitutional power by virtue of a memorandum addressed to the Clerk. That memo will accompany the governor's proclamation.

The Clerk of the House traditionally reads the governor's proclamation. In the same tone with Order 2(2) - (a) of the Bayelsa State House of Assembly:

(2) members having assembled, the Clerk of the State House of Assembly shall:

>> (a) read the proclamation for the holding of the first session of the House.

iv. *Roll call and return of writs*

The Clerk of the House of Assembly will then proceed to the roll call of all the members-elect in alphabetical order. These members-elect will, in turn, present the copies of the writ of their election to the Clerk for confirmation.

This vital duty of the Clerk of the House is detailed by Order 2(2) (b) of the Bayelsa State House of Assembly in these words:

>> Call the House to order and proceed to the roll call and confirmation of writs or copies of writs of election of members in alphabetical order.

This confirmation exercise is very important since it requires the presentation of the authenticated writ of election issued by the Independent National Electoral Commission (INEC) to the newly elected members. Thus, it is a *prima facie* evidence of the electoral success of the members-elect and the basis for their swearing in.

v. *Call for the nomination of the Speaker and Deputy Speaker of the House*

The Clerk of the House, as the presiding officer of the inaugural proceeding will, in fulfilment of the provision of Section 92 (1) of the Constitution, call for the nomination of members-elect for the election of the Speaker. Order 3(2) (a) of the Bayelsa State House of Assembly dealt with this subject matter thus:

>> A member, addressing the Clerk, shall propose another member from the House to be Speaker and shall move that such member 'Do take the chair of the House as Speaker'.

The nomination of any member must be seconded by another member.

The member who has been duly nominated and seconded must acknowledge or accept the nomination on the floor of the House. As held by Order 3 (2) (b) of Bayelsa State House of Assembly:

>> A member when nominated and seconded shall inform the House whether he or she accepts the nomination.

There is provision in Order 3(2)(c) of the Bayelsa State House of Assembly for the Speaker nominee to address the House for a period of five (5) minutes.

If there is no other nomination, the Clerk shall declare the proposed member-elect as the elected Speaker of the Bayelsa State House of Assembly (Order 3(2)(d)).

> But if there is any other nomination(s) which is (are) duly seconded, the Clerk will take official notice of the nomination(s) and formally ask:'Are there any further nominations'?

If there are no other nominations, the Clerk will officially close the nomination If there are only two candidates nominated and seconded for the position of Speaker, the voting shall be conducted by the Clerks-at-the-Table, making use of the proposers and seconders of the nominees as Tellers. The Clerks-at-the-Table will employ the division list of the House in the presence of the tellers. The procedure is that the Clerk's assistants as the returning officers shall submit the result of the division to the Clerk of the House. The onus then lies on the Clerk to declare the member who scored the greater number of votes from that division (election) as the Speaker of the House.

When there are more than two nominees for office of the Speaker, the same division procedure shall be adopted in the conduct of the election. Hence, the nominee who receives the majority of the votes shall be declared the Speaker of the House.

But if no nominee receives a majority of the votes in the division, the name of the candidate who secured the smallest number of votes shall be excluded from further or subsequent divisions. This division shall continue until a candidate secures the majority of the votes and thereby emerges and can be declared as the Speaker of House.

When there is a tie of votes, the Clerk of the House shall cause further division to be held as provided by Order 3(2)(h).

Withdrawal of candidates
vi.

The Standing Orders of Bayelsa State also provide for the withdrawal of any nominee after the first division and before the commencement of a second or subsequent division. In this wise, the nominee may withdraw his or her name from the election list. Hence, the election will proceed as if the withdrawn candidate was never nominated. The standard practice is that at any stage where the withdrawal leaves only one candidate vying for the office of the Speaker, that remaining sole candidate, shall without further division be declared elected the Speaker of the House.

The election of the Speaker is a vital issue to which the Standing Orders accord precedence over any other business of the House. As aptly posited by Order 3(2)(j):

> During the election of a Speaker, there shall be no debate and no question of privilege may be raised.

The importance of this first assignment of a new legislature, was further elucidated by Order 3(2) (l) that:

> The election of Speaker shall take precedence over all other business and no motion for adjournment nor any other motion shall be accepted while it is proceeding and the House shall continue to meet if necessary beyond its ordinary daily time of adjournment, notwithstanding any standing or special order, until a Speaker is declared elected.

vii. *Voting procedures for the Speaker and Deputy Speaker of the House*

The nomination of two or more members-elect for the position of the presiding officer of the House of assembly of a state (Speaker) or his deputy, opens the contest to voting.

The voting under the supervision of the Clerk of the House, shall be conducted by a roll call of all the members-elect, who shall declare the member of their choice.

The voting and recording exercise must be diligent and transparent, based on simple majority of the votes. The nominee with the highest number of votes cast by his fellow members-elect will be declared the Speaker of the House.

In the event of a tie of votes by two or more of the nominees, there will be recourse to further voting. The nominee with the least number of votes amongst the contestants will be excluded from the election.

There is also provision for the withdrawal of any candidate from the election before or in the course of the election.

The nominee who polls the highest number of votes cast in the subsequent election or who remains after the withdrawal of the other nominees, will be declared as the Speaker of the House.

The same procedure governs the election of the deputy speaker of the House. As aptly held by Order 4 of the Bayelsa State House of Assembly:

> The procedure for the election of the Deputy Speaker shall be the same as that of the Speaker.

viii. Oath of membership and allegiance of the Speaker and Deputy Speaker

The newly elected Speaker and his Deputy will then subscribe to their oaths of membership, office and allegiance before the Clerk-of-the-House.

This is in fulfilment of the mandatory provision of Section 94 of the Constitution, and Order 6(1) of the Standing Orders of Bayelsa State:

> The Speaker and Deputy Speaker shall declare their assets and liabilities and subsequently take and subscribe the Oath of Allegiance and Oath of Membership as prescribed in the Constitution before the Clerk to the State House of Assembly.

Subject to the convenience of the House and the schedule of the opening session, the newly elected Speaker and his deputy can then robe ceremoniously. Then, they will be led to assume the chair by their two proposers.

On the new Speaker's assumption of the chair, the mace which is the symbol of authority of the House will be 'raised' (lifted and placed on the dais from the hook of the bracket). Thus, heralding the formal constitution of the House with the emergence of a presiding officer.

ix. Oath of membership and allegiance of other members of the House

The other members of the House shall, subject to the provisions of Section 94 of the Constitution, declare their assets and liabilities. They will then take the oath of allegiance and membership prescribed in the seventh schedule to the Constitution before the Speaker of the House.

This exercise can be performed in batches at the convenience of the House.

The unmistakable admonition of Order 7 of the Standing Orders is that:

> Every member shall, before taking his seat, declare his assets and liabilities, and subscribe the Oath or Affirmation of Allegiance and membership as prescribed in the seventh schedule to the Constitution of the Federal Republic of Nigeria before the Speaker.

ix. *Speaker-elect's acknowledgment address*

It is customary for the Speaker-elect to express his gratitude to his fellow members for the high honour done to him. He will also state his resolve to live up to the expectations of that office and protect, defend and preserve the Constitution as well as the independence of the legislature.

This commendable gesture is the essence of Order 6 (2) that:

> Having been sworn, the Speaker returns his acknowledgment to the House for the honour conferred upon him...

x. Motion for adjournment

At this juncture, a member of the House will rise and congratulate the Speaker-elect and at the same time, move the motion for the adjournment of the House. The motion will be seconded and followed up with few congratulatory comments by the members. The question for adjournment will be put and the House will formally resolve and rise accordingly.

This provision of the Bayelsa State House of Assembly Standing Orders that ranks members for the post of the Speaker is unconstitutional. The position of the Constitution, as well as the law of the state, is that all the members are on the same status, it does not matter if you have served an earlier term of office.

Therefore, any previous membership of the House of Assembly terminates with the dissolution of that assembly. Thus, their current eligibility stems from their success at the general election. In the face of the Constitution, their equal status as members-elect cannot be overturned by the provision of the Standing Orders or orders of the legislature. The Constitution being the *grundnorm* of the country, overrides any other law or subsidiary legislation.

xi. The day-to-day order of business

After the inauguration of the House of assembly has been completed, the House must follow a particular order in conducting its daily business. Most of the standing orders or rules for the state houses of assembly prescribe the following:

1. Formal entry of the Speaker
2. Prayers
3. Approval of votes and proceedings
4. Oath of Allegiance and Oath of Membership for new members
5. Message from the governor
6. Other announcements by the Speaker
7. Petitions
8. Matters of urgent public importance
9. Personal explanations and
10. Order of the day.

xii. Rules of debate

These are parliamentary precedents derived from age-old practices that guide the temperament and civilized conduct of a legislature. The purpose of these traditional legislative rules is to maintain decorum and orderly processes and procedures that will lead to the attainment of the desired needs, expectations and goals of the citizenry represented in that assembly.

The standard practice provides for a procedural manner in the sitting arrangement, whereby members must sit in their officially allotted seats. Moreover, basic ethical standards and rules of etiquette, such as the prohibition of eating, smoking, and the use of offensive and insulting language about members, are highlighted.

The rules guide against the improper conduct of moving around in the chamber in the course of House deliberation, or committee session. It also frowns at two members standing or speaking at the same time. A member can only indicate his interest to speak and have the floor to speak when chosen to speak by the presiding officer.

The rules also set a time limit and the sequence of addresses by the members. All members must show respect to the 'chair' in all matters. Each member is expected to dress formally (traditional or western) during attendance of the House session or committee.

The rules traditionally forbid the interruption of a member in the course of his/her speech, but accommodate these salient exceptions:

a. to call attention to a point of order or privilege suddenly arising;

b. to call attention to the want of a quorum;

c. to call attention to the presence of strangers; or

d. to move a closure motion.

The same subject matter is treated in Chapter VIII, Rules 53- 62 of the Senate, and Order IX of the House of Representatives.

Chapter 18

Principal Officers of the National and State Houses of Assembly

Parliamentary procedure does not have to be complicated and mysterious. As long as the presiding officer conducts meetings fairly and judiciously, and members learn the basic principles and procedures of parliamentary procedure, business can be transacted democratically and efficiently.

Ned A. Sheader

*T*he Constitution recognizes the President of the Senate, the Deputy Senate President, Speaker of the House of Representatives, Deputy Speaker of the House of Representatives and the Clerk of the National Assembly. These offices are provided for in sections 50(1) (a) and (b) and 51 of the Constitution. Similarly, only the Speaker, the Deputy Speaker and the Clerk of the House of Assembly are recognized as principal officers of the state assembly by virtue of Sections 92 and 93 of the Constitution.

There is no provision in the Constitution for the position of majority leader, minority leader, or that of party whips. The exponents of these party posts may, however, find favour with the provisions of Sections 60 (National Assembly) and 101 (State House of Assembly) of the Constitution. These Sections empower the national assembly and the state Houses of assembly to regulate their own procedures, including the procedures for summoning and recesses of the House. The implication is that the creation of these posts is supported by these Sections.

For example, the preamble to the Bayelsa State House of Assembly Standing Orders emphatically holds that:

> *In exercise of the power conferred by Section 101 of the Constitution of the Federal Republic of Nigeria 1999 and of all other powers enabling it in that behalf, the Bayelsa State House of Assembly hereby makes the following Standing Orders.*

i. Speaker of the House of Assembly

The origin of this office can be traced to England in 1377, when Sir Thomas Hungerford was appointed as the Speaker, although there had been presiding officers before him as from 1258, who were known as *'parlour'* or *'prolocutor'*. The Speaker bears the onerous responsibility of presiding at any sitting of the House as contained in Section 95(1) of the Constitution. The general control of the House and the assurance that the rules laid down by the House for the carrying on of its business are observed, are all duties of the Speaker.

Therefore, the guidance and direction of House debates, the taking of votes and the roll call of members during House sessions fall into the Speaker's schedule. The Speaker, as the political head of the legislature, signs all acts, addresses, joint resolutions, writs, warrants and subpoenas issued by the order of the House.

He also decides all questions of order, subject to an appeal by any member, on which appeal, no member shall speak more than once, unless by permission of the Speaker. He is the principal representative of the House in dealing with the other arms of government, as well as international bodies and foreign governments. He is expected to be impartial, tactful and mature in order to balance the varying interests within the legislature, especially the minority and opposition groups.

Erskine May's insightful remark is that:

> *Confidence in the impartiality of the Speaker is an indispensable condition of the successful working of procedure, and many conventions exist which have as their object not only to ensure the impartiality of the Speaker but also to ensure that his impartiality is generally recognized.*

This foremost officer of the legislature, by virtue of Section 190 of the Constitution, becomes the custodian and trustee of the state's executive powers when the governor is on vacation or unable to discharge his official duties. The governor's written memo to the Speaker, to that effect, empowers the deputy governor to act on the governor's behalf. The governor's written notification to the Speaker to resume duties after his vacation, restores his executive powers.

More so, in the situation where the posts of the governor and the deputy governor of a state are vacant in line with Section 191(2) of the Constitution, the Speaker shall hold the office of the governor for a period of not more than three (3) months during which there shall be an election of a new governor.

This constitutional provisions came to the fore in Kogi, Adamawa, Bayelsa, Sokoto, Cross River and Ekiti states, where the Speakers of the respective state Houses of assembly were sworn in as acting governors based on the nullification of the April 14, 2007 governorship election by the Election Petition Tribunals and the Court of Appeal.

The Supreme Court affirmed the importance of the Speaker and the Deputy Speaker in the case of *Inakoju* v. *Adeleke*. The apex court emphatically held that:

> ... *Having regard to the importance attached to the office of the Speaker of the state House of assembly in Section 95 of the 1999 Constitution by which the Speaker is mandatorily required to preside at the sitting of the House of assembly; and in his absence, the Deputy Speaker 'shall preside'. The two officials are therefore entitled to preserve the rights attached to their offices, as long as they have not been removed from office by a resolution of the House of assembly passed by the votes of not less than two-thirds majority of members of the House, as prescribed by Section 92(2)(c) of the said Constitution.* [1]

The Bayelsa State House of Assembly Standing Orders (vide Order 22), highlighted the duties of the Speaker as the foremost principal officer of that legislature.

---

[1] [2007] 2 MJSC pg 5. para 5.

He shall preserve order and decorum in case of disturbances or
disorderly conduct in the galleries, or in the lobby, may cause
same to be cleared.

The Speaker can be removed from office by a resolution of the House of
Assembly, supported by the votes of not less than two-thirds majority of the
members of the House by virtue of Section 92(2) (c) of the Constitution. The
Speaker will equally vacate his office if he ceases to be a member of the House
of Assembly or by reason of the dissolution of the House vide Section 92 (2) (a).
He also vacates his office when the House first sits after any dissolution of the
House as contained in Section 92 (2) (b) of the Constitution.

ii. Deputy Speaker of the House of Assembly

The same constitutional provisions govern this office and that of the Speaker
(Section 92). The Deputy Speaker performs the role of the Speaker in his absence
(especially in presiding at sittings of the House) as endorsed by Section 95 (1) of
the Constitution.

iii. Speaker Pro-tempore

The pro-tempore Speaker is a member of the House elected by his fellow
members (legislators) to preside over the sitting of the House in the absence of the
Speaker and the Deputy Speaker. This legislative rescue mission role is provided
for in Section 95(2) of the Constitution.

Order 24 of the Bayelsa State House of Assembly affirmed this position
thus:

In the absence of the Speaker and Deputy Speaker, such member
of the House as the House may elect, for the purpose shall
preside. Such member shall be known as 'Speaker Pro-tempore'.

However, Order 28 of the Bayelsa State House of Assembly, which requires that
any member must serve one tenure before being eligible for election as a principal
officer, is contrary to the intent of the Nigerian Constitution. The provision of the
Constitution is that all elected members are of equal status, and as such can vote
for and be voted for any office.

iv. Clerk of the House of Assembly

British parliamentary history reveals that the office of the Clerk came into being in 1325. The status of the office improved impressively with its occupation by men with vision and creativity like John Hatsell (1743-1820). Hatsell's impact became ingrained in British political history with a book[2] he wrote on parliamentary procedures.

The most outstanding Clerk in the history of the British House of Commons was Sir Thomas Erskine May, who laid the solid foundation on which the Clerk's department and parliamentary procedure has stood up to this day. Sir Thomas edited nine editions of parliamentary practice in his life time, which are still regarded as the alpha and omega of modern legislative practices and procedures. The office of the Clerk of the House of Assembly and his support staff are provided for in Section 93 of the Constitution. The Clerk is the chief administrative officer of the legislature. The appointment of the Clerk and the other staff of the House of assembly shall be prescribed by a law enacted by the assembly for that purpose. That law is the State House of Assembly Service Commission Law.

The Clerk is the head of the secretariat of the House of assembly. He provides the legislature with the basic administrative services that enable the House to meet the yearnings and expectations of the citizenry. This principal officer, from his vantage position on the table of the House, enters the decisions and proceedings into the minute book for publication in the votes and proceedings and also the journal. He reads out the title of the order of the day.

This chief permanent officer of the House of Assembly in the estimation of Erskine May bears these responsibilities:

> *The Clerk has the custody of all records or other documents, and is responsible for the conduct of the business of the House in the offices within his department. He assists the Speaker, advises members in regard to questions of order and the proceedings of the House.*[3]

---

[2] Hatsell's book on *Precedents of Proceedings in the House of Commons*, 1820.

[3] Erskine May, Ibid p. 189.

The political neutrality and impartiality principle of the public service guides the Clerk and his support staff. They are expected to refrain from partisan politics and taking sides in any political cleavage among members of the House. The Clerk to the House, as the administrative overseer of the legislature, coordinates and controls all the departments that constitute the House of Assembly.

v. Deputy Clerk and the Clerk Assistant

The responsibilities and duties of the Clerk to the House as the principal permanent officer of the legislature, is shared by other subordinate officers within the administrative hierarchy.

Thus, in the absence of the Clerk of the House, the Deputy Clerk of the House assumes his duties.

Orders 30 and 31 of the Bayelsa State House of Assembly describe this subject matter clearly:

> In the case of the unavoidable absence of the Clerk, his duties shall be performed by the Deputy Clerk or, should the latter be absent, by the Clerk Assistant.
>
> During any vacancy in the office of the Clerk, all powers, functions and duties of the Clerk shall be exercised and performed by the Deputy Clerk.

The level of legislative process and procedural awareness, has resulted in operative structures that recognizes the Clerk Assistant and Clerks-at-the-Table as principal permanent officers. These permanent officers bear supportive functions and duties that aids the Clerk and the entire legislature to achieve their constitutional objectives.

The Clerk Assistant who sits at the left hand of the Clerk-of-the-House at the Table is saddled with the keeping of the minutes of the proceedings, receives and keeps in order, notices of motions, questions and amendments. He also prepares the Notice Paper and Order Book for future sittings of the House of Assembly.

The increasing demands of modern governance on the office of the Clerk of the House of assembly as the administrative hub of the legislature, has resulted in far reaching innovations. The trend has led to the creation of vital departments under the overseeing umbrella role of the Clerk as the chief administrative coordinator of the House.

Hence, the emergence of principal Clerk in charge of designated departments or offices. The underlying motive of that initiative is explained by Erskine May in these words:

> *The essential function of the Department is to provide the procedural assistance necessary for the orderly conduct of the work of the House, and its committees, but Clerks also perform a number of administrative tasks and assist in the drafting of reports.*[4]

Therefore, the Clerks-at-the-Table ensure the preparation of the Order Paper, the Notice Paper and Order Book. It is equally their responsibility that any legislative question that appears on the Notice Paper, complies strictly with the Rules or Standing Orders of the House.

In the same vein, the Journal Office undertakes the compilation of the daily votes and proceedings and also the annual volumes of journals of the House.

Other Principal Officers of the State House of Assembly

The practical necessity of the House makes the engagement of these officers who are not listed in the Constitution imperative.

i. *Majority party leader*

The majority leader who is elected by the majority party members in the House is the chief strategist and floor spokesman of the ruling party. He serves as the party's legislative programme director through his management of the business and legislative schedule of the House. He plays a very prominent role in the executive or government-sponsored bills. He works to ensure the successful passage of proposals, especially for appropriation bills and motions relating to the commendation of the executive arm of government as his party's interest.

The majority leader performs a unique liaison function as the link between the legislature and executive. He exhibits impressive '*legislative bargaining*' skills and the uncommon ability to convince the minority or opposition parties to support his party or the government's proposals.

---

[4] Ibid. p. 194

The majority party leader plays the same liaison role among all the committees and the other principal functionaries of the legislature in rallying support for his party's goals. The majority leader personifies his party's manifesto and programmes in the legislature. He leaves no stone unturned in garnering the support of opposition parties for his party's policies. The tedious budget and appropriation sessions of the House task the temperament and ability of the majority leader to the extreme.

Order 25 of the Bayelsa State House of Assembly, deals with the office and duties of the Majority Leader. Hence:

25 (1) The Leader of the House shall be a member nominated from the party with the highest number of members in the House.

(2) His functions shall be:

(a) to lead the business of the House;

(b) to manage the legislative schedule of the House;

(c) to liaise with committee chairmen and other functionaries of the House;

(d) to perform such duties as the Speaker may assign to him;

ii. *Deputy Leader*

The Deputy Leader of the House shall be a member nominated from the party with the highest number of seats in the House. His functions shall be (Order 26):

(a) Assisting the Leader of the House in the performance of his functions

(b) He deputizes for the leader of the House in his absence

(c) Any other actions as may be assigned to him by the Leader of the House.

iii. *Minority Leader*

The Minority Leader is elected by his party members in the House. There will be as many minority leaders as the number of the parties in the House outside the ruling majority party. A Minority Leader preserves, defends and protects his own party's interests in a similar fashion to the role of the Majority Leader to his party. There is also the possibility for the creation of deputies for the above cited offices. These deputies merely assist the parties leaders in the execution of their duties.

iv. *Party whips (majority/minority parties)*

Party whips are elected by their respective political parties in the assembly. They bear the unique responsibility of maintaining control of their party members in the legislature and ensuring the successful execution of their party's agenda on the floor of the House. Party whips are also chamber facilitators who marshal the required political forces to support their parties' strategies and programmes. They work closely with the party leaders and the executive to bargain fruitfully for their parties interests

Hence, party whips organize their party caucuses and keep their fellow members informed about the House's business and political development. In Hilaire Barnett's assessment:

> *Much of the organization of the business of the House is in the hands of the Whips, including planning the parliamentary timetable and advising on practice and procedure. Whips of all parties are also responsible for recommending candidates for membership of Parliamentary Committees.*[5]

Erskine May illustrated further that:

> *Certain duties are common to whips of all parties. They keep their members supplied with information about the business of the House, secure the attendance of members, arrange for their members who are unable to attend divisions to pair with members of the opposite side of the House so that their votes may be neutralized and not lost and suggest members to serve on standing and select committees. They also act as intermediaries between the leaders and the rank and file of their parties in order to keep each informed of the views of the other.*[6]

---

[5] Barnett, 586.

[6] May, 202.

The Chief Whip is saddled with the responsibility to chair the Ethics and Privileges Committees and also to notify the Speaker to enforce the Orders relating to Ethics, Privileges, Orders of Debate and Decorum.

Principal functionaries of the National Assembly

The Constitution and National Assembly Service Commission Act, Rules of the Senate and the Standing Orders of the House of Representative recognize key officers of the National Assembly as follows:

i.   *President of the Senate*

The presiding officer of the Senate has his office constitutionally endorsed by Section 50(1) (a) of the Constitution. He is elected to that office by the members of the Senate. He directs and regulates the proceedings of the Upper House. He presides over any sitting of the Senate as contained in Section 53(1) (a) of the Constitution. The President of the Senate also presides over the joint sittings of the National Assembly in accordance with Section 53(2) (a) of the Constitution.

In a situation where the posts of the President and the Vice-President of Nigeria becomes vacant (Section 146 (2) of the Constitution), the President of the Senate shall hold the office of the President for a period of not more than three (3) months during which there shall be an election for a new president. The President of the Senate serves as the political head and principal liaison officer of the National Assembly.

He is also the chief emissary of the National Assembly in international engagements. The Senate President and the Speaker of the House of Representatives also become the custodians of the executive powers of the federation. By virtue of Section 145 of the Constitution, the President will transmit to them his intention in writing to proceed on vacation, with the Vice-President empowered to act on his behalf. The presidential powers will revert on similar notification in writing to the President of the Senate and the Speaker of the House of Representatives.

Rule 25 of the Senate contains the functions of the President of the Senate. There:

> (1) The president shall preside at sittings of the Senate:
>> (a) He shall sign the votes and proceedings after confirmation by the Senate;

(b) He shall be responsible for the observance of order in the Senate and Committee;

(c) He shall receive all communications addressed to the Senate;

(d) He shall have general control, except as provided by rule or law, of the chamber of Senate, and its corridors and passages;

(e) he shall sign all acts, addresses, resolutions, writs, warrants and subpoenas issued by order of the Senate;

(f) He shall be responsible for the observance of the Orders of debate. He shall give rulings on points of order or of Constitution raised during debate;

(g) He shall have a casting vote to avoid equality of votes but shall not vote in any other case;

(h) He shall interpret the rules.

The President of the Senate can be removed from office by a resolution of the Senate supported by the votes of not less than two-thirds majority of the members of the Senate (Section 50 (2) (c) of the Constitution).

ii. Deputy-President of the Senate

The office of the Deputy President, like that of the President of the Senate, is provided for in Section 50(1) (a) of the Constitution. He is equally elected by his fellow senators. He will preside in any Senate sitting where the President of the Senate is absent by virtue of Section 53(1) (a) of the Constitution.

He shall preside over the joint sitting of the National Assembly in any situation where the President of the Senate and the Speaker of the House of Representatives are absent. This is subject to the provisions of Section 53 (2)(b) of the Constitution. The same procedures and provisions in the Constitution that govern the removal and vacation of office as the President of the Senate govern the Deputy President.

Rule 26 of the Senate emphatically holds that:

In the absence of the President of the Senate, the Deputy President of the Senate shall perform all the duties and functions of the President of the Senate.

iii. *Speaker of the House of Representatives*

The Speaker of the House of Representatives is elected by fellow members of the House. The limits and responsibilities of this office are found in Section 50(1) (b) of the Constitution. He presides over any sitting of the House of Representatives. The duties and functions of this principal officer are covered by Order VII, Rule 1 of the House of Representatives.

He shall preside over the joint sitting of the National Assembly in the absence of the President of the Senate as provided by Section 53(2) (a) of the Constitution. He plays a significant role in the relationship between the House of Representatives and the other arms of government. The customary Speaker's role are all the general responsibilities of this principal office holder. The conditions for his removal and vacation from office are the same as those for the President of the Senate.

The duties and functions of the Speaker of the House of Representatives is covered by Order VII of the Standing Orders of the House of Representatives. These duties and functions, which are similar to those of the President of the Senate, were highlighted in ten different Orders, including Order VII, Rules 1 (2) and (3) to the effect that:

> 1(2) He shall preserve order and decorum and, in the case of disturbances or disorderly conduct in the galleries, or in the lobby, may cause the same to be cleared.
>
> 1(3) He shall have general control, except as provided by rule or
>
> law, of the chamber of the House, and of the corridors and passages.

iv. *Deputy Speaker of the House of Representatives*

The office of the Deputy Speaker of the House of Representatives is created alongside that of the Speaker, vide Section 50(1)(b) of the Constitution. He is also elected by the members of the House. He will preside over any sitting of the House of Representatives in the absence of the Speaker as stated in Section 53(1) (b) of the Constitution.

This principal officer will also preside over the joint sitting of the National Assembly in the absence of the President of the Senate, the Speaker of the House of Representatives and the Deputy President of the Senate (Section 53(2)(b) of the

Constitution). His removal and vacation from office follow the same procedure as that of the Speaker.

Order VII, Rule 2 (1)to (2) of the House of Representatives affirmed the duties of the Deputy Speaker as:

> 2 (1) In the absence of the Speaker, the Deputy Speaker shall perform all the duties and functions of the Speaker;
>
> 2(2) The Deputy Speaker shall be the Chairman of Committee of the whole House, save when the House goes into the Committee of supply or ways and means.

v. 'Pro-tempore' position in the National Assembly

The Constitution through Section 53 (3) empowers the members of the Senate or the House of Representatives to elect any member to preside, in the absence of all the aforementioned functionaries. Senator John Mbata played this role in the proceedings which ushered in Anyim Pius Anyim as the replacement for Chuba Okadigbo in 2001.On October 30, 2007, the House of Representatives elected Terogu Tsegba as the Speaker Pro-tempore, who presided over the affairs of that chamber until the emergence of Dimeji Bankole on November 1, 2007 as the substantive Speaker.

Order VII, Rule 3 of the House of Representatives upholds this position thus:

> In the absence of the Speaker and Deputy Speaker, such member of the House as the House may elect for the purpose shall preside. Such member shall be known as 'Speaker Pro-tempore'.

Rule 27 of the Senate, accounts for the position of 'President Pro-tempore'.

vi. Party leaders in the National Assembly

The proceedings of the National Assembly as ordained by the National Assembly Services Commission Act and Operative Rules, recognize the positions of party leaders and whips. Order VII, Rule 4(2) (a) – (d) of the House of Representatives therefore states the duties and functions of the leader of the House as follow:

> a. to lead the business of the House;
>
> b. to manage the legislative schedule of the House;
>
> c. to liaise with committee chairmen and other functionaries of the House;

d. to perform such other duties as the Speaker may assign to him.

Order VII, Rule 5 (1) - (2) of the House of Representatives deals with and covers the functions of the 'whip' of the House. In this vein, Order VII, Rule 5 (2) states that:

(2) His functions shall be:

(a) in conjunction with other officers, ensure the attendance of members, order, decorum and discipline in the House;

(b) organize members in debates and divisions and persuade them on voting one way or the other.

The positions of party leaders and whips of the Senate are treated under Rules 28-32 of the Upper Chamber.

Rules 1(2) and 1(3) detail the relief duties of the Deputy Clerk in course of the absence of the Clerk of the House. Meanwhile, the Principal-Clerk-Assistant will assume same role, when the Clerk and his deputy are absent.

Similarly, Rules 33-35 of the Senate, state the functions of the Clerk and also the replacement role of the Deputy Clerk in his absence – or in the case of vacancy.

vii. *The Clerk of the National Assembly*

The office of the Clerk of the National Assembly is provided for by Section 51 of the Constitution. This principal officer whose appointment, confirmation and removal from office are subject to sections 10 and 11 of the National Assembly Service Commission Act Cap N7 LFN 2004 performs the general functions of the Clerk of the House.

The peculiar administrative necessities of the National Assembly make it inevitable to assign a clerk and deputy separately to each chamber. Hence, the designated constitutional Clerk to the National Assembly plays an overseeing role and mans the Clerk's table mostly during joint sittings and on very important occasions. Order VII, Rule 11 of the House of Representatives deals with the duties of the Clerk of the House. Order VII, Rule 11 (2) provides that:

The Clerk shall keep minutes of the proceedings of the House and of committee of the Whole House, and shall circulate a copy of such minutes to be known as the votes and proceedings, on the day following each sitting of the House or as soon as possible thereafter.

viii. The Sergeant-at-Arms

The origin of the office of the sergeant-at-arms is traced to the regime of the Lancastrian kings in England. The regime appointed the sergeant-at-arms as royal body guards to attend the House of Commons. The members of the House of Commons seized the opportunity to use him in the protection of their privileges. Thus, with his service, they could arrest and imprison offenders without court proceedings.

In Nigeria, the tradition is maintained through the office that ensures orderly conduct within the chamber and throughout the precincts of the House. The sergeant-at-arms is usually a retired officer of the armed forces who bears the mace and controls even the police team sent to guard the legislative building. The legislature relies on the services of this office for the actualization of its powers and privileges on the issue of summons and warrants to compel attendance of persons before it (Sections 89 and 129 of the Constitution). Thus, the sergeant-at-arms executes the Speaker's warrant for contempt and can, on order, bring a person before the House. He or his assistants can serve processes of the legislature. He can also keep a person in custody until further arrangements are made for his transfer.

The sergeant-at-arms or his assistant stays in the chamber throughout the sitting of the House. He records attendance on the instruction of the presiding officer and ensures orderliness on the floor of the House and the gallery. He sees to the departure or ejection of a member suspended from the House.

Chapter 19

House Committees

The main function of standing committees has been to consider and amend public bills, thus doing what the House could do if it had time. Select committees do the kind of things that the House as a whole could not easily do.

O . H ood Philips & Paul Jackson

A committee is a subdivision of the legislature which is mandated on its own behalf to make rules, review draft legislation, investigate issues or any other assignment. It is usually based on matters that are constitutionally the responsibility of that House of assembly. The calendar of the legislature is made in such a way that committees are imperative for it to fulfill its constitutionally allotted duties to the electorate. The tedious and technical details of lawmaking processes and procedures, including the volume of human and material resource demands, make the division into specialized units or committees inevitable.

It is pertinent to note that no committee can take a definite decision on a matter which constitutionally is the prerogative of the House. Therefore, a committee is constitutionally bound to report its findings to or make recommendations for the House, upon which rests the onus for the final decision. This reportorial duty of the committee is emphatically spelt out in Section 103(3) of the Constitution, which reads that:

> Nothing in this section shall be construed as authorizing a House
> of assembly to delegate to a committee the power to decide
> whether a bill shall be passed into law or to determine any matter
> which it is empowered to determine by resolution under the
> provision of this Constitution, but such a committee of the House

may be authorized to make recommendations to the House on any such matter.[1]

The Supreme Court based its decision in *AG Bendel State v. AG Federation* (supra) on the premise:

> *That until the two houses of the National Assembly, sitting either separately or jointly as the case may be, pass the money-bill, or the version of the joint committee on finance set up thereon, into law, it is not a bill passed by the National Assembly and cannot, therefore, be assented to by the president of the Federal Republic of Nigeria*[2]

In a strongly worded disapproval of the action of the Joint Finance Committee in passing a bill without due recourse to the National Assembly, Fatayi Williams (CJN) said:

> *I cannot conceive of a situation in any country with parliamentary democracy where legislative powers generally, and those relating to money bills in particular, could be handed over by the elected representatives of the people to a committee of twenty four of such elected members, no matter how eminent they may be.*[3]

This issue re-echoed in 2001 through the controversial Electoral Act, which was not referred back to the National Assembly after committee's deliberation.

Principal House Committees

The Constitution conferred on the legislature the discretion to form committees and determine the number of their membership (Section 62 – for the National Assembly, and Section 103 – for state houses of assembly). Therefore, section 62 (1) and (2) of the Constitution emphatically holds that:

> (1) The Senate or the House of Representatives may appoint a committee of its members for such special or general purpose as in its opinion would be better regulated and managed by means of such a committee, and may by resolution, regulation or otherwise, as it thinks fit, delegate any functions exercisable by it to any such committee.

---

[1] See also Section 62 (4) for the National Assembly.

[2] [1981] ANLR p.103 para.9.

[3] [1981] 10 SC p. 33.

(2) The number of members of a committee appointed under this section, their terms of office and quorum shall be fixed by the House appointing it.

The state houses of assembly derive their powers on this subject matter vide Section 103 (1) - (2) of the Constitution:

(1) A House of Assembly may appoint a committee of its members for any special or general purpose as in its opinion would be better regulated and managed by means of such a committee, and by resolution, regulation or otherwise as it thinks fit delegate any functions exercisable by it to any such committee.

(2) The number of members of a committee appointed under this section, their term of office and quorum shall be fixed by the House of Assembly.

The Constitution, however, mandatorily prescribes only two committees for the National Assembly – the Joint Finance Committee and the Public Accounts Committees (Sections 59(2) and 85(5)). The Public Accounts Committee of state houses of assembly is provided for in Section 125(5).

The financial capacity of and the available human resources to a legislature determine the number of committees it can establish and operate within its jurisdiction. The size of a legislative House is also a notable determinant in its committee arrangement. Section 91 of the Constitution states that no state House of assembly will be composed of less than twenty four members, but not more than forty members.

The situation in the National Assembly, where the Senate of 109 members has fifty standing committees, however, is disquieting. In stark contrast, the House of Commons, with 651 members, has only sixteen select committees, while the US Congress has fifteen committees. The following committees have been regular features of most democratic legislatures, as contained in their standing orders and rules:

    i.   special committees

    ii.   standing committees

    iii.   select/ad hoc committees

    iv.   committee of the whole House

    v.   joint committees

Special Committees

These are mostly broad-based, and usually continue for the life of the assembly or parliament which created them. In this category are:

     a. committee of selection

     b. rules and business committee

     c. House services committee

     d. public petitions committee

     e. public accounts committee

In general the state houses of assembly, take as their first order of business, (after the election of the Speaker and other statutory members) to appoint the membership of the following special committees. This must be done within 10 days after the first sitting:

     (a) Committee of Selection

     (b) Rules and Business Committee

     (c) House Services Committee

     (d) Public Petitions Committee

     (e) Public Accounts Committee

Rule 96 of the Senate is to the effect that within the first fourteen (14) legislative days following the first sitting of the Senate, the membership of the following special committees shall be appointed:

     i.   Committee of Selection

     ii.   Committee on Rules and Business

     iii. Senate Services Committee

     iv. Committee on Ethics, (code of conduct and public petitions)

     v.   Public Accounts Committee

     vi. Committee on National Security and Intelligence

i.   Committee of Selection

This foremost committee of the House of Representatives is usually constituted by the presiding officer and other elected principal officers. The function of this committee as ordained by Order 78 (4) (a) - (c) includes:

     (a) Nominating members to serve on any ad hoc or special committee;

     (b) to consider any special matter brought before the House; and

(c) Such members as may be going on parliamentary delegation other than committees.

The Committee of Selection in compliance with Order 78 (2) shall consist of the Speaker, as chairman, the deputy speaker, who may take the chair in the absence of the Speaker, all House officers and two (2) nominees of the political parties in accordance with their numerical strength in the House.

The vantage position of the Speaker and the president of the Senate in the selection and removal of members from committees should be reviewed. It has been transformed into a personal instrument of the presiding officers, to compensate their supporters and victimize their opponents in the House. Nigeria's democratic experience since 1999 has seen a manifestation of abuse in this process, through incessant replacement of committee chairmen and members based on personal patronage, especially in the Senate.

ii. *Rules and Business Committee*

The business committee is put in place at the commencement of every full calendar session of the legislature. The members of this committee are nominated by the committee of selection. This strategic committee schedules the House programmes and calendar. It regulates the House business through the determination of dates and timetables for debates on bills, motions and other related business agenda of the House.

Order 78 advises the Rules and Business Committee with its functions. Thus:

> 3(1) There shall be a committee to be known as Rules and Business Committee appointed at the commencement of the life of the House consisting of the parties represented in the House in accordance with their numerical strength.
>
> 3(2) The Committee's functions or jurisdiction shall cover:
> - (a) scheduling the business of the House and causing them to be printed on the order paper.
> - (b) allocation of time for the business of the House.
> - (c) House organization relative to rules and procedure of the House.

Rule 97 (2) (a) - (i) of the Senate highlights the Rules and Business committee. It further saddled the committee from (g) - (i) with:

> (g) Interaction with state houses of Assembly relative to Rules and Business of the Senate.

(h) workshops and seminars in respect of parliamentary practice and procedure for senators

(i) Gazetting of Bills

iii. *Public Petitions Committee*

The public petitions committee is nominated by the committee of selection. It receives, considers and reviews all petitions referred to it and reports its findings and recommendations to the House.

This Committee is covered by Order 78 (4) (1) - (2) which state that:

> There shall be a committee to be known as the Public Petitions Committee consisting of five (5) members appointed at the commencement of the life of the House.
>
> (2) The Committee's jurisdiction shall:
>
> (a) consider the subject matter of all petitions referred to it under the provisions of Order 36 (Petitions) and shall report from time to time to the House its opinions of the action to be taken thereon together with such other observations on the petitions and signatures attached thereto as the committee may think fit.

This committee is covered by Order XVII Rule 5(1)-(2) of the House of Representatives which states that:

> (1) There shall be a committee to be known as the Public Petitions Committees consisting of not more than 15 members appointed at the commencement of the life of the House.
>
> (2) The committee's jurisdiction shall:
>
> (a) consider the subject matter of all petitions referred to it and shall report from time to time to the House its recommendations on actions to be taken thereon, together with such other obser-vations on the petitions.

The Senate operates through a combination of ethics, privileges and public petitions committees (vide Rule 97 (4) (a) - (d)).

iv. *Public Accounts Committee*

The public accounts committee performs the onerous legislative duty of examining and scrutinizing the annual accounts of the states and the federation. This oversight responsibility is based on the report of the auditor-general to the House (Section 85(5) for the National Assembly, Section 125(5) for state houses of assembly). The auditor-general is constitutionally required to make the report within 90 days of his receipt of the accountant-general's financial statement and annual accounts of the state. This committee has the power to send for persons, papers and records, with regard to the appropriation of the sums granted by the House to meet public expenditure. It reports its findings from time to time to the House and sits during any adjournment of the House.

The public accounts committee has the power to examine any account or report of statutory corporations and boards after they might have been laid on the table of the House. It is obligatory for the committee to report its progress regularly to the House. The primary function of this committee is to ensure that public funds are spent prudently, for the purposes intended and appropriated by the legislature. As aptly observed by Hilaire Barnett:

> *By critically examining the expenditure of departments and assessing the extent to which expenditure produces value for money, the public accounts committee exerts considerable influence on the government.*[4]

The 'Public Accounts Committee' in most of the state houses of assembly comprises five (5) members appointed at the commencement of the life of the House. It is the duty of the committee to examine the accounts showing the appropriation of the sums granted by the House to meet 'Public Expenditure', together with the Auditor's report thereon. The committee shall for the purpose of discharging that duty have power to send for persons, papers and records to report to the House from time to time and to sit notwithstanding the adjournment of the House.

In furtherance of the unique jurisdiction of Public Accounts Committee, the auditor-general shall bring to the attention of the committee any pre-payment audit queries raised by the internal auditors of a ministry, department or agency but overruled by the chief executive.

More importantly as the legislative financial watchdog of state, this committee is empowered to examine any accounts or reports of statutory corporations and boards after they have been laid on the Table of the House and to report thereon from time to time to the House and to sit notwithstanding any adjournment of the House.

The unique role of this committee demands the representation of all the political parties in its membership. It is also important that experienced accountants and seasoned technocrats serving as legislators are placed in the

---

[4] Barnett, 631.

committee. The chairmanship of this committee in some advanced democracies is conceded to the opposition party or any other minority party. This measure will aid the attainment of the deserved probity and fairness intended by the Constitution.

v. House Services Committee

Membership of the House Services Committee is also nominated by the Committee of Selection. This committee has the duty of informing the Speaker on issues concerning the comfort and convenience of the members of the House. It is simply the welfare committee of the House.

Order 78 (3) (1) detailed the composition and duty of this committee thus:

> There shall be a committee to be known as House Services Committee consisting of five (5) members appointed at the commencement of the life of the House to look after the welfare of members.

vi. Standing or Select Committees

The fundamental legislative duty of conducting investigations and supervising the activities of the executive arm of government (including ministries and agencies) requires the service of standing or select committees. The oversight role conferred on the legislature by Section 88 of the Constitution (for the National Assembly) and Section 128 (for state houses of assembly) can only be actualized through standing or select committees. These committees are usually named after the ministries or agencies whose activities they supervise and scrutinize. In this regard, the works committee, health committee, foreign affairs committee, agriculture committee and sundry, become synonymous with legislative activities bordering on each committee's jurisdiction.

vii. Ad hoc Committees

The legislature can set up a special committee for the purpose of checking on an unexpected circumstance or sudden occurrence within its jurisdiction. Such a committee is called an *ad hoc committee*. The legislature accords a specific purpose to an ad hoc committee as the basis of its terms of reference. The purpose of the committee will be geared towards the realization of the intended objective of the House. This will be traditionally set out at the committee's inauguration. The tenure of an ad hoc committee terminates on the submission of its report to the House on whose mandate it operated.

viii *Committee of the Whole House*

Based on certain circumstances, a legislative House could resolve its entire membership into a committee. The required constitutional quorum of the House equally satisfies the condition for constituting this committee. A unique trait of this committee is that the presiding officer of the House (Speaker, or president of the Senate) leaves his seat and assumes the chair of the Clerk. The mace is then lowered below the dais and placed into hooks or brackets. The Speaker is then referred to as chairman throughout the proceedings of the committee.

As aptly noted by Erskine May:

> *It is in fact, the House itself in a less formal guise, presided over by a Chairman instead of the Lord Speaker and conducting its business according to more flexible rules of procedure.* [5]

In furtherance of the unique flexibility of this committee, some of the Standing Rules/ Orders, concede its chairmanship to the deputy presiding officer. There shall be a resolution praying that the House should immediately or on a future day resolve itself into a Committee of the Whole House.

The chairman who then becomes responsible for the conduct of the proceedings, and directs the debate. Although the rules of the House in terms of debate govern the committees deliberation, but with notable slight differences. Hence, a member can be allowed to speak more than once on the same subject matter.

The tradition, is that a motion will be moved by a member that the chairman do report progress and seek the leave to sit again. If that motion receives the desired support, the chairman will leave the chair and on resumption of the House, report the progress of the committee to the Speaker and also pray for leave for the committee to sit again.

Joint Committee of the National Assembly

The Constitution gave approval for the inauguration of the Joint Finance Committee of the National Assembly vide Section 59 (2). The exigencies of national issues, can also lead to the setting up of joint committees comprising of equal number of members of each chamber of the National Assembly.

This initiative is appreciated as a time- saving strategy which will speedily harmonize the eventual outcome of the deliberation rather than the duplicity of time, effort and resources which separate sessions provoke. It then becomes a

---

[5]Erskine May, 572

solution to the traditional harmonization conference that emerges when there is conflict in the resultant stance of both chambers over a particular proposal.

When a chamber considers it expedient that a particular bill, proposal or issue should be subjected to joint committee deliberation, it will declare that intention by the passage of a resolution. That resolution and a message will be conveyed to the other chamber which in turn will manifest its agreement through a supportive resolution.

The trend is that the second chamber will also send its approval resolution and message to the originating chamber. The originating chamber will then appoint a committee of a certain number of her members and communicate same to the second chamber. The list of the committee members will be accompanied by a message requesting the second chamber to appoint her own equal number of committee members. When the second chamber complies with that request and informs the originating chamber with the list of members attached, the originating House will then send a conclusive proposal of time and place of the joint meeting.

Joint committees usually operate with the same powers and procedures of the standing and select committees.

Sub-committees

A subcommittee operates on the delegated authority of the House, to which it remains accountable. Therefore, it requires a leave of the House as its appointing authority in order to divide itself into sub-committees to achieve its desired target.

Hence, such a division and apportion of delegated authority, facilitate the process and efficiency of the committee.

The consent power of the House authorizing the creation of the subcommittee, also prescribes the quorum and deliberative procedure of the subcommittee.

The Bayelsa State House of Assembly Order 84 (1) (ii) provides that:

> Each subcommittee is a part of that committee and is subject to the authority and direction of that committee and to its rules as far as applicable.

Proceedings in Committees

The operating rules of the House govern the committees although some of the Standing Orders /Rules, prescribe that each committee can adopt its mode of operation. Hence, the quorum, voting and report standard can be tailored to suit its urgent purpose.

It is in this light that Order 84 (1) (a) (i) provides that:

The Rules of the House are the rules of its committees and sub-committees so far as applicable except in connection with a motion of high privilege in committees and sub-committees.

A committee of the House is empowered to undertake official inquiries, investigations and studies into issues, departments or agencies as well as subject matters that fall within its jurisdiction.

The procedure is that the chairman of the committee at an investigative hearing shall publicly declare the subject and purpose of their assignment at the opening session.

In furtherance of the underlying fair hearing objectives, witnesses before committees are allowed to engage the services of learned counsel to guide them in course of their testimony.

Meanwhile, the counsels are subject to the privileges and rights of the House. If these privileges are breached it can also lead to contempt of the legislature and attendant reprimand.

The chairman at an investigative hearing shall announce in the opening statement the subject of the investigation. Any witnesses at an investigative hearing may be accompanied by their own counsel for the purpose of guiding them concerning their constitutional rights. The chairman may punish breaches of order and decorum and of professional ethics on the part of counsel, by censure and exclusion from the hearing; and the committee may cite the offender to the House for contempt.

Traditionally, the testimony of witnesses should be rendered in open session, but the committee reserves the right to convene an executive session based the sensitivity of the subject matter. The committee can also request written statements from the witnesses.The committees are mandated to have printed and bound testimony and other data presented at its hearing.

The eventual report of the committee's assignment shall be presented to the House. The committee's report will be endorsed by the whole members or majority of the members. There is also room for dissenting members to file their own report and state the reasons for their dissenting view.

It is pertinent to note that the House must have been formally in session before resolving into a Committee of the Whole House. And the House cannot be adjourned from the committee, it must resolve formally into a traditional session, with the mace rising to its place on the table and the Speaker returns to his chair. It is only then, that a motion for adjournment can be validly moved. The decision of the House, based on the sensitivity of the subject under discussion in the course of the committee holding, can only be resolved through members voting in the formal sitting.

Ad-hoc sub-committees

The consenting power of the House authorizing the creation of the ad-hoc sub-committee, also prescribes the quorum and terms of reference of the sub-committee.

A standing or ad-hoc sub-committee may be created by the Speaker in conjunction with the selection committee and each sub-committee of a committee is a part of that committee and is subject to the authority and direction of that committee and its rules as far as applicable.

Chapter 20

Treatment of Motions in the Legislature

A motion is a proposal initiated by a legislature or a group of legislators urging that the Assembly take certain actions or that it expresses itself as holding certain views.

H enry N . Robert

A motion is an expression of the legislature over an issue it considers of utmost importance. It is a 'legislative prayer' to the legislature or the executive arm of government. It is a member's or some members' proposal to the House to act on a matter of interest to the mover(s). A motion can be a proposal, made to one or other House by a member, that the House do something, order something to be done or express an opinion with regard to some matter.

According to Erskine May: *A motion is a proposal made for the purpose of eliciting a decision of the House.* [6]

A diligent legislator can herald his constituency's need for water or molestation by armed bandits through a motion. This will now be a medium to call on the police or the executive arm of government to take urgent steps to arrest the worrisome situation.

Types of Motion

The daily operation of the legislature dictates the employment of many forms of motions. These mechanisms include:

---

[6] Erskine May, op cit., 321-322.

i. *Substantive or main motion*

This is a self-contained motion stressing the subject which the member (mover) intends to bring to public knowledge. A main motion requires notice to the legislature, although, this can be waived.

ii.   *Subsidiary motion*

This kind of motion treats and refers to an existing substantive motion, reminding the House to immediately consider the substantive one. It may also serve as a motion for modification, disposal or to delay action on the substantive motion. A motion for adjournment that deals with particular reference to treat, as a matter of utmost importance, a motion already before the House, is an example of a subsidiary motion.

Erskine Mays' remark is that:

> *Subsidiary motion may be (1) ancillary motions dependent on an order of the day, such as the motion that a bill be now read a second time, or that the House agrees with the report of committee, (2) motions made for the purpose of superseding questions, such as motions for the adjournment of a debate; (3) motions dependent on other motions such as amendments."*[7]

iii. *Privileged motion*

A privileged motion takes precedence over all other motions and other business subjects before the House. Even when it has no relation to the pending business or issue before the House, it is still accorded preference. The traditional motion on issues of 'urgent public importance or interest' qualifies as a privileged motion.

The state houses of assembly holds delicately and guides jealousy, its privileges. Thus, any breach of that hallowed status, is treated with considerable attention.

A matter of privilege at any time arising shall, until disposed of or unless the debate on a motion thereon is adjourned, suspend the consideration and decision of every question. Provided that precedence of every other business shall not be given to any motion, in the opinion of the Speaker a prima facie case of

---

[7] Erskine May, p. 321

breach of privilege has not been made and or the matter has been raised at the earliest opportunity.

Any matter of urgent public importance shall be communicated to the Speaker before the commencement of the day's sitting. The Speaker's discretion shall prevail to refuse or allow the prayer (claim) if the matter is definite and urgent.

If the claim is allowed by the Speaker and the leave of the House is given by at least one-fifth of all the members of the House, the matter shall be debated on that legislative day. No more than one of such motion may be made at the same sitting.

This subject matter is also contained in Order VIII, Rule 4 of the House of Representatives.

An important development or a mishap of prominent dimension can easily be accorded preference over all other businesses of the House. The customary motion *on* adjournment and motion *for* adjournment satisfy this classification.

iv. *Incidental motion*

This kind of motion arises out of other motions that are pending before the House. It is a subsidiary motion, mostly used to challenge and object to the consideration of the House on a pending motion.

Legal status of a motion

A motion passed by a legislature has no force of law. A motion is at best 'a legislative prayer' to the legislature, the executive or any agency, to act as a solution to a public problem. It is not a potential law. A motion merely reflects the moral authority of the legislature as the supreme lawmaking organ of the nation, state or local government. Thus, it is not a substitute for a bill, as a constitutional instrument of legislation. As was strongly held by Asobie:

> *Therefore, no legislature should, by the use of motions, give away its primary role in the act of governing – that of initiating legislation.*[8]

---

[8] H. Assisi Asobie. 'Legislative proposals, motions, questions and debates'. Paper presented at the Legislative Workshop for Honourable Members of Anambra State House of Assembly, Enugu (1981) p.11.

It is, therefore, imperative that the legislature concentrates on its lawmaking role and guides its independence jealously. This can only be achieved by thorough initiation and passage of bills rather than undue reliance on endless treatment of motions. In short, ceaseless debates on motions portray laziness and ignorance of legislators. Legislators should strive to avoid unnecessary distractions from their primary duty. The executive arm has professed more zeal in the initiation of bills in most democracies in the world, at the expense of the legislature. Professor B.O. Nwabueze's stance is remarkable:

> *Indeed, a motion involving no exercise of constitutional power need have no factual basis at all apart from the strong feeling that something needs to be done about a given issue.*[9]

Application of a motion

The fact that a motion is an instrument of the legislature that expresses its views and moral judgement cannot be overlooked. However, a motion must be specific and be supported with the right procedures in order for it to attract deserved attention. The important position of the legislature in government demands that its motions be timely, definite and specific. They must be targeted, usually, to pressurize the executive or other agencies to initiate policies for the betterment of the society.

Democratic tenets and legislative advocacy demand that motions be presented in concise language and its purpose explicitly stated. Thus, the worrisome state of insecurity, endless hike of the price of petroleum products, incessant strike actions, especially by academic and non-academic staff of universities, road traffic accident rates, as well as the disquieting state of public infrastructures are salient issues for motions from all tiers of houses of assembly. These motions can be consolidated with the inauguration of ad hoc liaison committees with the executive and law enforcement agencies.

Issues of urgent national importance, however, require well-fashioned motions from the National Assembly and resolutions from the states. The support of motions with flawless resolutions will check against the high incidence of 'hanging motions'. The latter weakened considerably the entire legislative process in Nigerian since 1999.

---

[9] B.O. Nwabueze. *Presidential Constitution of Nigeria* (C Hurst & Co,. London & Nwamife Publishers, 1982), p. 233.

Motions and resolutions

The constitution requires a resolution of the House for the determination of certain issues. A resolution is a formal declaration of a legislature, decided by vote, expressing opinion of the House on a matter it considers of great essence. A resolution must be anchored on a substantive motion, duly moved and seconded before the House vote or decision.

A resolution is required for the removal of the presiding officer of a state House of assembly, House of Representatives and the Senate (Section 50(2)(c) for the National Assembly; Section 92(2)(c) for state houses of assembly). The legislature can also employ a resolution to express its opinion on some social issues, such as congratulatory messages to members of a successful national or state contingent. The resolution can also convey a House's deep sympathy to victims of disasters.

A model resolution should take this format:

> *Whereas we consider that security of lives and properties are basic functions of government: and whereas, there is a frightening rate of armed robbery and attendant loss of lives and properties throughout our country or state, therefore:*

Resolved: that it is the view of this House that adequate security be provided immediately in all local government areas throughout this state: and resolve that:

> *. . . A committee of seven members be appointed by the House to present these resolutions to the governor of this state, the commissioner of police of this state and members of the security council of this state and other relevant authority urging upon their prompt action in the matter.*

Notice of motion

The customary practice is that notice must be given of any motion or amendment that will be treated before the House. But the rules guiding the proceedings of the legislature can provide otherwise in certain cases, and the House can also waive such requirements for formal notice.

In general, a notice shall be given of any motion or amendment which is proposed to be moved with the exception of the following:

(a) a motion or amendment made or offered in Committee of the Whole House;

(b) a motion for the adjournment of the House or of any debate;

(c) motion that the report of a select committee be referred to the Committee of the Whole House;

(d) a motion for the withdrawal of strangers;

(e) a motion for the suspension of a member;

(f) a motion arising out of the business of the day made immediately after that business is disposed of and before any fresh matter is entered upon; and

(g) an amendment to a motion which has been moved without notice either under this rule (see also Order VIII, Rule 8 of the House of Representatives).

Rule 47 of the Senate demands that notice of motion must be written and signed before it submission to the president of the Senate. The same rule specifies that submission must be on a day on which the Senate is sitting, but allows same between the hours of 9 a.m. and 3 p.m. on the day when the Senate is not sitting. It prohibits submission of notice on Saturdays, Sunday and public holidays.

All notices of motion must be submitted to the Speaker (a) On the day in which the House is sitting or (b) On the day when the House is not sitting between the hours of 9.00 am and 3.00 pm, except on Saturdays, Sundays and public holidays

The onus lies on the Speaker to peruse the content of the motion and subject to his discretion, approve or reject the motion. If the Speaker is satisfied that the there are cogent grounds for support of the motion, he will then cause the notice of the motion to be numbered and published in the 'Schedule of Notices of Motions'. It will be then assigned to the Rules and Business Committee not later than seven days for scheduling. .

The procedure of the House of Representatives on the notice of motions, differ slightly from that of the Senate. Thus, Order VIII, Rule 9, empowered the Speaker on the receipt of the notice, to cause it to be numbered and published in schedule of 'Notices of Motions'. The Speaker will then assign the notice of motion to the relevant committee of the House not later than seven (7) days after the publication in the schedule.

The relevant committee is saddled with the review of the substance of the motion, and on approval, shall forward its recommendations to the Rules and Business Committee of the House. It is the Rules and Business Committee that will schedule the motion for debate in the House.

In state houses of assembly, all notices of motions must be submitted to the majority leader or in his absence, the deputy majority leader. The responsibility for the notices of motions to be numbered and published in the schedule of notices of motions, is that of the chairman, committee on Business Rules and Standing Orders.

Notices and relevance of amendment

The enabling flexibility of legislative procedure, accommodates amendment of motions under specified guidelines. Erskine May captured the necessity of this parliamentary devise in these glowing words:

> *The object of an amendment may be[10] either to modify a question in such a way as to increase its acceptability or to present to the House a different proposition as an alternative to the original question?*

The position in most states houses of assembly requires that a notice of an amendment be given to the Speaker not later than five days after the publication of the schedules. The Speaker is also saddled with the responsibilities to cause the intended amendment to be forwarded to the relevant committee along with the motion.

Likewise in the Senate, the notice of amendment to a motion must be given to the president of the Senate not later than five (5) days after the publication of the schedule (see Rule 47 (6)). Similarly, in the House of Representatives, all the notices for the amendment of motions must be given to the Speaker not later than five (5) days after the publication of the schedules (See Order VIII Rule 9 (5)).

The procedure demands a strict standard of relevance for the application for amendment of a motion to succeed. Any amendments proposed to any motion or Bill under consideration in the House or a committee, shall only be in order if they are relevant to the question or matter then under discussion.

---

[10] ibid, 326.

The National Assembly proceedings is guided by the same test of relevancy as posited by Order VIII Rule 10 (1)-(2) of the House of Representatives, and Rule 48 (1)-(2) of the Senate.

Moving a motion

The legislative practice standbard is that a motion of which notice has been given may be moved only by the member who proposed it, or by one of the members in whose names it stands.

The proposer or the member called to move a motion may highlight and speak in favour of his motion. This is to enable him to convince the House of the usefulness and importance of his proposal. He will conclude by proposing his motion formally and urging his fellow legislators to lend their weight of support to his thoughtful proposal or motion.

Therefore, Order 42 categorically holds that:

> The mover of any motion shall move his motion on any day it is so scheduled unless a cogent and compelling reason is given otherwise it shall be struck out by the Speaker without debate.

Seconding of motion

It is the parliamentary practice, for the presiding officer to call on another member to second a motion after it had been moved by the proposer. The seconder has the opportunity for that affirmative pronouncement before proposing the question.

But the prime sponsor (proposer) or co-sponsor of a motion cannot be allowed to second the motion.

In the state houses of assembly the question on any motion or amendment shall not be proposed from the chair unless it shall have been seconded, but in committee, a secondment shall not be required.

The same subject matter is covered by Order VIII, Rule 2 of the House of Representatives and Rule 49 of the Senate.

Proposing the question from the chair

The parliamentary tradition is for the presiding officer of the House to read out the question. He will preface it with the words:

> 'The question is that . . .'

It is this question format that is known in parliamentary parlance as 'proposing the question from the chair'.

It is after the question has been proposed and read to the House, that the House assumes the possession of the motion and the debate begins.

Order 47 graphically illustrates the proposing of question method. Hence:

That those words be there inserted or added (Order 47 (1)).

'That those words be left out'. (Order 47 (2)).

It is after this proposal from the chair that the other members can freely contribute to the motion affirmatively or otherwise. The legislative procedure offers the proposer of the motion the first chance of debate. This is to enable him to convince the House of the usefulness and importance of his proposal. At the conclusion of the debate on a motion, the presiding officer will read the motion once again to the House and propose the question from the chair.

The Speaker will then direct that members who support the motion 'say aye'. He is expected to pause long enough to enable the supporters of the motion to loudly say 'aye'. The presiding officer will then direct members who do not support it 'say no'. This loud calling and answering process is known in parliamentary language as 'collecting the voice'.

The presiding officer will then, based on the loudness of the 'ayes' or '*noes*', decide on what the majority is (that is, he judges the louder voices as the majority). This is known as '*voice vote*' in legislative proceedings. But if some members disagree with the presiding officer's decision on the '*voice vote*', he will resort to 'roll call'.

A motion can only be withdrawn with the permission of the House. In this vein, the potential mover of the motion will adduce reasons to the House and consequently seek permission for the withdrawal of his intended motion.

Withdrawal of a motion

A motion or an amendment may be withdrawn at the request of the mover by leave of the House or committee before the commencement of debate. A motion or an amendment so withdrawn may be represented but in the case of a motion, notice is required.

If an amendment has been proposed to a question, the original motion cannot be withdrawn until the amendment has been disposed of. See Order VIII, Rule 13 (1) - (2) of the House of Representatives and Rule 51 (1) - (2) of the Senate.

Waiver of the requirement for notice

The flexible attitude of the legislature, can reflect in its powers to attend to urgent issues by dispensing with the required notice for substantive motion.

Thus, with the sanction of the presiding officer and supportive concurrence of the House, the requirement of notice can be waived for a substantive motion.

Motion *for* adjournment

This daily motion suspends the day's sitting of the House. It signifies an intention to terminate the proceedings of the House on a particular day and also announces the next sitting date and time.

Motion *on* adjournment

This is a proposal by a member after the motion for adjournment has been moved and seconded. It is the customary adjournment debate. It may not be resolved before the adjournment of the House, but can reemerge as a substantive motion. The tradition is that most members use the opportunity of a motion on adjournment to highlight grave social problems or sensitive matters that might be affecting their constituencies directly or the country generally.

It is settled that once the House adjourns with a definite date and time of next sitting, it cannot be officially reconvened for business, unless by agreement of the members. The members can equally be put on notice, to attend a sitting, even while on recess, if there is an urgent national issue.

Therefore, the removal of Evan Enwerem as president of the Senate in 2000 comes to question. He was removed from office on the same day he had formally adjourned the Senate, due to the lack of a quorum. To make this removal valid, the Senate should have been formally convened on the adjourned date and time, because it was *functus officio* until the agreed adjourned date and time. However, to actualize the provision of the Constitution (Section 50(2)(c)) on the matter of the removal of the presiding officer of the Senate, members deserve ample notice on the order paper for the day's business.The decision of the Federal High Court in the case of *Enwerem v. Okadigbo*[11] was to the effect that it was an internal affair of the Senate to which the court had no jurisdiction. Moreso, the case was statute barred in line with the Public Officers Protection Act Cap 379, Laws of the Federation of Nigeria 1990.

In the emphatic words of Olatoregun J[12]

In this case, cause of action arose when on the I[st] of November, 1999 on the floor of the House that is the Senate, Senator Evan Enwerem was removed by a 2/3rds majority of the Senate. He filed this action on the 27[h] of June, 2000 more than six clear months.

Thus, while relying on the case of *Fred Egbe v. Adefarasin*,[13] he restated the court's verdict that:

Where a statute provides for the institution of an action within a prescribed period ... any action that is instituted after the period stipulated by the statute is totally barred as the right of the plaintiff or the injured person to commence the action would have been extinguished by such law.

---

[11] [2001] 1 FHCLR. 102.

[12] ibid. p. 114.

[13] [1985] 1 NWLR Pt 3, p. 549.

Chapter 21

Passage of Bills and Appropriation Bills in a State House of Assembly

Your representative owes you, not his industry only, but his judgement; and he betrays instead of serving you if he sacrifices it to your opinion.

Edm und Burke (1729-1797)

Section I. The Passage of Bills

T he State House of Assembly derives its power to make laws from the Constitution. Thus, the prescribed mode of exercising state legislative power, as stated by section 100 (1) of the Constitution is:

> The power of a House of Assembly to make laws shall be exercised by Bills passed by the House of Assembly and, except as otherwise provided by this section, assented to by the Governor.

The prominent position of the legislature in actualisation of the democratic expectation of each state was re-echoed in section 100 (2) of the Constitution:

> A Bill shall not become law unless it has been duly passed and subject to subsection (1) of this section, assented to in accordance with the provisions of this section.

Each state house of assembly has the power to regulate its affairs vide section 101 of the Constitution. As such, all executive Bills emanating from the governor shall be forwarded to the Speaker under a cover letter personally signed by the governor of the state.

In the same vein, all Bills emanating from the judiciary shall be forwarded to the Speaker under a covering letter personally signed by the chief judge of the

225

state. Bills from members of the state house of assembly shall also be forwarded to the Speaker.

Official Notice of Bills

The notice for an executive or government Bill shall be given via the publication of the provisions proposed to be embodied in such Bill in an issue of the official Gazette or Order Paper or House Journal. Mr. Speaker can direct otherwise as regards the above publication whereby a copy of the Bill has been sent to every member.

The proposer of a member Bill shall give notice of the provisions proposed to be embodied in the Bill to the Clerk of the House. The Clerk will then cause the proposal to be published in three successive issues of the Official Gazette or Order Paper or House Journal. The Speaker can also direct otherwise and a copy of the first of such issues be sent to every member and above publication waived.

The procedure demands a compendium of background information and financial implication of the Bill be delivered to all members. In the case of amending a Bill, the procedure requires that an up-to-date consolidation of the law or laws to be amended shall be delivered to all members unless the Bill intends to amend a law amended previously in the session. A compendium of the financial cost and implications as well as the consolidation of amended laws is contained in the standing orders or rules for each state house of assembly.

The parliamentary tradition is that every Bill must pass through three stages: the first, second and third readings, before it can become law. An example of this legislative precedence is affirmed by Bayelsa Standing Order 71 (10)[1] that:

> Every Bill shall receive three readings previous to its passage,
> which readings shall be in three different days, unless the House
> unanimously directs otherwise and the Speaker shall give notice
> at each reading whether it is first, second or third.

i.   First reading

A Bill slated for introduction to the House, will be on the Order paper of that

---

[1] All of the following references are taken from the Bayelsa State Standing Orders (2007).

particular day. This stage is merely the formal declaration of the short title of the Bill. If the Bill is an executive or government Bill, the majority leader of the House will move a motion for the presentation of the Bill for first reading. The Clerk of the House then reads aloud the short title of the Bill. Order 71 (9) bares this issue that:

> Upon the short title of the Bill being read aloud by the Clerk, the Bill shall be deemed to have been read the first time.

The Speaker will in turn repeat the short title of the Bill and declare the Bill as having been read the first time. A copy of the Bill will be symbolically laid on the table of the House by the sponsor (the member introducing the Bill or by the Clerk of the House).

It is then the responsibility of the Rules and Business Committee to schedule the deliberation of the next stage of the Bill. As captured by Order 71(10) (b)

> At the conclusion of the proceedings on the first reading or on any subsequent stage of a Bill, a day to be named by the committee on Rules and Business shall be appointed for the next stage.

ii. *Second reading*

The second reading gives the members the ample opportunity to deliberate on the general principles of a Bill (its merits and demerits). In this wise, the legislators can then decide to approve or reject the Bill.

As aptly held by Order 71(11) (a):

> On the order for the second reading of a Bill being read a motion may be made 'That the Bill be now read a second time' and a debate may arise covering the general merits and principles of the Bill.

The motion for the second reading of the Bill will be moved by the sponsor of the Bill which is the majority leader for every government Bill; or a member of the House for a privately sponsored Bill.

But a member can object to the passage of the Bill by strategically introducing an amendment to the Bill.

There is also room for genuine amendment to a Bill after the second reading. At the conclusion of the debate for the second reading of the Bill and introduction of amendment(s) if need be, the Speaker shall put:

That this Bill be now read a second time.

If the question is agreed to by a required majority of the members, the Clerk shall then read aloud the long title of the Bill. The Speaker will in turn repeat the long title of the Bill and declare that the Bill has been read a second time

Committee Stage

The standard legislative practice, is that a Bill after the second reading shall stand committed to a standing committee for thorough scrutiny. But the House can rule otherwise through a motion without notice that commits the Bill directly to the committee of the Whole House.

An eloquent testimony of this phase is detailed by Order 71 (12) that:

When a Bill has been read the second time, it shall stand committed to a Standing Committee unless the House on motion made commits it to the committee of the Whole. Such motion shall not require notice, but must be made immediately after the Bill is read a second time and must be proposed by the Majority Leader of the House or a member acting in that capacity. Bills committed to a Standing Committee shall be allocated to a particular committee by the Speaker whose discretion in this matter is final. X

It is in the Standing Committee, that the Bill will be subjected to far reaching deliberations including public hearing and the contribution of experts on the subject matter of that proposed law. The committee will make its recommendations to the House after an exhaustive deliberation and consideration. It can suggest salient areas of improvement and amendments to the Bill.

A Bill, due to its content, may touch on the jurisdiction of two or more committees. The practice, is that the committee with the dominant jurisdiction will be assigned the responsibility for the Bill's treatment and deliberation, while the other committee(s) with less jurisdiction will constitute the sub-committee(s) of that principal committee:

Report Stage

The Standing Committee that treated and deliberated on the Bill, will through its chairman and the involvement of the Business and Rules Committee, slate a date to present its findings to the House. The members are usually given about five days subject to the administrative convenience of the House to consider the report. The members of the House can introduce an amendment and contribute to the Bill during the report stage. It is the chairman of the Standing Committee with the dominant jurisdiction who deliberates on the Bill, who reports the Bill to the House.

Committee of the Whole House

Here, the Speaker or whoever will preside, will leave the chair and take the seat of the Clerk. The Clerk in turn, will take the place of one of his assistants. The mace will be lowered and the presiding officer will be referred to as chairman.

The chairman shall call the number of every clause in succession or the first and last number of a group of clauses. If there are proposed amendments, he shall put forward the question.

The prevalent parliamentary practice is to take up the identified new clauses where they fit into the Bill without bothering to consider them, item by item, after the whole Bill has been appraised. The standard practice is that it is only relevant additional new clauses that can be added to a Bill. Hence, new clauses shall not be inconsistent with a previous decision of the committee that is not substantially the same as a clause which the committee had previously decided that should not stand as part of the Bill.

At the conclusion of the proceeding of the Committee of the Whole House, a motion shall be moved: That the chairman does report the Bill. The question shall be decided without an amendment or debate.

The chairman, if he is the Speaker, will go back to the chair. But if he is not the Speaker, he will go back to his seat. The mace will once again rise and the House becomes formally reconstituted. The Chairman shall then put the question:

'That I do report the Bill or the Bill as amended to the House'

iii. *Third reading*

After the Bill has been reported to the Committee of the Whole House, it will proceed to the third reading. But if a motion emanates from a member for its recommital and the motion succeeds, the Bill will then go back or be recommitted to the Committee of the Whole House.

When a Bill has been reported from a Committee of the Whole House it shall be ordered to be read the third time, which could be immediately or on a day which Rules and Business Committee may appoint. However if a member gives notice of his intention to move the recommittal of the Bill, it may not be read the third time until the motion for recommittal has been taken care of.

If there is no motion for recommittal or if that has failed, the Bill will be ordered for the third reading, subject to the convenience of the House and the schedule of the Rules and Business Committee. There will be room for correction and amendment if there are errors or oversights highlighted in course of the journey of the Bill. These amendments and corrections can be effected only with the permission of the Speaker.

The motion will then be moved that the Bill be read the 'third time'. The Speaker will put the question:

'That the Bill be now read the third time'.

This question will be without debate and if supported by the requisite number of members, the Speaker will then call upon the Clerk to read aloud the long title of the Bill. The Speaker will also repeat the long title of the Bill and declare the Bill read the third time and passed.

Clean Copy and Engrossment of a Bill

A printed copy of a Bill incorporating all the amendments and endorsed by the Clerk of the House and the Speaker is known as a 'Clean Bill'. Engrossment involves the production of a final 'Clean Copy' of a Bill by the legal department after the embodiment of all the amendments agreed to by the House. The Bill will be drawn up in the proper legal drafting format and sealed with an authenticated certificate endorsed by the Clerk of the House.

Thereafter, the Bill will be presented to the governor for his assent. At which time the governor may assent, reject or propose an amendment to the Bill. If the governor withholds his assent of the Bill, the house can override his dissent with two-thirds majority that the Bill shall become law without the governor's assent. If the governor proposes an amendment, the House may however, consider the governor's amendment, and return the Bill thus amended for the governor's signature.

Withdrawing a Bill

A Bill can be withdrawn by the sponsor through a motion without notice before the commencement of public business or on the order of the day for any stage of the Bill.

Bills of the same subject matter cannot be proposed after the second reading of the first Bill during the same session. There are special requirements for the treatment of Bills affecting private rights.

Section II: Passage of the Appropriation Bill

The legislature bears the constitutional duty to scrutinize and approve the financial plan of the governor of the state for a specified year or supplementary measure. It is the responsibility of the governor to prepare and lay before the house of assembly (at any time before the commencement of each financial year) estimates of the revenue and expenditure of the state for the next following financial year.

The heads of expenditure contained in the estimates, other than expenditure charged upon the consolidated revenue fund of the state shall be included in a Bill to be known as an Appropriation Bill.

The underlying constitutional standard is that no money should be withdrawn from the State Consolidated Revenue Fund except in the manner prescribed by the House of Assembly (see Section 120 (2) - (4) of the Constitution).

Presentation of the Appropriation Bill

The governor of the state will forward the Appropriation Bill to the Speaker accompanied with an official letter personally signed by him. There will be a motion moved by the majority leader praying that the governor of the state will attend the House to present the Appropriation Bill.

At the beginning of each financial year the governor shall introduced into the House an Appropriation Bill which shall contain the estimated financial requirements for expenditure on revenue accounts on all services of the government for the succeeding financial year. The details of these requirements shall be contained in the estimates which shall be presented at the same time.

The time of presentation of the Appropriation Bill offers the governor the opportunity to dwell on the economic, social and political condition of the state. Hence, he informs the legislature and the entire state of the exact financial state of the government, previous year(s) performance, prospects and initiatives for the forthcoming year. The presentation forum is usually an appraisal or stocktaking session of the government and also an announcement of the expected promising programmes. The ceremonial Appropriation Bill is usually a financial summary of the recurrent and capital expenditure of the state.

The governor's budget speech and the annexed estimates dealing with ministries, departments and agencies (MDAs) with total figures and breakdowns are voluminous. They run into intimidating number of pages that put the members of the House and other officials to an enormous task. The governor's budget speech as the financial and economic plan of the state is concluded with the request to the house of assembly to approve the chief executive's submission. Therefore, to authorize the appropriation of funds for the financial execution of government's programme (Appropriation Bill) and also to levy taxes, duties, levies etc. to realistically achieve the set programmes (Finance Bill).

The Debate Procedure

i. *First reading*

In every state house of assembly the governor's budget speech, is the *first reading* of the Appropriation Bill. Thus, the budget speech annexed to the Appropriation Bill and officially laid on the Table and accepted by the Speaker before it is handed over to the Clerk, symbolises the first reading of the Bill.

The tradition is to adjourn the House 'sine dei' after the governor's appropriation presentation. It is also expected that the governor's speech, the Appropriation Bill and estimated details will be circulated to each member of the House in readiness for legislative deliberation.

Motion of Thanks

Parliamentary courtesy demands that the next sitting day order paper of the House will bear the 'Budget Address and motion of thanks'. This motion of thanks by the majority leader to the governor usually heralds an invitation by the other members to comment and discuss the governor's budget speech. The House based on the discretion of the Speaker may resolve to convene into a Committee of the Whole House. This will enable the members to have a more liberal treatment of the budget speech.

Deliberation Calendar

The Rules and Business Committee will embark on the tasking assignment of drawing up a House calendar for the deliberation of the Budget and Appropriation Bill. A realistic calendar will take into account the various stages which the Appropriation Bill will undergo before its eventual passage into an appropriation law each state. The calendar will allocate adequate days to each stage.

In general, the Rules and Business Committee shall determine the number of days to be allotted for the *second reading* of the Bill. At the hour appointed for interruption of business on the last of such allotted days, Mr. Speaker shall put the question to bring the proceedings on the second reading to conclusion. Provided that the question on the second reading may be agreed to on a day earlier than the last day so allotted.

The Appropriation Bill will be attached with a schedule of allocation of funds proposed for each 'Head of Expenditures' which the state house of sssembly is requested to approve. The Bill will be further accompanied with a revenue profile that will detail the source, procedures and means of government to raise funds to finance the proposed expenditure.

It is remarkable that two separate Bills will emerge as the outcome of the governor's budget presentation before the House of Assembly. The first is the Appropriation Bill which details the allocation of funds for public administration and social services for that financial year. The second is the Finance Bill that targets the sources of government revenue through direct and indirect taxes to finance the projected services within that given year.

ii. *Second Reading*

The majority leader bears the duty to move that the Appropriation Bill be read a second time. Once the motion receives the required support and is successful, the House will dissolve into a Committee of the Whole House. This phase offers the members a conducive opportunity to discuss the affairs of the state. During the second reading, the debate shall be confined to the financial and economic considerations and the government's financial policy. Detailed items in the estimate may not be debated on the second reading.

The majority leader will announce the close of the debate on the date scheduled for the conclusion of the second reading

Appropriation Committee

At the demanding stage in the parliamentary journey of the Appropriation Bill, all standing committees of the House of Assembly will constitute sub-committees for the Appropriation Committee. The Appropriation Committee will then sub-delegate to these sub-committees aspects of the estimates containing the affairs of the ministries, departments and agencies (MDAs) within their jurisdiction.

Hence, the Education Standing Committee will handle the estimates and budgetary allocation for the Ministry of Education.

When a Bill has been read the second time, it shall be committed to the Appropriation Committee. The standing committees of the house shall for this purpose be deemed to be sub-committees of the Appropriation Committee and shall sit-in with the Appropriation Committee to consider estimates for the ministries, departments and agencies which come under their charge.

It is pertinent that some sub-committees will insist on the personal appearance of commissioners and some principal officers under their domain. This personal attendance will enable the legislators to have more insight and ask questions on the operation and need for certain allocations.

The sub-committees will submit their report and the proposed amendment to the Appropriation Committee after their deliberation. The Appropriation Committee will amalgamate and consider all the reports and finally present a conclusive report officially to the House.

Committee of Supply

The House will resolve into a Committee of the Whole House to be known in the standing orders as the 'Committee of Supply'.

The Speaker of the House shall preside over the Committee of Supply or the deputy speaker in the absence of the Speaker. The Rules and Business Committee will allocate specific days for the deliberation of the Committee of Supply. The operative pattern is that the Bill stands postponed until after the consideration of any schedule to the Bill. The import of this parliamentary rule, is that a resolution must be passed on each item under the Head of Expenditures inclusive of amendments thereto.

The Speaker (chairman) in the course of the Committee of Supply shall call the title of each Head of Expenditure in turn and shall propose the question:

> That the sum of X.... naira for Head X . . . do stand as part
> of the schedule to the Bill).

When all 'Heads of Expenditure' with proffered amendments have been resolved in like manner, the chairman shall put the question:

> That the schedule or schedules as amended do stand part of the
> Bill.

The next stage entails the listing of the Appropriation Bill as the first 'Order of the Day' on a date specifically allotted for that   procedure. Once the Appropriation Bill is passed by the Committee of Supply, the Appropriation Committee shall within three working days prepare its final report. That report will entail a detailed incorporation of a summary of all amendments agreed to by the House, and also state the total amount of money approved for each Ministry, Department or Agency by resolution of the House. Once the Appropriation Committee report is approved, the majority leader shall move the motion that the Bill be read a ***third time***. The third reading motion does not need to be seconded, and shall be decided without amendment or debate.

When the Appropriation Bill has passed the Committee of Supply, the Appropriation Committee shall within three working days prepare and submit a summary of all amendments agreed to by the House. The report shall also show clearly the total amount approved for each ministry, department or agency. Upon approval of the committee's report the member in charge shall move the third reading of the Bill forthwith which motion shall not require to be seconded and shall be decided without amendment or debate and if decided after the hour appointed for the adjournment of the House, the Speaker shall immediately on that decision being reached, adjourn the house without question put.

iii. *Third reading*

If the motion succeeds, the debate and proceedings on the Appropriation Bill will be concluded. The affirmative vote of the required majority of members will conclusively set the stage for the engrossment of the Bill and consequent governor's assent. After the third reading, the laid down procedures for Bills shall be followed.

Finance and Supplementary Appropriation Bills

The tradition is that on the presentation of the budget speech, the Appropriation Bill is attached with a revenue profile. But when the Appropriation Bill is referred to the Appropriation Committee, the revenue profile will be detached and sent to the Finance Committee. The Finance Committee will now constitute a sub-committee of the Appropriation Committee assigned with the role to consider the revenue profile.

The revenue profile notwithstanding, there may be need for a Finance Bill which may not be tabled or presented with the Appropriation Bill on the same day. There may also be a need for a supplementary Appropriation Bill or even virement based on an unpredictable outcome of the economic and political environment.

The finance and supplementary bills are subjected to the same procedural standard of three readings like any other Bill.

Chapter 22

Passage of Bills and Appropriation Bills in the National Assembly

In every situation the quality of the budgetary outcome is contingent upon the nature of the political environment, the magnitude of available resources and the level of integration among the budgetary actors.

H um phrey N w osu

Section I: Passage of Bills

*T*he legislature derives its power to make laws from the Constitution. Hence, the prescribed mode of exercising federal legislative power, as provided by Section 58(1) of the Constitution is: The power of the National Assembly to make laws shall be exercised by bills passed by both the Senate and the House of Representatives and except as otherwise provided by subsection (5) of this section, assented to by the president.

In appreciation of the National Assembly's power to regulate its own procedures (vide Section 60 of the Constitution), each chamber adopts its standing rules. Hence, the lawmaking processes and procedures are strictly governed by these rules. Order XII of the House of Representatives deals with procedures on bills.[1]

The National Assembly

An executive Bill initiated from the presidency shall be accompanied by a covering letter personally signed by the president and sent to the President of the

---

[1] Also see chapter XI of the Senate Rules.

Senate and the Speaker of the House of Representatives (Order XII Rule 2(1)(a) of the House of Representatives, and Rule 78 (1) (a) of the Senate).

A Bill emanating from the judiciary shall be forwarded to the speaker of the House of Representatives and the President of the Senate under a covering letter personally signed by the Chief Justice of the Federal Republic of Nigeria (Order XII Rule 2(1)(b) of the House of Representatives, and Rule 78 (1) (b) of the Senate).

> The President of the Senate and Speaker of the House of Representatives will then send a copy of the proposed Act (law) to their respective rules and business committees. An executive Bill is presented on behalf of the executive arm of government by the majority party leader of the House of Representatives or Senate, who would also sponsor the motion for the three readings of the Bill.

For a private member Bill, the sponsor forwards the draft to the Speaker of the House of Representatives if it proposed in that chamber. The office of the Speaker will then send it to the Rules and Business Committee. In the Senate, the sponsor of a Bill shall forward his Bill to the president of the Senate (Rule 78 (2)). The president of the Senate shall forward the Bill(s) to the Committee on Rules and Business for registration in the Register of Bills and for publication in the schedule of Bills in the Order Paper (Rule 78 (3)).

> Similarly in the House of Representatives, the Speaker shall cause the Bill forwarded to him to be numbered and published in the Schedule of Bills (Order XII Rule 2 (3).

In each case, a copy of the proposed law (Bill) will be sent to the Clerk of the House whose responsibility it is, to assign a number to it. In the Upper Chamber (Senate), the number is prefixed by the letters 'SB' meaning Senate Bill; In the lower Chamber (House of Representatives), the number is prefixed by the letters 'HB' meaning House Bill.

A printed copy of the Bill shall be sent to every member as soon as possible (See Order XII Rule 2(4) of the House of Representatives and Rule 78(4) of the Senate).

The private sponsor of a Bill shall undertake the motions for its readings (these must be seconded) and also canvass for the support of other legislators towards the successful passage of the Bill. The Rules and Business Committee then schedules a date for its consideration by the respective chambers.

Structure of a Bill

Every Bill has a unique format, although there is no uniformity as regards the length, clauses and schedules. However, it must have a short title.

i. A short title – this is the citation title which deals with the specific area of policy it hopes to address;

ii. A long title – which is the descriptive title that gives a concise summation of its objectives;

iii. The enacting words – 'Be it enacted by the . . . as follows':

iv. The body – this can be divided into parts or clauses.

There may be need to insert schedules into laws based on the peculiar feature of the subject matter. In some laws, a preamble may be interpolated between the title and the enacting words.

Official notice of a Bill

A Bill may originate in either the Senate or the House of Representatives (Section 58(2) of the Constitution). But it cannot become law unless it has been passed by both chambers.

At the House of Representatives, all government or executive bills must be published (once) in the official gazette or house journal by the office of the clerk. However, a private Bill must be published twice in the official gazette.[2]

At the Senate, executive or government bills requires printed notification in an issue of the official gazette or the National Assembly journal;[3] but a private Bill requires two successive publications in the official gazette or house journal.

---

[2] See Order XII Rule 1 (1) - (2) of the House of Representative.

[3] See Rule 77 (1) - (2) of the Senate.

Generally, a sponsor of a Bill is required to accompany his Bill with a motion of the intent to introduce the Bill. It is apposite, that a copy of the first of these publications must be sent to every member of the affected chamber.

The procedure also demands background information on the proposed draft law, which is systematically arranged in clauses. This methodical format makes the debate and amendment of the Bill very easy.As upheld by Rule 77(3) of the Senate:

> A compendium of the background information and financial implications shall accompany every Bill.

Before a Bill can become law, it must pass through three stages: the first, second and third readings. This procedural tradition is ordained by Rule 79(1) of the Senate that:

> Every Bill shall receive three readings previous to its passage, which readings shall be in different days, unless the Senate unanimously directs otherwise and the president of the Senate shall give notice of each reading whether it is first, second or third.

Similar provisions guide the House of Representatives (vide Order XII, Rule 3(1)).

i. *First reading*

A Bill slated for introduction will be on the order paper of the House for that particular day. This stage is the formal declaration of the short title of the Bill. If the Bill emanates from the executive, the majority leader will move a motion for the presentation of the Bill for first reading. The Clerk to the House then reads aloud the short title of the Bill; the presiding officer will in turn repeat the short title of the Bill and declare the Bill as having been read the first time. A copy of it will be symbolically laid on the table of the House by the sponsor (the member introducing the Bill) or by the Clerk to the House.This stage requires no debate (Order XII, Rule 2(6)) of the House of Representatives and Rule 78 (6) of the Senate which clearly states that:

> Upon the short title of the Bill being read aloud by the Clerk, the Bill shall be deemed to have been read the first time.

The Bill will then be subjected to the scrutiny and appraisal by the Bill Office to ensure its compliance with the basic statutory and enactment requirements.

ii. Second reading

This stage offers the members of the House the opportunity to deal adequately with the general principles of the Bill (its merits and demerits). They can then decide to approve or reject the proposal provisionally. In Hilaire Barnett's analysis:

> *It is at the second reading that a Bill will receive the first in-depth scrutiny. The scrutiny occurs in the form of a debate, generally on the floor of the House, and is confined to matters of principle rather than detail.*[4]

On the day scheduled for the second reading, the majority leader, if the Bill originates from the executive, will move the motion:

That the Bill be now read a second time.

The sponsor of a private Bill, will move the same for the furtherance of his proposed law. The motion must be seconded.

In course of the consequent debate, a member may object to the passage of the Bill. The objection can be in the form of an amendment. He can employ the subtle parliamentary ploy of moving:

That the Bill be now read a second time upon this day six months.

The objection can emphatically be introduced as a 'reasoned amendment', thereby, eloquently stating why the Bill should not receive a second reading. If the House resolves in favour of the amendment, the Bill will be rejected.

But if the House rejects the amendment, then the motion for second reading will succeed.

After the successful motion, the sponsor of the Bill then canvasses for the support of his fellow legislators, in order to gain the prerequisite majority for the passage of the Bill. Sometimes, there are suggested amendments, which can be effected by the House. The consequent debate may take additional days or weeks

---

[4] Hilaire Barnett, 586.

to conclude. The House will then vote to approve its passage to the next stage or to reject it.

The support of the required majority of the members of the House is necessary for the passage of the Bill to the next stage. But if it is rejected (or killed) by the House, it will be dropped; it cannot be re-introduced during the same session. If the Bill receives the required support, the presiding officer will declare that it has been read a second time, and it will be moved to the committee stage. The age-long format is that the presiding officer shall put the statement:

That this Bill be now read a second time.

If the statement is agreed to by the required majority of the members, then, the presiding officer will call upon the clerk to read the long title of the Bill. The presiding officer then in turn reads the long title of the Bill and declares that the Bill has been read a second time (See Rule 80 (3) of the Senate and Order XII Rule 4(3) of the House of Representatives).

iii. Committee stage

The Bill, having passed the second reading stage, is referred to the appropriate standing committee for a detailed scrutiny. The committee can at this stage invite the public and private contributors, especially experts and practitioners in the subject area of the Bill. After all necessary deliberation and due consideration, the committee makes its recommendation to the House. It can also suggest areas of improvement or amendment on the Bill.

The nature of a Bill may lend it to touch on the jurisdiction of two or more committees. In such cases, it is the committee which has the dominant jurisdiction, that will be assigned the responsibility of the scrutiny and treatment of the Bill, the other committees with less jurisdiction, will be constituted into sub-committees to undertake their aspects of the Bill and report to the main committee (Rule 81(2) of the Senate and Order XII Rule 5(2) of the House of Representatives).

Public hearing

The issue of public hearing may be determined by the nature of the Bill. If it is controversial or of immense public interest such that it warrants the contribution of other interest groups, it is required of the committee to make a public announcement advising the date, venue, subject matter and time of the public hearing with at least advanced notice of one week.

The House, can through a motion without notice by the Senate leader or House of Representatives leader, immediately after the second reading of a Bill, waive its committal to a standing committee and assign the Bill directly to the Committee of the Whole House (Rule 81 (1) of the Senate and Order XII Rule 5(1) of the House of Representatives).

iv. Report stage

The chairman of the standing committee that handled the Bill and the Rules and Business Committee of the House will then pick a date for the presentation of their findings on the Bill to the whole house. Members are given about five days, subject to the convenience of the house, to consider the report. The house can amend and contribute to the Bill at this stage.

The Business Committee has the duty of allotting a date for the consideration of the entire committee report and amendment, if any. Individual contributions will also be included in the review of the committee.

The Standing Orders of the House of Representatives (vide order VII Rule 2(2)) accords the deputy speaker the chairmanship of the Committee of the Whole House, except when the whole house becomes the Committee of Supply or Ways and Means. The president of the Senate still operates as the chairman of the Committee of the Whole Senate.

Thus, the chairman assumes the seat of the Clerk, and the Clerk occupies the place of one of his assistants. The mace will be lowered beneath the table and placed at the bracket. This parliamentary ritual symbolizes the beginning of session.

The chairman shall call the number of each clause in succession or the first and last number of a group of clauses. If there are proposed amendment(s) or not, he shall then proceed to put the question:

That the clause (or clause as amended, do stand part of the Bill.

(See Rule 85 (1) of the Senate and Order XII; Rule 9(1) of the House of Representatives).

The current legislative practice is to take up the identified new clauses where they fit into the Bill without bothering to consider them after the Bill has been appraised.

It is only relevant additional new clauses that can be added to a Bill. The standard test, is that the new clause shall not be inconsistent with a previous decision of the committee nor substantially the same as a clause which the committee had previously decided that should not stand part of the Bill.

Postponed clauses shall be considered after the remaining clauses of the Bill have been treated before the introduction of new clauses.

At the conclusion of the proceedings, the leader of the House shall move the motion:

That the chairman does report the Bill.

The question shall be decided without any amendment or debate.

Finally, the chairman if he is the presiding officer shall return to the chair. But if he is not the presiding officer, he will go back to his seat. The mace will once again rise and the House becomes formally re-constituted. The chairman shall then put the question:

That I do report the Bill (or the Bill as amended) to the Senate or the House of Representatives.

v. Third reading

It is suggested that an accurate record of votes is taken by voice or rollcall of all the members present and voting (usually, the best approach is rollcall, which effectively checks the controversies that trail some Bills).[5]

After the Bill has been reported to the Committee of the Whole House, it will proceed to the third reading. But if a motion for its re-committal is moved and it succeeds, the Bill will then go back or be recommitted to the Committee of the Whole House.

If there is no motion of re-committal, the Bill will be ordered for the third reading subject to the convenience of the House and the schedule of the Rules and Business Committee. There will be room for correction and amendment if there are errors or oversights highlighted in course of the journey of the Bill. These amendments and corrections can be effected only with the permission of the presiding officer of the House.

---

[5] In 2002, the Child Rights Bill, which was taken by voice vote, generated a lot of controversy. The adoption of this method of voting was considered by many experts as unfortunate

The leader of the House will then move the motion that the Bill be read the 'third time'. The presiding officer will put the question:

That the Bill be now read the third time.

This question will be without debate and if agreed to by the requisite number of members present, the presiding officer will then call upon the Clerk to read the long title of the Bill. The presiding officer will also repeat the long title of the Bill and declare the Bill read the third time and passed. (See Rule 86(1) - (4) of the Senate and Order XII Rule 10(1) - (4) of the House of Representatives).

The Court of Appeal affirmed these stages in the case of *National Assembly v. President,*[6] in which Oguntade J.C.A. declared that:

> *Having gone through the first, second reading, the committee stage and the third reading. In the course of these readings and committee stage the Bill is examined in detail and amended if necessary. Law making is therefore a serious business. The court is enjoined to take judicial notice of the course of proceedings in the National Assembly.*

vi. A Clean Bill

A printed copy of a Bill incorporating all the amendments endorsed by the Clerk to the House and the presiding officer is known as a 'Clean Bill'. Usually, the Clerk in the chamber from which a Bill originated sends the 'Clean Bill' to the Clerk to the other chamber, accompanied with a memorandum requesting the concurrence of that other chamber.

If the Bill is acceptable in its entirety to the receiving house (ie, without any amendment at the various stages), the Clerk sends a memorandum informing the originating house that his chamber has agreed to the Bill without any amendment. But where both chambers fail to agree on the content and amendments of the Bill, a conference of both chambers becomes inevitable.

---

[6] [2003] 9 NWLR pt 824 p. 104.

Conference of both chambers

This is a meeting between selected members of the House of Representatives and the Senate. The object is to resolve and reconcile the differences between both houses over the provisions of a Bill. Section 58(3) of the Constitution provides for this conference. This is to ensure that a Bill is passed by both houses of the National Assembly and that they agree on the amendments.

The constitutional intention is that a Bill must be passed in identical form by both chambers of the National Assembly before it is sent to the president for his assent.

In that perspective, a conference committee comprising the same number of members from each chamber, as ordained by provisions of the rules of the respective chambers, will consider areas of disagreement between both chambers in a Bill before engrossment. The conference(s) should include some members of the committee which considered the Bill originally, who will be joined with other members nominated by their respective chambers for the harmonization of amendments and conflict areas in the Bill that are not acceptable to both chambers.

It is appropriate to note that the conference committee's jurisdiction is limited specifically to the areas of disagreement between the Senate and the House of Representatives. As emphatically held by Rule 87 of the Senate:

The conference committee shall deliberate only on areas of disagreement between the Senate and the House of Representatives. The conference committee shall not insert in its report any matter not committed to it by either Senate or House of Representatives nor shall it be in order to strike out from the bill matter agreed by Senate or House of Representatives.

The proceedings of the conference are usually open, except when a majority of the members vote for a closed session. It is only the decision of the majority of the conference in the form of an agreement or compromise on the two versions of the Bill from both chambers, that can be forwarded to the floor as the conference report. If both chambers disapprove of the agreement reached by the conference committee, the Bill will be sent back to the conference committee constituted by newly appointed conferees.

But if the report of the second committee is rejected by both chambers, then the Bill can be committed to a joint sitting of both chambers. The outcome of the joint sitting is usually to strike a compromise and reach desired agreement.

Engrossment of a Bill

Engrossment involves the production of a final 'clean copy' of a Bill, by the legal department after the embodiment of all the amendments agreed to by both chambers of the National Assembly. The Bill will be drawn up in the proper legal drafting format and sealed with an authenticated certificate endorsed by the Clerk to the National Assembly. Thereafter, the Bill will be presented to the President of the Federal Republic of Nigeria for his assent or otherwise.

In conformity with the provisions of section 2(1) of the Acts Authentication Act Cap A2 Laws of the Federation of Nigeria 2004:

> The Clerk to the National Assembly shall forthwith after enactment, prepare a copy of each Bill as passed by both house of National Assembly embodying all amendments agreed to, and shall endorse on the Bill and sign a certificate that the copy has been prepared as prescribed by this section and is a true copy of the Bill.

The duplicate copies of the Bill and attached schedules are then sent to the President of the Federal Republic of Nigeria for his consent. If the president consents and signs, it becomes an Act. It will then be returned to the Clerk so that he can facilitate the publication of the Act in triplicate.

The government printer will publish the Act on vellum and return the copies to the Clerk to the National Assembly, who will retain a copy for official records and send a copy to the president. The third copy is sent to the Chief Justice of Nigeria, where it will be enrolled in the Supreme Court as an Act of the National Assembly.

However, if the president withholds his assent and the Bill is passed by two-thirds majority of each house of the National Assembly, the Bill becomes law without the president's assent (Section 58(5)).

But the legislature requires three fresh readings of the Bill before it can override the president's veto as stipulated by Section 58(5). This was the decision of the Court of Appeal in *National Assembly* v. *President*.[7] In the words of the

---

[7] ibid.

Court of Appeal: for a Bill to become law without presidential assent, it must fulfil the following conditions:

> a. *It must, once more, pass through all the seven stages which it went through before it was sent to the president for his assent, and*
>
> b. *The repeat passage must be by two-thirds majority of the total number of members in each house of the National Assembly.*
>
> *There is no room in the Constitution for the National Assembly to override the veto of the president by a mere motion. The whole process of the initial legislation must again be undertaken.*[8]

The departure from this constitutional procedure has resulted in some notable court actions challenging some enactments. The decision of the Supreme Courts in *AG Bendel State v. AG Federation*[9](supra), made abundantly clear the position of the law :

> *That a Bill whether a money Bill or a non money Bill, does not and cannot become a law made by the National Assembly unless and until it has been passed by the Senate, the House of Representatives and, except where the provisions of Section 54(5) of the 1979 Constitution (now Section 58(5)) apply, assented to by the President of the Federal Republic of Nigeria.*[10]

In this case, the Supreme Court also settled the issue of employing the Clerk's authentication certificate as a shield for irregularity. The stance of the Court was:

> *That the issue of a certificate by the Clerk to the National Assembly with respect to any particular enrolled Act, pursuant to the provision of Section 2 of the Act Authentication Act, 1961, does not preclude the court from going behind the certificate in order to make necessary inquiry in proceedings which specifically*

---

[8] ibid.

[9] [1981] ANLR p.102, para.3.

[10] [1981] ANLR p.101 para.3.

> *seek a declaration by the court on the constitutional validity of such an Act.*[11]

The controversy trailing the 2001 Electoral Act and the 2005 Appropriations Act by the National Assembly hinged on this issue. Among the various allegations were: one, that some portions or clauses were introduced into the Electoral Act, in addition to what was passed by the National Assembly; and two, the National Assembly claimed that an entirely different Act emerged from what the legislature passed as 2005 Appropriation Act.

Money bills and budgetary processes

The generation and distribution of public funds, is the compelling factor in public administration. Hence, the official document which contains the words and figures that propose the expenditure for items on an annual basis, becomes an inevitable part of every administration. Therefore, budget as the financial plan which aims to translate the financial resources of a country, state or local government into human purposes or advantage, constitute an integral part of the society's expectations and advancement.

In appraising the realistic application of legislative powers over money and budgetary matters, section 59 of the Constitution becomes relevant. The provisions of this section 59 (1) shall apply to:

> (a) an Appropriation Bill or a supplementary Appropriation Bill, including any other Bill for the payment, issue or withdrawal from the consolidated revenue fund or any other public fund of the federation of any money charged thereon or any alteration in the amount of such a payment, issue or withdrawal; and

> (b) a Bill for the imposition of or increase in any tax, duty or fee or any reduction, withdrawal or cancellation thereof.

The import of the combination of the above cited section 59(1) (a) - (b) will give birth to money Bills. But the eventual outcome of section 59 (1) (b) is traditionally known as the Finance Bill. Hence, while the object of section 59(1) (a) is on authorization of public expenditure, that of section 59(1) (b), is on taxation or

---

[11] [1981] ANLR p.101 para.6.

sources of finance, for the expenditure raised in 59(1) (a). The power of the National Assembly with respect to money Bills can be appreciated through a combined review of Section 59, 80-83 of the Constitution.

The president of the Federal Republic of Nigeria is charged by Section 81(1) of the Constitution to prepare and lay before each House of the National Assembly, at any time in each financial year, estimates of the revenue and expenditure of the federation for the following financial year. The heads of expenditure contained in the estimates (other than expenditure charged upon the Consolidation Revenue Fund of the federation)shall be included in a Bill to be known as the Appropriation Bill (Section 81(2)).

In short, the Constitution emphatically holds that no money(s) shall be withdrawn from the consolidation revenue fund or any other public fund of the federation, except in the manner prescribed by the National Assembly (Section 80(4)).

Likewise, the state governors are required to perform the same duties to the state houses of assembly in line with the provisions of Section 121 (1) of the Constitution. The same medium via an Appropriation Bill is also required by Section 121 (2) of the Constitution. The same conditions guide the operation of state funds. There is an imperative prescription by the state houses of assembly before a state's money could be withdrawn (Section 120 (4)).

Section II: Presentation of an Appropriation Bill

The president is expected to forward the Appropriation Bill to the presiding officers of both chambers of the National Assembly along with an official covering letter personally signed by him. The state governors perform the same process accompanied with their signed official covering letter sent to speakers of their respective houses of assembly.

There will be a motion moved by the majority party leaders in each house. It will be resolved that the president, in the exercise of his rights, under Section 81(1) of the 1999 Constitution of the Federal Republic of Nigeria, be admitted to attend and present to the joint session of the National Assembly, the Appropriation Bill and budget message. The same motion will occasion each governor's presentation under Section 121(1) of the Constitution in the various state houses of assembly. The tradition has been that the president or state governor use the appointed date for the presentation of Appropriation Bills to deliver their budget speech.

The time of presentation of Appropriation Bills offers the president the opportunity to give an account of the state of the nation; likewise each state governor will present the condition of his state. The president, for the sake of convenience, normally addresses a joint session of the National Assembly before presenting the Appropriation Bill.

The exact financial state of the governments' previous year(s) performance, prospects and initiatives for the forthcoming year are thus highlighted. It is usually an appraisal or stocktaking session of the performance of the government and an announcement of the expected future programmes. The actual Appropriation Bill is usually a financial summary of the recurrent and capital expenditure of the federation or the states in a few pages. The president's or state governor's budget speech and the annexed estimates, dealing with ministries, departments and agencies (MDAs), total figures and breakdowns are voluminous. The Appropriation Bill runs into an intimidating number of pages and places an enormous task on the desk of the legislators.

The president's or state governor's budget speech, as the financial and economic plan of the country or state, is concluded with the request to the National Assembly or State House of Assembly to approve the chief executive's submission. Hence, to authorize the appropriation of funds for the financial execution of government's programmes (Appropriation Bill) and also to levy taxes, duties, levies, etc to realistically achieve the set programmes (Finance Bill).

This agelong tradition of the president's personal presentation of the money Bill to the joint session of the National Assembly was not performed for the 2010 Appropriate Bill. Instead, on 24 November 2009, the president's special adviser to the National Assembly, Mohammed Abba Aji, placed two copies the 2010 Appropriation Bill before each chamber of the National Assembly on behalf of the president, without reading it.

Debate procedure of an Appropriation Bill

i. *First reading*

The standing orders or rules of most states as well as those of the National Assembly, assumes that the president's or the governor's budget speech, is the first reading of the Bill. The budget speech is annexed to the Appropriation Bill and officially laid on the table and accepted by the presiding officer, before it is handed over to the Clerk to the house. This presentation symbolizes the first reading of the Appropriation Bill. Order XII, Rule 16(1)(b) of the House of Representatives presents that:

> On presentation, the Bill shall be deemed to have been read the first time and a date be fixed for commencement of the second reading.

The House normally adjourns 'sine dei' after the president or governor's exhaustive budget speech and the attendant ceremonies. The president's or the governor's speech, the Appropriation Bill and estimated details are circulated to the legislators in readiness for actual legislative deliberation.

ii. *Motion of thanks*

The next sitting day order paper of the house will bear 'the budget address and motion of thanks'. This motion of thanks will be by the majority leader to the president or the state governor, as the case may be. The motion of thanks by the majority leader usually heralds an invitation to his fellow legislators to comment and discuss the president's or governor's budget speech. The House, based on the discretion of the presiding officer, may resolve to convene into a Committee of the Whole House. This will enable them to have a more liberal treatment of the budget speech.

iii. *Deliberation calendar*

The Business and Rules Committee will embark on the herculean task of drawing up a house calendar for the deliberation of the budget and Appropriation Bill. A realistic calendar will take into account, the various stages which the Appropriation Bill will undergo before its eventual passage into an Appropriation Act of the National Assembly or an Appropriation Law of a state. The calendar will allocate adequate days to each stage.

The Appropriation Bill is attached with a schedule of an allocation of funds proposed for each Head of Expenditure which the National Assembly or state house of assembly is requested to approve. The Bill as current practice has revealed, will further be accompanied with a revenue profile that will detail the source, procedure and means of government to raise funds to finance the proposed expenditure. This revenue profile initiative is notable with the National Assembly.

The age-long tradition, is that the Ministry of Finance will publish and announce a detailed breakdown of the government's revenue scheme to meet the proposed expenditure. Thus, the details of new tax measures, import duty regulations and other relevant measures that constitute the Finance Bill, will be released. These outlined measures will remain in abeyance until the passage of the Finance Bill and its consequent assent by the president and enlistment as the Finance Act of the Federal Republic of Nigeria for that specified year. It can only come into effect when it has been duly passed by the National Assembly and assented to by the President.

It is pertinent to note, that two separate Bills will emerge as consequence of the budget speech of the chief executive. The first is the Appropriation Bill which details the allocation of funds for public administration and social services for that financial year. The second is the Finance Bill that targets the sources of government revenue through direct and indirect taxes to finance the projected services within that given year.

iv. *Second reading*

The majority leader will move a motion that the Appropriation Bill be read a second time. Once the motion is passed, the House will dissolve into a Committee of the Whole House. This phase offers the members ample opportunity to discuss the affairs of the state or the nation. Order XII, Rule 16(3) of the House of Representatives affirms this position thus:

> During the Second Reading, the debate shall be confined to the
>
> financial and economic state of Nigeria and the government's financial policy. Detailed items in the estimate may not be debated on the second reading.

It is equally the responsibility of the majority leader to announce the close of the debate on the date scheduled for the conclusion of the second reading.

v. *Appropriation Committee*

At this crucial stage in the legislative journey of the Appropriation Bill, all standing committees of the assembly will constitute subcommittees for the Committee on Appropriation, who will subdelegate to these subcommittees, aspects of the estimates containing the affairs of the MDAs within their domain.

Hence, the health standing committee will handle the estimates and budgetary allocation for the Ministry of Health.

As stated in Rule 92(4) (a) of the Senate:

> When the Bill has been read the second time, it shall be committed to the Appropriation Committee. The standing committees of the Senate shall for this purpose be deemed to be subcommittees of the Appropriation Committee and shall consider estimates for the ministries, departments and agencies which come under their charge.

It is customary that some subcommittees will insist on the physical appearance of certain ministers and other principal officers before them to answer questions on their budget and to justify their request for certain allocations. The same level of personal attendance can also be expected from state commissioners and their principal officers before committees in the state houses of assembly.

The subcommittees will submit their reports and the proposed amendments to the Appropriation Committee after their deliberation. The Appropriation Committee will amalgamate and consider all the reports and finally present a conclusive official report to the House.

vi. *Committee of Supply*

The House will resolve into a Committee of the Whole House referred to in some standing orders or rules as 'Committee of Supply' (See Order XII Rule 16(4) (b) of the House of Representatives). The Rules and Business Committee must slate specific days for the deliberation of the Committee of Supply. The operative pattern as ordained by Order XII Rule 16(7) of the House of Representatives, is that the Bill stands positioned until after the consideration of the schedules to the Bill. The import of this legislative rule is that a resolution must be passed on each item under the Head of Expenditures inclusive of amendments thereto:

Thus, the presiding officer of the Committee of Supply shall call the title of each Head of Expenditure and in turn shall propose the question:

> That the sum of x X . . . billion for Head X do stand part of the schedule to the Bill.

When all heads of expenditures with proffered amendments have been resolved in like manner the chairman shall put the question:

> That the schedule or schedules (as amended) do stand part of the Bill.

The next stage will entail the listing of the Appropriation Bill as the first 'Order of the Day' on a date specifically allotted for that. The procedure is that once the Appropriation Bill is passed by the Committee of Supply, the Appropriation Committee shall within three working days prepare its final report. That report will entail a detailed incorporation of a summary of all amendments agreed to by the House and also state the total amount of money approved for each ministry, department or agency by resolution of the House. Once the Appropriation Committee report is approved, the majority leader shall move the motion that the Bill be read a third time. The third reading motion does not require to be seconded and shall be decided without amendment or debate.

vi. *Third reading*

If the motion succeeds, the debate and proceedings on the Appropriation Bill will be concluded. The affirmative vote of the required majority will conclusively set the stage for engrossment processes and consequent chief executive assent.As held by Rule 92(18) of the Senate:

> After the third reading, the laid down procedures for bills shall be followed.

National Assembly Appropriation strategy

The National Assembly in exercise of her constitutional powers to regulate her affairs vide section 60 of the Constitution, has fashioned out an appropriation mechanism. This device, aimed at facilitating the Appropriation Bill processes, has been in vogue, for some years in that parliament.

Thus, after the second reading of the Appropriation Bill and its referral to the two chambers appropriation committees, both committees meet in a combined effort and understanding to treat and consider the schedules to the Bill. In this respect, the sub-committees of the Senate and the House of Representatives to whom the heads of expenditure have been assigned, now sit together in a joint meeting to treat and consider their assigned heads of expenditure. Hence, the ministry of education head of expenditure will be considered by joint meeting of the Senate and House of Representatives sub-committees.

At the conclusion of this exercise, the joint sub-committee will then report to the joint meeting of the Appropriation Committee. It is this Joint Appropriation Committee of the Senate and the House of Representatives that will prepare the report which will be submitted to the two chambers of the National Assembly.

The beauty of this new practice, is that it saves time and proffers common ground to harmonize differences.

National Assembly Joint Finance Committee

If only one chamber of the National Assembly passes the Appropriation Bill and the other chamber does not within two months from the financial year, the president of the Senate shall, within fourteen days (14 days), convene a meeting of Joint Finance (Appropriation Committee) to review and resolve the differences (vide Section 59 (2) of the Constitution).

If the Joint Finance Committee fails to resolve the differences, then the Bill will be presented to the National Assembly at a joint meeting. If the Bill is passed at this joint sitting, it shall be presented to the president for his assent (Section 59 (3).

This constitutionally ordained Joint Finance Committee, is different from the above cited combination of appropriation committees of both chambers and sub-committees therein for the facilitation of consideration of heads of expenditure and attendant budgetary processes.

Authorized withdrawal before the passage of the Appropriation Bill

Meanwhile, before the passage of the Appropriation Bill, the president can authorize the withdrawal of money from the Consolidated Revenue Fund of the Federation to meet necessary expenditure and service. The authority shall not exceed the period of six months (Section 82). A state governor can exercise precisely the same authority through Section 122 of the Constitution.

Finance and Supplementary Appropriation bills

The practice is that on the presentation of the budget speech, the Appropriation Bill is attached with a revenue profile. But when the Appropriation Bill is referred to the Appropriation Committee, the revenue profile will be detached and sent to the Finance Committee. The Finance Committee will now constitute a sub-committee of the Appropriation Committee assigned with the role to consider revenue profile.

The revenue profile notwithstanding, there is room for a Finance Bill which may not be tabled or presented on the same day as the Appropriation Bill. There is also room for a supplementary Appropriation Bill or *virement* based on the unpredictable outcomes of the economic and political environment.

In this sphere, the Finance Bill and supplementary Appropriation Bill, will pass through the same procedural route as a normal Bill. Hence, they will be subjected to the conventional first, second and third readings. For a Finance Bill, the other standing committees of the House will not constitute sub-committees of the Finance Committee and as such do not partake in its committee stage deliberation.

The practice is that a Finance Bill will be introduced and slated as an item on the other paper by the majority leader who bears the responsibility for the introduction of executive bills. Thus, the majority leader is saddled with the task to move the motion for the three readings of the Bill.

On the second reading of a Finance Bill, it will be exhaustively debated by the members, as any other Bill. The contentious subjects typically border on tax measures. The Bill will then be referred to the Finance Committee after the second reading.

The urgent need for the passage of this Bill, so that the government can get on with its business, has manifested in the creation of a Joint Finance Committee of both chambers.

The Joint Finance Committee will then subject the Bill to a thorough in-depth, critical scrutiny, especially the tax proposals in the attached schedule to the Bill.

The public policy spirit and attendant interests, demand a public hearing that will involve private and public stakeholders, experts and other shades of interest groups. Therefore, financial consultants, the manufacturers' association, trade unions, chambers of commerce, industrialists, as well as the organized private sector should contribute in line with their practical experience and expertise on the subject matter.

The Joint Finance Committee will then be properly informed and adequately equipped after such holistic contributions to write a comprehensive and realistic report and make dynamic recommendations to the House. The committee, based on the stark realities of the evidence and findings presented by aforestated interest groups, may recommend an increase or decrease in the items of taxation listed in the schedule to the Finance Bill.

The consequent report and recommendations of the Finance Committee, will be debated in the Committee of the Whole House known traditionally for this purpose as the 'Committee of Ways and Means'. This committee will be chaired by the presiding officer of the house.

Hence, on the completion of the treatment of the Finance (or money) Bill by the Finance Committee, the report as well as attendant recommendations and amendments to the Bill and schedules to the Bill, will be presented to each chamber in the Committee of Ways and Means (Committee of the Whole House).

At the conclusion of the Committee of Ways and Means, the Bill will now follow the traditional route to a third reading, engrossment, authentication and presentation to the president for his assent.

But where the president withholds his assent within thirty (30) days after the presentation of the Bill to him, the Bill shall be presented again to the National Assembly. There, the passage of the Bill by a two-thirds majority of the members of both Houses of the National Assembly sitting at a joint meeting, will transform the Bill into law. In this case, the president's assent will not be required (See section 59(4) of the Constitution).

The state houses of assembly do not have a joint finance committee, therefore their appropriation procedures do not entail any conflict resolution.

Appropriation Bill and the Future of Nigerian Democracy

This subject has raised disquieting controversies at the federal level since the year 2000. In short, it is an issue that has exposed the unhealthy relationship between the executive and the legislative arms of government as from year 2000.

The truth is that constitutional and other guidelines pertaining to the raising, spending and accounting for public funds, have been discarded in all tiers and sectors of governance. Budgetary discipline, transparency and strict adherence to policy guidelines, which democratic governance demands, are alien to the country's shoddy financial system and a culture of mismanagement.

Hence, approved budgetary allocations are hardly released to the specific ministry department or agency even many months after the enactment of the Appropriation Act. It is startling and disturbing that legislators arrogate to themselves the powers of appropriation of funds such as meant for constituency projects, over which they control the disbursement. The disheartening scenario in our public service where salaries are owed, irrespective of approved allocation, confirms this.

Anambra State typifies this ugly situation from 1999 – 2003. Salaries and arrears of almost two years were outstanding to public servants irrespective of receipts of normal allocation from the Federation Account. This pathetic state of affairs presents a picture of porous public coffers, where individuals have been able to withdraw millions of naira with impunity.

The constitutional checks ordained by the creation of the offices of the accountant-general and auditor-general, have been neutralized beyond comprehension. Indeed, the positions of these officials have been reduced to that of mere helpless lackeys of the chief executives in all the three tiers of government. The alarming state is such that the numerous corporations, parastatals and other agencies have operated without audited accounts for almost one decade. The accounting ethic as a standard procedure has long fizzled out in the public service.

The reprehensible fashion with which legislators sanction Appropriation Bills, especially supplementary Appropriation Bills, smacks of impropriety. There have been cases where the executive presented an Appropriation Bill to the legislature, and such was approved and assented to a few days or even hours to the end of the financial year.

The Way Forward

The present constitutional and statutory measures, if adhered to, will go a long way toward safeguarding the public coffers and restoring confidence and sanity in governance. The following salient initiatives can be introduced to strengthen the already existing mechanisms.

i. *Public enlightenment and adequate publicity*

The palpable ignorance of Nigerians on finance and appropriation bills is incontestable. Thus, public awareness seminars and campaigns on Appropriation Bills must be intensified. It is obvious that many Nigerians are still in a dilemma of differentiating between the military era budget speech and the intervention of the present democratic era in monetary affairs.

The lackluster presentation of appropriation bills in the media also widens the ignorance gulf and deepens public apathy on the subject. The system demands a more colourful ceremonial presentations to attune the minds of the populace to the affair.

ii. *The establishment of a budget review office*

The establishment of a 'budget review office', akin to the Office of Management and Budget (OMB) in the United States[12] will be of great technical and administrative help to the executive and the legislative branch of government in considering and evaluating presented budgets. This office will collate and publish the internal budget of the ministries, departments and agencies (MDAs) before presentation to the legislature. The OMB will also publish the approved sums through the Ministry of Finance, after the assembly has deliberated on the quarterly allocations in respect of the ministries and other projects. The budget review office, should be established in all the three tiers of government.

iii. *Project identification initiative*

Approved projects and the sums of money allocated in the budget must be advertised with signposts on the particular approved site. The budget review office will be responsible for this. Uganda applied this method, and it checked considerably the controversy of project allocation and attendant corruption in diverting public funds.

It is startling that most of the estimate profiles attached to our Appropriation Bill lack a descriptive profile. In short, the sums are merely lumped and assigned without a specific description of the items.

Thus, project identification, tenure, duration as well as accompanying revenue profile, are hardly highlighted in the presentation to our law makers.

iv. *Collective vigilance*

The beauty of democracy lies in the popular participation of various pressure groups and activists. Therefore, professional bodies, civil society organizations and sundry, must practically engage themselves in public affairs. Hence, public hearing sessions of the assembly must be utilized and the legislators be made accountable for their acts through public opinion.

v. *Introduction of civic education in the school curriculum*

---

[12] H.N. Nwosu. The Budgeting Process in the Presidential System. Presented at the workshop for legislators. Anambra State House of Assembly, Enugu (1981), p.6.

The syllabuses of current secondary and tertiary institutions, must be reviewed to accommodate civic education. Hence, the inculcation of history and civic education in general studies programmes will enhance the growth of our democratic culture.

There is an urgent need to introduce legislative procedures as well as pubic accounting and budgetary processes as a core course in the general studies programmes in our tertiary institution syllabus. This initiative will boost the consciousness of citizens and pubic accountability advocacy.

vi. *Establishment of a legislative budget office and dynamic advocacy*

The uneasy controversy between the executive and the legislative arms of government especially at the federal level since year 2000, demands an institutional remedy. Hence, our legislative houses need a legislative budget office to acquaint them with technical information about the economy, budgetary processes involving public expenditure and revenue profile statistics.

This office was introduced into the United States in 1976, and is anchored to the Budget or Appropriation control law. It will check effectively, the ceaseless non-release of appropriated funds and abuse of office that has characterized our pubic spending for the past eight years. [13]

Our lawmakers must also emulate the legislative industriousness of their counterparts in the United States by initiating proactive legislation. The abiding efforts of outstanding United States congressmen through historic legislation, is pertinent. Hence, the Landrum-Griffin Act, the Sherman Anti-Trust Law, The Taft-Hartley Act and others, were memorable laws sponsored by seasoned law makers for the well-being and advancement of their country and the citizenry.

---

[13] It is not possible to know the amount of inappropriate spending during military rule.

Chapter 23

The Legislature and Public Hearing

If groups within the society do not find open channels through which to express their interests and needs, these demands are likely to remain unsatisfied. The resultant dissatisfaction may erupt in violence, or may require suppression by the elites.

A lm ond & Pow ell

---

*T*he lawmaking organ of the state in the performance of its role as the society's 'errand boy' or 'post office' has a more direct link with the populace. In serving the interest of its catchment's area, as the elected representatives, the legislature typifies the slogan of 'power to the people'. The legislature makes use of the following methods in taking care of the needs of the citizenry:

i. *Instrument of petition*

A petition enables interest groups, organizations, communities and private individuals to convey and express their support or disapproval of a particular policy or legislation. The common form of complaint to the legislature usually takes the form of a petition by members of the public or person(s) seeking redress from the assembly. Public officers who feel unjustifiably removed from office can apply through petition to the legislature for consideration and redress.

The petition will be addressed to the petitioners representative in the legislature or to any other member. It is that addressee who will formally present the petition to the house on the agreed date. The house rules require no debate on the immediate presentation of a petition. But it can be read to the house and be placed on the table before being referred to the Public Petition Committee.

The legislature must pay adequate attention to petitions because it serves as a measure for the electorate to judge the sensitivity of their representatives. The legislature on the receipt of complaints against certain government agencies can check and control the management of such agency. Meanwhile, the legislature must thoroughly review a petition before establishing an official stance on the issue. The legislature has to consider the legal issues involved, it must investigate the petitioner's background and it must also ascertain if the issue is already before a competent court of law or administrative tribunal. Hence, the legislature lacks jurisdiction to interfere with a case before a court or tribunal. These salient factors must be appraised before an official pronouncement by the house on a matter before it.

In order to avoid the misuse and abuse of the petition the state houses of assembly will not entertain any petition for which there is a judicial remedy for which an application has been made, and for which provision is made in Section 33 (2) of the Constitution.

It is usually the public petitions committee that recommends the legislature's position on a case directed through a petition.

ii. *Press briefing/conference*

The legislature occasionally organizes question and answer sessions for the general public. There, the principal officers render account of their stewardship. These sessions, provide answers to questions already sent to the legislature and enlighten the public considerably. These fora also serves as stocktaking sessions on the performance of the legislature within specified period.

iii. *Public hearing*

During the progressive advancement of a bill to the committee stage, the interested public has a right to contribute its ideas/opinion on the proposed law. Likewise, the legislature in the exercise of its constitutional power of investigation can seek expert guidance from the public. This contribution can be rendered orally or by written memorandum. It materializes in the contribution of experts, professional bodies and the affected local communities where the proposed law will take effect.

Any new piece of legislation manifests the yearnings of a defined territorial area and its citizens. For example, the need for an effective anti corruption law in Nigeria was deemed necessary and desirable by a vast majority of Nigerians. Nevertheless, the Senate repealed the anti-corruption (ICPC) Act (2002)without any public hearing. Such flagrant abuse of the citizens' fundamental right to public hearing is outrageous. Subsequently the Senate organized a public hearing on the bill. But to what purpose, as the Act had been repealed?

iv. *Special session by eminent statesmen*

The legislature occasionally hosts eminent statesmen of national and international repute. The presence of such dignitaries and their uncommon delivery act as a guiding and inspirational beacon to the legislators. The speech usually hinges on public interest and general expectations from the lawmakers. The address of the joint sitting of the National Assembly by former President Bill Clinton in year 2000, was in this light.

The special guest may be a former legislator with a wealth of practical experience in parliamentary proceeding and politicking. The current legislators will benefit from such rare interaction. This class of statesmen, symbolizes a remarkable transition phase between the past, present and future generations of a country and continent.

Therefore, their presence re-echoes national goals and refreshes the patriotic exigency in the mind of the current legislators.

v. *Constituency office and forum*

The expectation and objective of constituency office by legislators, is to bring the breath, dream and reality of government to the doorsteps of the citizenry. This office is the actual communication link between the populace, their representatives and the government.

The conventional role of a constituency office is that it keeps the electorate and their representative continuously aware of the needs and yearnings of the constituency. In short, it is the ultimate database for the realization of the constituency's expectations. The spirit of participatory democracy, demands periodic meeting between the legislators and their constituency members. It should be devoid of party affiliations.

This exchange of ideas enables the legislators to appraise the basic needs of the electorate. In turn, the constituency members will also appreciate the official and unofficial challenges of their representatives. But unfortunately, the general political apathy of the Nigerian public and the selfishness of their elected officers, have frustrated the effectiveness of this democratic mechanism.

The lobby system

A lobby is the large hall in the legislative building (parliament) that is open to the members of the public so that they can have interviews with the legislators. Lobby also means the act of a group of people who try to influence and persuade lawmakers to support or oppose a proposed law. The persuasion or agitation can also be directed at an existing law that requires an amendment or repeal. It is also the act of trying to convince a politician to assume a favourable stand on a particular interest or a public issue.

Professional lobby groups

The complex nature and intricacies of law-making processes as well as the professional demand of some legislation have created more responsibilities for the legislature. This has resulted in the employment of professional lobby groups into the legislative fold in most democracies.

The established professional lobbyists operate through offices equipped with computers and huge databases to amass and assess unlimited amounts of information. They possess respectable contacts within the executive and the legislative arms of government. They also command an appreciable level of media clientele.

The specialized and well established network of the professional lobbyists, place them ahead of the research and statistics department of the legislature. Lobbyists engage in detailed research from whence they proffer scientifically convincing evidence in support the causes of their clients.

The inexhaustible database of seasoned lobbyists will reveal many incontrovertible facts on various legislative sub-ject matter, such that the information can stun legislators into an unquestionable adoption to their submissions. Nigeria needs the services of professional lobby groups in her current socio-political situation. The crippling conflict between the executive and legislature, demands trained professionals who can remedy this ugly rift.

The placement of liaison officers in the legislature has not shown any appreciable impact, which strengthens the point for professional lobbyists. Added to this, poor staffing and the absolute lack of basic infrastructures in most legislative buildings, can only be redressed through sophisticated services which professionals can offer.

It is unfortunate that lobbying has been associated with bribery in Nigeria. Hence, it has been accorded a deplorable status. Thus, the executive arm of government has remained the most prolific initiator of Bills in the legislature at all levels of government in the country. In fact, it enjoys almost an absolute dominion in this sphere.

The current legislators labour mostly on motions which have no legal effect. The lack of legal drafting skills handicaps the legislature. The professional lobbyists could fill this gap and re-awaken the expected democratic output from the legislature.

The legislature and alternative dispute resolution (ADR) mechanisms

The legislature in performing its public hearing role, has a lot to benefit from the services of alternative dispute resolution mechanisms. The public petition committee and any other ad hoc/ select committee whose terms of reference border on conflict resolution, can benefit immensely from these mechanisms. They are now popular trends in most democracies.

Alternative dispute resolution mechanisms are a well-articulated range of processes and strategies prepared for the purpose of helping disputing parties to resolve their conflicts. These alternative dispute resolution mechanisms include:

i. *Arbitration*

Arbitration is a voluntary reference of a dispute between two or more parties to a neutral third party decision maker. The arbitrator is usually knowledgeable in the subject matter on which he renders a binding decision based on the consent of the disputants. C. W. Moore defined arbitration as:

> *a generic term for a voluntary process in which people in conflict*
>
> *request the assistance of an impartial and neutral third party to*
>
> *make decisions for them regarding contested issues.*[1]

---

[1] C.W. Moore, *The Mediation Process: Pratical strategies resolving conflict*, 3rd ed. Jessey-Bass, San Francisco, 2003.

This mechanism is applied after the failure of initial attempts to resolve a conflict. As aptly posited by Oluwale Albert:

> *Arbitration is resorted to when past efforts to reach a common ground by the disputants proved abortive though both of them want the conflict to be resolved quickly.*[2]

There is also non-binding arbitration which enables the disputants to accept or reject the arbitrator's decision.

ii. *Mediation*

This is an informal, voluntary process in which a neutral, trusted and acceptable third party assists the disputants to attain a mutual settlement of their conflict. The mediator's role is to bring the disputing parties together so that they will on their own, proffer a solution to their dispute.

In J.E. Beer and E.Stief's assessment, mediation is:

> *. . . any process for resolving disputes in which another person helps the parties negotiate a settlement.*[3]

The mediator cannot render a binding decision on the disputing parties. Hence Albert's submission that:

> *The mediator is simply an authorized 'go between' in the process of getting the parties to resolve their differences under non-adversarial setting.*[4]

iii. *Conciliation*

The conciliation process involved a conciliator who is a neutral third-party trusted by the disputants. He/she proffers a solution to the conflict by drawing terms of

---

[2] Isaac Oluwale Albert, *Introduction to Third Party Intervention in Community Conflict.* (Archives Publishers, Ibadan 2001), p.34.

[3] J.E. Beer and E. Stief, *The Mediator Handbook.* (New Society Publishers Gabriola Island, B.C. Canada 1997), p.3.

[4] Albert, 83.

settlement as a compromise measure after consultations with the disputing parties. In the revealing words of Albert:

> *The main goal of conciliation is to reduce hostility; it provides a good opportunity for trust-building and positive relationship necessary for sincere negotiation of the issues in the conflict.*[5]

iv. *Negotiation*

This is an informal, unstructured process employed by the disputing parties without the involvement of any third party. It is aimed at the realization of a mutually acceptable resolution of their conflict. C. W. Moore sees negotiation as:

> *A process of establishing and building relationships, through which participants jointly try to reach agreement on issues of individual or mutual concern.*[6]

The legislature applies these mechanisms while performing her fact-finding responsibilities. They can neither serve as the equivalent of nor supplementary measures to the constitutionally ordained roles of the executive and judicial arms of the government.

---

[5] Albert, 36.

[6] Moore, op cit.

Chapter 24

Impeachment Procedures, Resignation, and Recalling a Legislator

Power will intoxicate the best of hearts as wine the strongest heads. No man is wise enough nor good enough to be trusted with unlimited power.

C harles C aleb C orton

---

*T*he constitution can act as a check against the abuse of office by government officials through the instrumentality of impeachment. Legislators are also subject to constitutional checks through the mechanism of *recall*. The Court of Appeal, in the case of *Jimoh v. Olawoye*,[1] defined impeachment as:

> *The act, by a legislature, of calling for the removal from office of a public official accomplished by presenting a written charge of the official's alleged misconduct.*

These constitutional checks and balances position the legislature as the watchdog of the government for society. The mechanisms of impeachment and recall, and the code of conduct is to ensure that political officeholders posses the needed integrity and command public confidence.

There is also room for voluntary disengagement by public officeholders – through the instrument of resignation. Therefore, there is no justification for any government official, including legislators, to be indifferent to his duty or function. Suffice it to say, most of these elected officials, especially the legislators, have fallen short of the expectations of the electorate. This has been described by political observers as a worrisome development.

---

[1] [2003] 10 NWLR Pt 828. 307 CA, p.313.

Aderemi' JSC's uncompromising comment in *Dapianlong v. Dariye* [2]follows here:

> *I shall end this discourse by saying that the allegation levelled against the 1st respondent as contained in the records, are despicable to the highest degree. If proved in accordance with the laws of our land, by the cardinal principle of morality, justice and democratic government that an offender guilty of crime should be sentenced by the court to such penalty as his crime merits, the 1st respondent must not be allowed to run away from justice. But before this can be done, due process of law must be followed from the beginning to the end.*

Removal of the president and/or the vice-president from office

Section 143 of the 1999 Constitution provides for the removal of the president and vice-president from office. The procedure starts with a written notice of the allegation against the officer, which shall state, among others, that the officer is guilty of gross misconduct in the performance of the functions of his office.

The particulars of the misconduct must be detailed and specific. The notice of allegation must be signed by not less than one-third of the members of the National Assembly and presented to the President of the Senate [Section 143(2)(a)].

The president of the Senate is required, within seven days of the receipt of the notice, to cause a copy of it to be served on the holder of the office and on each member of the National Assembly. The reply to the allegation will equally be served on each member of the National Assembly. The Constitution states that within 14 days of the presentation of the notice to the Senate, whether there is a reply or not from the officeholder, in respect of the allegation, each chamber of the National Assembly must resolve, without any debate, whether the allegation should be investigated or not [Section 143(3)].

The motion for the investigation of the allegation must be supported by a vote of not less than two-thirds majority of all the members of each house of the National Assembly [Section 143(4)].

The Chief Justice of Nigeria shall, at the request of the President of the Senate, within seven days of the passage of the motion, appoint a panel of seven persons to investigate the alleged act of misconduct. In the opinion of the Chief

---

[2] [2007] 4 SC (Pt 111) at page 217 para 10-20 .

Justice, the seven persons must be of unquestionable character, and should not be public servants, legislators or members of any political party [Section 143(5)].

The affected officeholder under investigation has the right to defend himself in person and can, at the panel of investigation, be represented by legal practitioners of his choice [Section 143(6)]. The National Assembly will determine the powers and jurisdiction of the panel of investigation. This panel will submit the report of its findings to each house of the National Assembly within three months of its appointment.

If the report of the panel to each house of the National Assembly is to the effect that the allegation could not be proven, the matter will be closed without further proceedings [Section 143(8)]. But if the allegations, according to the report, have been proved, each house of the National Assembly shall, within fourteen days of the receipt of the report, consider and resolve the matter. If the report is adopted with the support of a two-thirds majority of all the members of each house, the holder of the office shall stand removed as from the date of the adoption of that report.

The court has no power over the proceedings or the determination of the panel of the National Assembly in this matter. As was held by the Court of Appeal in *Abaribe* v. *Abia State House of Assembly*:

> *It is the house of assembly that has the power to determine what constitutes gross misconduct or a conduct that will lead to impeachment proceedings.*[3]

The Court of Appeal equated the power of the National Assembly and state houses of assembly in this matter with that of a court. Thus, it was declared in the same case of *Abaribe* v. *Abia State* . . .(supra) that:

> *A state house of assembly is not an inferior tribunal but is equal*
>
> *to the judiciary or the court in the power-sharing characteristic of a federal constitution where there is separation of powers.*[4]

Removal of a state governor and /ora deputy governor from office

The procedure for removing state governors and deputy governors from office is similar to that of the president and the vice-president. This is provided for in

---

[3] [2002] 14 NWLR Pt. 788. 466 CA. p.474, para.9.

[4] ibid, para. 7.

Section 188. In this respect, the notice of any allegation against the governor or the deputy governor of a state must be in writing and signed by not less than one-third of all the members of the assembly (section 188 (2)). The signed notice must be delivered to the Speaker of the house of assembly stating that the affected officeholder is guilty of gross misconduct in the performance of the function of his office. The detailed particulars of the misconduct must be specified ((section 188 (2) (a)-(b)).

The Speaker of the House shall, within seven days of the receipt of that notice, cause a copy of that notice to be served on that governor or deputy governor; as well as each member of the house of assembly. It is also the responsibility of the Speaker, to ensure that any statement in reply to the allegation from the holder of the office, based on the notice of allegation, will be served on each member of the house (proviso to section 188 (2)(a) -(b)).

The House shall resolve by a motion within fourteen days of the presentation whether or not the allegation contained in the notice shall be investigated. This motion shall be made without any debate, whether or not the allegation will be investigated. The motion for the investigation of the allegation, must be supported by the vote of not less than two-thirds majority of all the members of the house of assembly (section 188 (4)).

The Speaker of the House, shall within seven (7) days of the passage of the motion for the investigation of the allegation, request the chief judge of the state to appoint a panel of seven persons to investigate the allegation. The seven persons in the opinion of the chief judge, will be of unquestionable integrity, not being members of any public service, legislative house or political party (section 188 (5).

The governor or the deputy governor under investigation has the right to defend himself in person or be represented by legal practitioner of his choice before the panel(section 188 (6)). The house of assembly will prescribe the procedure for the deliberation of the panel. The panel has a period of three months to investigate and report its findings to the house from the date of its appointment (section 188 (7) (a)- (b)).

If the panel's report to the house, is to the effect that the allegation has not been proved, no other proceedings shall be taken in respect of the matter (section 188 (8)).

But where the allegation has been proved based on the panel's report, then the assembly will consider the report within fourteen (14) days of its receipt. If the report is adopted by a resolution supported by not less than two-thirds majority of all the members of the house, the holder of the office shall stand removed from office as from that date (section 188 (9)).

The proceedings and determination of the house and the panel shall not be questioned in any court (section 188 (10)).

The provision of Section 188 (11) just as Section (143 (11), fortifies the strong position of the National Assembly and state houses of assembly on this subject matter through a wide definition of 'gross misconduct'. The eloquent provision run thus:

> . . . In this section – "gross misconduct" means a grave violation or breach of the provisions of this constitution or a misconduct of such nature as amounts in the opinion in the House of Assembly to gross misconduct.

Case of impeachment in Oyo State

The lingering question with regard to the removal of Rashidi Ladoja as the governor of Oyo State was the satisfaction of the 'two-thirds majority of all the members of the house' as required by the constitution – in this case, only 18 out of 32 members of the house supported the removal.

The Court of Appeal dealt extensively with this subject matter in the case of *Adeleke & Ors* v. *Inakoju & Ors* which was decided on 1 November 2006. That case nullified the alleged impeachment of Rashidi Ladoja as the governor of Oyo State. The thrust of that decision which was upheld by the Supreme Court on 7 December 2006, hinged on the procedural compliance with Section 188(1)-(9) of the 1999 Constitution.

When the appellate court ruled in favour of Governor Rashidi Ladoja, it did so in recognition of the constitutional role of the Speaker of the house of assembly in the impeachment of a governor or deputy governor of a state. In this wise, the mandatory circulation of the notice of impeachment to all the members of the house of assembly by the Speaker was not done.

In the instructive words of the appellate court:

> *It is clear from the constitutional provisions that the House of Assembly of a state is comprised of all the elected members of the House sitting in an official capacity in its designated chamber as the house of assembly of a state with the speaker or deputy speaker presiding. Its legislative functions including impeachment of a governor or even a Speaker must be carried out in its plenary*

session open to all members in an atmosphere that is free from fear, intimidation and violence.[5]

On that premise, the Court of Appeal declared unconstitutional, the factional meeting of the 18 members of the Oyo State House of Assembly in a hotel complex on Ring Road, Ibadan!

The beauty of the decision of the Court of Appeal was that it debunked the erroneous view that Section 188(10) of the Constitution is an ouster clause, ie, that the court of law lacks jurisdiction on impeachment proceedings of the legislature. In rejecting and denouncing the lower court's rejection of jurisdiction on this matter, the appellate court specifically held that:

> *Indeed he had jurisdiction to examine the claim in the light of section 188 subsections 1-9 of the 1999 Constitution and if he was not satisfied that the impeachment proceedings were instituted in compliance thereof, he has justification to intervene to ensure compliance. If on the other hand there was compliance with the pre-impeachment process then what happened thereafter was the internal affairs of the House of Assembly and he would have no jurisdiction to intervene.*

The Supreme Court upheld the ruling of the appellate court and held that, with regard to Section 188 of the Constitution:

> *. . . The whole section must be taken into account. Subsections 1-9 thereof clearly state what must be done before a governor may be removed from office. It is only when these conditions are religiously fulfilled will a governor be said to have been removed from office. When the governor has been constitutionally removed, then and only then, will subsection 10 come into play — it ousts the jurisdiction of the court to question such valid removal from office.*[6]

Therefore, the court has jurisdiction to examine the pre-impeachment process of a legislature and determine the court's position based on that *procedural*

---

[5] *The Nation* newspaper, 3 November 2006, pp. 43-44.

[6] [2007] 2 MJSC pp 10-11.

compliance. The same view was also upheld in nullifying the impeachment of Governor Peter Obi by a faction of the Anambra State House of Assembly. The High Court and Court of Appeal concurred, agreeing with the reasoning and decision in the Oyo State matter, (see *Balonwu v. Obi)*.[7] In a similar tone, the Court of Appeal and the Supreme Court nullified the unconstitutional removal of Joshua Dariye as governor of Plateau State. He was subsequently reinstated; he resumed duty on 30 April 2007 (*Dapienlong v. Dariye* (suipra).

Impeachment of a chairman and / or a vice-chairman of a local government council

The state government laws in respect of this subject matter are in consonance with Section 188 of the Constitution. The Court of Appeal upheld this view in the case of *Adeleke* v. *Inakoju* (supra). In reviewing the case of *Jimoh* v. *Olawoye*,[8] the appellate court confirmed that:

> . . . *In considering the removal of a chairman of local government council in an identical provision as Section 188 of the 1999 Constitution, it followed Ekpo's case to hold that before the ouster clause can apply, the preconditions in subsections 1-9 of Section 26 of the Kwara State Local Government Law 1999, must be satisfied.*

But some local government laws, contain slightly different procedural provisions. This is most remarkable in the presentation of the notice for the removal of the council chairman or vice chairman to the secretary of local government or the clerk of the council. In Lagos State, this subject matter is governed by the Lagos State Local Government (Administration Law 1999, vide Section 24).

Hence, the removal of a local government chairman or vice chairman, requires a notice in writing of the misconduct in the performance of his functions in office signed by not less than one-half of the members of the council. The notice which shall be specific, and shall state the detailed particulars of the misconduct and be presented to the secretary of the local government (section 24(1)).

The secretary to the local government shall within 7 (seven) days of the receipt of the notice shall cause a copy to be served on the holder of the affected

---

[7] [2007] 5 NWLR Pt 1028, 488 CA.

[8] 10 NWLR [2003] Pt. 282. p. 307.

office and on each member of the council. Similarly, any statement made in reply to the allegation by the affected office holder shall be served on each member of the council (section 24 (2)).

The council shall within 14 (fourteen) days of the notice in the absence of the holder of the office in course of its meeting, resolve by motion without any debate whether or not the allegation shall be investigated. This resolution will be irrespective of any statement made by the affected office holder in reply to the allegation. (Section 24(3)).

The motion of the council for the investigation of the allegation shall be passed if it is supported by the votes of not less than two-thirds majority of all the members of the council. (Section 24(4)).

Within 7 (seven) days of the passage of the motion for the investigation of the allegation, the secretary to the local government shall inform the chief judge of the state of the allegation. The chief judge of the state shall then appoint a panel of seven persons to investigate the allegation. The members of the panel in the opinion f the chief judge should be of unquestionable integrity, and not being members of any public or civil service, a legislative house or a political party (section 24(5)).

The holder of the office under investigation shall have the right to defend himself in person or be represented before the panel by a legal practitioner of his own choice (section 24(6)).

The panel in the exercise of its functions and power as prescribed by the law, shall within 3 (three) months of its appointment report its findings to the local government (section 24(7) (a) - (b)).

If the panel's report to the local government is to the effect that the allegation has not been proved, there shall be no further proceedings in respect of the matter (section 24(8)).

But where the report of the panel is that the allegation against the affected holder of the office has been proved, then, the council shall within 14 (fourteen) days of the report, consider the report in the presence of the affected holder of the office. If the report is adopted by the resolution of not less than two-thirds majority of all the members of the council, the affected holder of the office shall stand removed from office as from the date of the adoption of the report. (section 24(9)).

The law provides that 'misconduct' includes breach of the Oath of Allegiance or Oath of Office of chairman or vice chairman or a breach of the provisions of this law or a misconduct of such nature as amounts to bribery or corruption or false declaration of assets and liabilities or conviction for reasonable felony.

Therefore, the notice of the allegation of gross misconduct against the chairman or vice chairman in line with the local government enabling law of the state, must be in writing and signed by not less than one-third of all the members of the legislative council of that local government area.

The notice must be presented to the leader of the legislative council, stating that the chairman or vice chairman is guilty of gross misconduct in the performance of the functions of his office. The leader shall, within seven days of the receipt of that allegation, cause a copy of the notice to be served on the chairman or vice chairman and on each member of the local government legislative council.

If there is any statement in reply from the affected chairman or vice chairman, the leader shall cause same to be served on each member of the legislative council.

The legislative council shall within fourteen (14) days of the presentation of the notice to its presiding officer (leader) resolve by a motion without any debate, whether or not the allegation shall be investigated.

The motion of the legislative council for the investigation of the allegation, must be supported by a vote of not less than two-thirds majority of all the members of that legislative council.

The leader shall within seven days of the passage of that motion request the chief judge of the state to appoint a panel of seven persons of unquestionable integrity, who are not members of any public service, legislative house or political party (in his opinion) to investigate the allegation.

The chairman or vice chairman under investigation has the right to defend himself in person or be represented by a legal practitioner of his choice before the panel.

The panel, within three months, shall report its investigation to the legislative council. If the legislative council, based on the panel's report, resolves by a vote of not less than two-thirds of all the members, to remove the chairman or vice chairman, that office holder stands removed from office from the date of the adoption of the report. The proceedings and determination of the panel and the legislative council are not questionable in any court.

But the true position of the law as held by the Court of Appeal and Supreme Court in the case of *Adeleke & Ors* v. *Inakoju & Ors* (supra) is now settled.

The pre-impeachment process must be in compliance with all the afore-stated subsections and conditions therein. Therefore, the court is at liberty to exercise jurisdiction and establish compliance with the aforestated provisions of the enabling local government law.

The case of *Jimoh* v. *Olawoye* (supra) which elaborated on Section 26 (10) of the Local Government Law of Kwara State, 1999 also concurred with the Oyo State case of *Adeleke & Ors vs Inakoju & Ors*.at the Court of Appeal and the apex court. In the case of *Jimoh* v. *Olawoye*, the Court of Appeal also inferred the incidental powers of the legislative council to suspend the local government chairman through Section 26 (10) of the Local Government Law.

There was also a striking reference to the case of *Ekpo* v. *Calabar Local Government Council*[9] which detailed the identical provision for the impeachment of the local government chairman and vice chairman.

The impeachment process of the three tiers of government (federal, state and local government), are governed under the provision of identical checks and balances. Hence, the legislative constitutional power of impeachment must be in strict compliance with the spirit and letters of the Constitution. If it fails to satisfy the provisions of the Constitution or the enabling local government law on the subject matter, the court will declare it null and void. But once the process is in line with the relevant pre-impeachment procedures and constitutional provisions, the court will regard the matter as an absolute legislative affair, and as such, will not intervene.

Vacation of legislative seats

The constitution provides for conditions apart from voluntary resignation and demise under which a legislator can vacate his seat. The constitutional conditions are almost identical for national and state legislators. The states have adopted similar provisions in their respective local government laws.

Members of the National Assembly

Section 68(1) provides that a member of the Senate or the House of Representatives shall vacate his seat of which he is a member if:

    a)   he becomes a member of another legislative house;

---

[9] [1993] 3 NWLR.

b) any other circumstances that can disqualify him for election as a member of the National Assembly;

c) he ceases to be a citizen of Nigeria;

d) he becomes president, vice-president, governor, deputy governor or a minister of the government of the federation, a commissioner of the government of a state or a special adviser;

e) If he becomes a member of a commission as provided by Section 68(1)(e) of the constitution;

f) If without just cause he is absent from meetings of the house of which he is a member for a period amounting in the aggregate to more than one-third of the total number of days during which the house meets in any one year.

g) If he becomes a member of another political party before the expiration of the period for which that house was elected.

This provision will not operate if he joined another political party due to a division in his previous party. Likewise if there is a merger of two or more political parties or factions by one of which he was previously sponsored, then, his seat cannot be declared vacant.

h) If the member of the National Assembly is recalled and the chairman of the Independent National Electoral Commission notifies the President of the Senate or Speaker of the House of Representatives by a certificate of that effect.

The enforcement of this provision requires satisfactory evidence from the presiding officers of both chambers of the National Assembly. The test also demands a written statement evidencing a just cause from these presiding officers. Therefore, it is a matter that can ultimately be settled by a court of competent jurisdiction. The case of *Oloyo* v. *Alegbe*[10] was settled on this premise. (See Section 68(2) and (3) of the Constitution).

The provision for the state house of assembly members is in Section 109 of the constitution.

---

[10] [1982] 3 NCLR p. 647.

Recall of a legislator

Legislators, just like other public officers, should observe the necessary requirements of the Constitution and the code of conduct. Indeed, the indifference and glaring recklessness of some of our legislators are classical examples of ignorance of the instrument of recall. In most cases, assembly attendance records are below average all over the country; where this is not the case, serious legislative procedures are ignored with impunity.

In *Ebiesuwa* v. *Commissioner of Police*,[11] the high court in then Bendel State held that:

> *It is unconstitutional for any member of a state legislature to*
>
> *engage or participate in the management of any private business,*
> *profession or trade. A member of a state house of assembly is on*
> *a full time appointment.*

The Constitution allows members of the National Assembly and those of state houses of assembly to be recalled by their constituencies. According to Sections 69 and 110, members of the National Assembly and state houses of assembly, respectively, can be recalled from the membership of the legislature if a petition alleging loss of confidence in such a member, is signed by more than a half of the registered voters in his constituency. The petition must be presented to the chairman of the Independent National Electoral Commission (INEC).

If the petition, which is subject to a referendum by the INEC within 90 days of its receipt, is approved by a simple majority of the registered voters in the affected legislator's constituency, he will be formally recalled as a member of the house. This terminates his membership of that assembly, and that seat becomes vacant until a bye-election is held for a replacement.

Immunity of political officeholders

The constitution has envisaged that the tasks of a public office need little or no distraction. Hence, it shields the president, vice-president, state governors and deputy governors from civil or criminal proceedings while in office (Sections 308(1) and (3)).

---

[11] [1982] 3NCLR 339.

Thus, in the case of *Tinubu* v. *IMB Securities Plc*,[12] the Supreme Court held that:

> *By virtue of Section 308(1)(a) of the 1999 Constitution which provisions are mandatory, no civil or criminal proceedings may be instituted or, if already instituted as in this case, shall be continued against any person holding the office of the president, vice-president, governor or deputy governor during his period of office.*
>
> *In this case, no civil proceedings may be instituted, or, if already instituted, shall be continued against the appellant who still holds the office of governor of Lagos State.*

However, it is noteworthy that this immunity is not forever and does not protect the officeholder against police investigation. This was expressed by the decision of the Supreme Court in *Fawehinmi* v. *IGP*:[13]

> *The main purpose of Section 308 of the 1999 Constitution is to allow an incumbent president, vice-president, governor or deputy governor mentioned in that Section, a completely free hand and mind in the performance of the duties and responsibilities assigned to the office which he or she holds under the constitution. But this is not intended to grant him or her immunity forever from full criminal investigation or any criminal proceedings in respect of any offence allegedly committed by him or her during the tenure of office.*

This standard of reasoning will check the excesses of public officers due to the underlying caution notice.

But this subject matter has attracted loud controversy due to the performance of some chief executives who have transformed that legal shield into an engine of fraud. The heartless looting of the public treasury by some of the chief executives, has placed a severe constraint on the underlying import of the immunity clause in the constitution. In view of the misuse and abuse of the immunity clause by past and current chief executives it should be expunged from

---

[12] [2001] 16 NWLR (Pt 740) 670 SC, p. 675.

[13] [2002] 7 NWLR p. 643.

the constitution to keep a check on these public officers.

The immunity option is intended to shield the executives from frivolous civil actions, however immunity does not extend to criminal actions while in office. Therefore, there will be no immunity in respect of criminal actions of incumbent chief executives.

Resignation of public officeholders

Section 306(1) of the constitution provides that:

> Save as otherwise provided in this Section, any person who is appointed, elected or otherwise selected to any office established by this constitution may resign from that office by writing under his hand addressed to the authority or person by whom he was appointed, elected or selected.

The resignation will take effect on the receipt of the written memo by the addressee authority or person appointed by that authority (Section 306(2)). The notice of the resignation of the President of the Senate and the Speaker of the House of Representatives shall, in each case, be addressed to the Clerk to the National Assembly. In the same vein, the notice of the resignation of the Speaker of a state house of assembly shall be addressed to the Clerk of the house of assembly (Section 306(6)).

However, the notice of resignation of a member of a legislative house shall be addressed to the President of the Senate or to the Speaker of the legislative house where the member belongs (Section 306 (7)).

Selected Readings

A braham , L.C . and S.C . H aw trey. *A Parliam entary D ictionary*. Butterw orths, G reat Britain, 1956.

A cts A uthentication A ct C ap A 2, *Laws of the Federation of Nigeria*, 2004.

A lbert, Isaac O law ale. *Introduction to Third-party Intervention in Com m unity Conflicts*. A rchives Publishers, Ibadan, 2001.

A lobo, Joshua E. *Election Petition in Nigeria (Cases and M aterials)*. Josin Publishing H ouse, A buja, 2007.

A ppadorai, A . A . *The Substance of Politics*. O xford U niversity Press, N ew D elhi, 1975.

A sobie, H . A ssisi. Legislative proposals, motions, questions and debates. A paper presented at the Legislative W orkshop for honourable m em bers of A nambra State H ouse of A ssembly, Enugu, 1981.

Ball, A lan and B G uy Peters. *M odern Politics and G overnm ent* 7th ed. Palgrave M acm illan, 2005.

Barnett, H iliare. *Constitutional and Adm inistrative Law* 3rd ed C avendish Publishing, London, 2000.

Beer, J.E. and S. Stief. *The M ediator H andbook*. N ew Society Publishers, G abriola Island, British C olum bia, C anada, 1997.

C onstitution of the Federal Republic of N igeria, 1999.

D e Tocqueville, A lexis. *D em ocracy in Am erica*. V ol 1. A lfred A . Knopf, N ew Y ork, 1948.

D icey, A .V . 1885. *Introduction to the Study of Law of the Constitution*, O xford, London.

Electoral A ct 2002 C ap E6 *Laws of the Federation of Nigeria* 2004.

Legislative H ouses (Pow ers and Privileges) A ct C ap L12 *Laws of the Federation of Nigeria* 2004.

M ay Erskine's Treatise on the Law, Privileges and U sage of Parliam entary Processes (23rd ed.) W . M ackay, M . H utton, M . Sandall, et.al, Butterw orths, London, 2004.

M oore, C .W . *The M ediation Process. Practical strategies for resolving conflict*, 3rd ed. Jessey-Basse, San Francisco, 2003.

N ational A ssem bly Service C om m ission A ct C ap N 7 *Laws of the Federation of Nigeria*, 2004.

N w abueze, B.O . *Constitutional H istory of Nigeria*. Christopher H urst, London, 1982.

N w abueze, B.O . *Federalism in Nigeria under the Presidential C onstitution*. Sw eet and M axw ell, London, 1983.

N w abueze, B.O . *Presidential Constitution of Nigeria*. C hristopher H urst & C o. (London) and N w amife Publishers, Enugu, 1982.

N w abueze, B.O . *Federalism in Nigeria under the Presidential Constitution*. Lagos State M inistry of Justice, Law Review Series, 2003

N w abueze, B.O . *H ow President O basanjo Subverted the Rule of Law*. G old Press,Ibadan, 2007.

N w ankw o, G . O nyekw ere. Legislative supervision of the adm inistration, a paper presented at the w orkshop for legislators, A nam bra State H ouse of A ssem bly, Enugu, 1981.

N w osu, H . N . The budgetary process in the presidential system . A paper presented at w orkshop for legislators, A nam bra State H ouse of A ssem bly, Enugu, 1981.

O laszek, W alter J. C ongressional procedures and the policy process. *W ashington D C Congressional Q uarterly* 1978.

Phillips, O . Hood. *Constitutional and Adm inistrative Law* 16 ed. ELBS Fletcher and Son, 1978.

Stiftung, Friedrich Ebert. *Constitutions and Federalism* . Friedrich Ebert Foundation, Berlin, 1997.

W heare, K.C . *The M odern Constitution*, 2nd ed. O xford U niversity Press, London, 1966.

Y ar'A dua, Shehu M usa. Forew ord. In: *Local G overnm ent Reform* , Federal G overnm ent Printer, Kaduna, 1976.

G overnm ent Publications

Bayelsa State, Standing O rders of the Bayelsa State H ouse of A ssem bly, Y enagoa, 2007

Standing Rules of the Senate, The N ational A ssem bly, A buja, 2003

Standing O rders of the H ouse of Representatives, N ational A ssem bly, A buja, (17 M ay 2007

TABLE OF CASES

Table of Cases

Table of Cases

INDEX

About the Author

Emmanuel Obusom Anyaegbunam was born in Port Harcourt and is a legal practitioner and consultant working in Lagos. He is a graduate of the University of Nigeria, Nsukka, and was formerly on the editorial board of *The Nation*. In addition to his passionate interest in educating the public on the vital role of the legislature in democracy, Mr. Anyaegbunam is a public commentator.

His other books include the *Origins of Football and the History of the World Cup* (1999) and *Faith, the Cornerstone of Success* (2002).

www.ingramcontent.com/pod-product-compliance
Lightning Source LLC
Chambersburg PA
CBHW070848290526
45795CB00001B/36